BLOOD MOON

BIBLICAL SIGNS OF THE COMING APOCALYPSE

S. DOUGLAS WOODWARD

Other Books by S. Douglas Woodward

Are We Living in the Last Days?

Decoding Doomsday

Black Sun, Blood Mood

Power Quest, Book One

Power Quest, Book Two

Lying Wonders of the Red Planet

Co-authored with Douglas W. Krieger and Dene McGriff

The Final Babylon

Participation in Defender Books' Publications

God's Ghostbusters

Pandemonium's Engine

Blood on the Altar

BLOOD MOON

Biblical Signs of the Coming Apocalypse

*Why the Gospel of Jesus Christ Mandates
Keeping Watch during Earth's Last Days*

*Watch therefore, for ye know neither the day
nor the hour wherein the Son of man cometh.*
(Matthew 25:13)

S. Douglas Woodward

FAITH HAPPENS
WWW.FAITH-HAPPENS.COM
OKLAHOMA CITY

BLOOD MOON
Biblical Signs of the Coming Apocalypse

Why the Gospel of Jesus Christ Mandates Keeping Watch during Earth's Last Days

©Copyright S. Douglas Woodward, 2014

Faith Happens, www.faith-happens.com. All rights reserved. Printed in the United States of America.

Scripture taken from the King James Version of the Bible unless otherwise noted.

All photographs of artwork used in this book or on the cover are public domain from the Wikimedia JPEG 'Commons' database unless otherwise noted.

Graphic on Ezekiel's temple courtesy of Bob Hall.

To order multiple copies of the book, please email **info@faith-happens.com** or **doug@faith-happens.com**.

For information about the author, including scheduling him for speaking engagements, please see **www.faith-happens.com.**

Prophecy/ Eschatology / Theology

Cover design by the author

ISBN-13: 978-1495239571

ISBN-10: 1495239578

CONTENTS

TABLE OF FIGURES xi
DEDICATION xiii
ACKNOWLEDGEMENTS xv
PART ONE: SIGNS OF THE COMING APOCALPYSE 1

1: INTRODUCTION JESUS: THE APOCALYPTIC RABBI 3
   SIGNALS IN THE SKY 3
   HOW JEWISH NATIONALISM KILLED THE MESSIAH 4
   THE UNEXPECTED END TO HIS MINISTRY 6
   IN THE VERY SAME WAY AS YOU SAW HIM LEAVE 9
   THE APOCALYPSE, A KEY ELEMENT TO THEIR MESSAGE 11
   KEEPING A KINGDOM MINDSET 14
   EVEN LIBERAL THEOLOGIANS TESTIFY TO THIS TRUTH 15
   EVANGELICALS DENY THE MESSAGE OF THE KINGDOM 18
   BLOOD MOONS AND THE SIGNS OF HIS COMING 20
   A 'KINGDOMLESS' GOSPEL HAS HAD LITTLE IMPACT 21
   EVEN SCIENCE TELLS US THE APOCALYPSE IS NEAR 24
   THE PURPOSE OF THIS BOOK 25

2: HEAVENLY PORTENTS OF THE APOCALYPSE 29
   WHAT THE WORD APOCALYPSE MEANS 29
   TODAY'S MOST POPULAR PORTENT 32
   WHAT DOES THE TETRAD MEAN FOR ISRAEL? 35
   ASCRIBING 'FULFILLED' STATUS TO BIBLE PROPHECIES 41
   GOD'S APPOINTMENT OF THE SUN, MOON, AND STARS 42
   HEBREW FEASTS AS PROPHECIES 45

3: THE QUEST TO DECIPHER THE FUTURE 49
   HUMANITY EAGERLY SEEKS TO KNOW THE FUTURE 49
   THE HISTORICAL BASIS FOR OCCULTISM 51
   FAILURE OF NEW AGE PROPHECY—2012 IS NOW HISTORY 54
   THE PROOF IS IN THE PROPHECY—IF FULFILLED, THAT IS 56
   PROPHECY MATTERS SINCE IT IMPLIES TRANSCENDENCE 56
   PROPHECY—FAITH IS MORE THAN WISHFUL THINKING 59

4: CHRISTIANITY—AN APOCALYPTIC FAITH 63
PORTRAYING THE KINGDOM OF GOD IN IMAGES 63
APOCALYPSE IMPLIES GOD'S INTERVENTION 65
FIVE THEMES CONFIRMING APOCALYPSE TO BE PRIMARY 67
- The Kingdom is at hand 67
- The Angels Charge: Waste No Time—Witness Now! 70
- Prepare for the Coming Cataclysms of the Apocalypse 71
- The Commandment to Watch Always 73
- Anticipate Salvation's Completion: Our Glorification 74

5: SIGNS AND WONDERS 77
SIGNS THAT CONFIRM THE COVENANTS 77
THE NOAHIC COVENANT 78
THE SIGN AS A TOKEN OF THE ABRAHAMIC COVENANT 80
THE NAME, THE PRESENCE, AND VOICE OF GOD AS A SIGN 81
THE MEANING OF OWTH OFTEN EQUATES TO OATH 84
SIGNS AND WONDERS 85
THE TESTIMONY OF DANIEL'S GENTILE KINGS 87
THE DISCIPLES WERE PROVEN BY SIGNS AND WONDERS 89
SUMMARY: THE VARIOUS TYPES OF SIGNS AND WONDERS 91

6: SIGNS OF THE TIMES 95
MANY EXPECT THE APOCALYPSE DRAWS NEAR 95
FOR UNBELIEVERS, NO SIGN OF DISASTER MAY BE COMING 98
THERE ARE ALSO SIGNS THAT GO UNDETECTED 101
JESUS CITES THE BIBLE'S BIGGEST WHOPPERS 104
DENYING THE INEVITABLE APOCALYPSE WE SEE COMING 106
LIVING AS IF THE END IS SOON—BECAUSE IT MAY BE 107

7: KNOWING THE END AT THE BEGINNING 109
FORESHADOWING: A TECHNIQUE IN TELLING A STORY 109
THE BOOK OF ENOCH—AN EARLY BOOK OF PROPHECY? 110
PATRISTIC REFERENCES TO THE BOOK OF ENOCH 112
THE BOOKS' EARLY HISTORY 114
ENOCH AND THE ELECT 115
ENOCH THE REPRESENTATIVE OF THE RAPTURE 118
GOD'S FOREKNOWLEDGE OF HIS ELECT 120
AND GOD REMEMBERED NOAH 122

8: *PAROUSIA*—JESUS' COMING AND ABIDING 125

- THE GOOD GHOSTS OF CHRISTMASES PAST 125
- ANTICIPATION—KNOWING IT IS WORTH THE WAIT 126
- WHY PAUL WROTE THESSALONICA A SECOND TIME 128
- *ERCHOMAI* CONTRASTED WITH *APOCALYPTŌ* 130
- PAROUSIA—A FORM OF COMING THAT CONTINUES 132
- AND SO SHALL WE BE TOGETHER FOREVER 134

9: DECODING SIGNS AND SETTING DATES 137

- CODE BREAKING AND CIPHER SOLVING 137
- SETTING A TIME LIMIT FOR WHEN IT ALL MUST HAPPEN 139
- THE LENGTH OF A BIBLICAL GENERATION 140
- THE BUDDING FIG TREE—A COUNTDOWN TO HIS COMING? 144
- DOES ISRAEL'S RETURN FULFILL END DAYS' PROPHECY? 146
- HAS THE TIME OF THE GENTILES COME TO AN END? 147
- WAS JESUS CONFUSED REGARDING WHEN HE RETURNS? 148
- AFFIRMING THE INEVITABLE WITHOUT SETTING A DATE 150

PART TWO: KEEPING WATCH UNTIL JESUS COMES 153

10: AFTER THE APOCALYPSE 155

- PARDON ME FOR REPEATING MYSELF 155
- THE MILLENNIAL REIGN—A WORLD REFRESHED 157
- THE AFTERLIFE AS A MOTIVE TO ENDURE 158
- THE FOUR PHASES OF THE AFTERLIFE 160
- A SHORTSIGHTED VIEW 162

11: DOOM AND GLOOM 165

- THE GOOD AND THE BAD GO TOGETHER 165
- KNOCKING ON WOOD 166
- GOING TO HELL IN A HANDBAG 167
- THE AFLOCKALYPSE OF 2011 168
- WHAT REALLY HAPPENED IN SODOM AND GOMORRAH? 170
- SALVATION AND JUDGMENT HAPPEN SIMULATANEOUSLY 174
- CHOOSE LIFE THAT YE MAY LIVE 175

12: FINDING MEANING IN DOOMSDAY 177

- EMBRACING DEATH RATHER THAN DENYING IT 177
- DESTROYING THREATS TO MEANING BEGETS EVIL 180
- WOULD GOD REALLY ALLOW US TO DESTROY OURSELVES? 181

WHEN BAD THINGS HAPPEN TO GOOD PEOPLE 182
WHAT WOULD THE UNIVERSE BE LIKE WITHOUT GOD? 184
WHY FAIRY TALES ARE NOT JUST FOR CHILDREN 185
HOW TO COPE WITH THE INEVITABILITY OF DOOMSDAY 186
LIKE NOAH, WE MUST PREPARE FOR THE RAINY DAY 188

13: LINKING OUR ORIGIN TO OUR DESTINY 191

STEP BY STEP, OUR LIVES SHOWCASE A GRAND DESIGN 191
A LIFE WELL-LIVED LIVES ON IN THE LIVES OF OTHERS 192
THE CONTROVERSIAL BOOK OF SECOND PETER 194
SEEING THE WORLD IN A FAR DIFFERENT LIGHT 195
IN THE BEGINNING, GOD CREATED. BUT THEN… 197
HOMO SAPIENS PRIOR TO ADAM AND EVE? 200
INTELLIGENT DESIGN AND OTHER CREATION THEORIES 202
NOT ONE FLOOD IN THE BIBLE, BUT TWO 204
SCOFFERS UNDERSTAND NOTHING ABOUT EITHER AGE 206

14: SEEKING THE IDENTITY OF ANTICHRIST 209

LOOKING OUT FOR THE ANTICHRIST 209
HOW THE APPEARANCE OF ANTICHRIST AFFECTS THIS 210
RESPONSIBLE STUDIES ON THE IDENTITY OF ANTICHRIST 213
OUTRAGEOUS ROOTS OF THE MAN OF SIN 214
AN APOLLO CREED: ANTICHRIST FROM THE PYTHON PIT 216
THE MINORITY REPORT—THE MUSLIM ANTICHRIST 219
ORION, GIZA, AND THE CULT OF THE ALL-SEEING EYE 221
MIGHT ANTICHRIST BE 'MORE THAN HUMAN'? 222
ANTICHRIST AS THE WOLFMAN—THE LYCOS FROM LYCIA 225
OTHER MANMADE BEASTS MAY BE COMING TO HAUNT US 226
LOOKING FOR THE ANTICHRIST: MORE THAN A CURIOSITY 227

15: ESCAPING THE WRATH TO COME 231

A REVERSAL OF FORTUNE, FOR ALMOST EVERYONE 231
GOD DESIRES TO HELP US MAKE ENDS MEET EVERYDAY 233
THE MEANING OF THE MILLENNIUM 234
FACING THE POSSIBILITY OF GREAT TRIBULATION 236
THE *DAY OF THE LORD*—TO WHAT DOES THIS REFER? 237
THE TIMING OF THE RAPTURE OF BELIEVERS 242
RESPONDING TO THE 'ESCAPIST' REBUKE 244
SO WILL CHRISTIANS GO THROUGH THE TRIBULATION? 245
BEING KEPT FROM THE HOUR OF TRIAL 250

    EMPLOYING A BIT OF LOGIC IN THE RAPTURE'S TIMING 251
    IS THE RAPTURE A FEAT TOO DIFFICULT FOR GOD? 252

16: WALKING WORTHY OF OUR VOCATION 255

    THE PRACTICAL IMPORTANCE OF THE APOCALYPSE 255
    COUNTING THE COST OF DISCIPLESHIP 257
    WHY WE MUST LIVE IN LIGHT OF THE APOCALYPSE 259
    LIVING SALTY LIVES THROUGH DOING GOOD WORKS 261
    WE ARE CALLED TO BE DISTINCTIVE—BUT NOT STRANGE 263
    MAKING THE MOST OF THE LITTLE TIME REMAINING 264

17: OBTAINING THE GLORY OF GOD 267

    TRANSFIXED BY THE TRANSFIGURATION 267
    THE PRINCE IN PAUPER'S CLOTHES 269
    THE GOSPEL SPEAKS OF A COMPLETE SALVATION 271
    WHAT DOES IT MEAN TO SHARE IN GOD'S GLORY? 273
    THE CREATION WAS SUBJECTED TO EVIL FOR OUR GLORY 275
    WHAT IT MEANS THAT JESUS CHRIST WAS MADE PERFECT 276
    THE TRANSFORMATION HAS ALREADY COMMENCED 278
    MOVING INTO A BRAND NEW HOUSE 279
    THE WEIGHT OF GLORY—WHAT DOES THAT MEAN? 280
    THE TRANSFIGURATION MADE OUR GLORY MORE SURE 283
    PRESENTING SALVATION TO OTHERS IN FULL MEASURE 285

18: CONCLUSION—FACING WHAT COMES NEXT 287

    GLOBAL CRISES, CATASTROPHES, AND CATACLYSMS 287
    WHAT'S THE WORLD COMING TO? 289
    FROM DEADLY DESPAIR TO THE DELUSION OF DIVINITY 290
    SIZING UP THE REAL AMERICA 292
    DO MYTHS AND MORAL LAPSES CAUSE OUR PROBLEMS? 294
    IS THERE CHANGE WE CAN REALLY BELIEVE IN? 296
    THE ONLY HOPE—THE KINGDOM OF GOD MUST COME 301
    THE LESSON OF ZACCHAEUS 303
    OCCUPY UNTIL I COME 304

APPENDIX ONE 309

    REASONS TO BELIEVE THE RAPTURE COMES SOMETIME BEFORE CHRIST'S RETURN AT ARMAGEDDON 309

APPENDIX TWO..313
   THE GREEK WORD APOSTASIA AND ITS IMPLICATIONS FOR THE RAPTURE OF THE CHURCH.. **313**

FOR FURTHER READING 317

ABOUT THE AUTHOR...319

TABLE OF FIGURES

FIGURE 1 - JESUS ENTERS JERUSALEM AND THE CROWDS WELCOME HIM BY PIETRO LORENZETTI, 1320 .. 5
FIGURE 2 - JESUS' ASCENSION TO HEAVEN DEPICTED BY JOHN SINGLETON COPLEY, 1775 8
FIGURE 3 – THE BLOOD MOON OF APRIL 15, 2014 30
FIGURE 4 – HALLEY'S COMET, 2010, OFTEN SEEN AS A HARBINGER OF DOOM 31
FIGURE 5 – OLD ORTHODOX WALL PAINTING OF THE APOCALIYPSE FROM OSOGOVO MONASTERY, REPUBLIC OF MACEDONIA 36
FIGURE 6 - NOSTRADAMUS ON THE HISTORY CHANNEL 50
FIGURE 7 - FREEMASON INTELLECTUAL MANLY P. HALL 52
FIGURE 8 - JACK PARSONS AND L. RON HUBBARD OF JPL, CIRCA 1950 53
FIGURE 9 – A MEDIEVAL ILLUSTRATION OF AUGUSTINE'S *CITY OF GOD* 60
FIGURE 10 - RUSSIAN ORTHODOX ICON, APOCALYPSE 66
FIGURE 11 - FOUR HORSEMEN OF APOCALYPSE, BY VIKTOR VASNETSOV. PAINTED IN 1887 75
FIGURE 12 - NOAH'S SACRIFICE BY DANIEL MACLISE 79
FIGURE 13 - MOUNT SINAI ON THE SINAI PENINSULA IN EGYPT (TRADITIONAL SITE) 82
FIGURE 14 - THE PILLAR OF FIRE IN THE MIDST OF THE HEBREW CAMP 84
FIGURE 15 - DANIEL IN THE LIONS' DEN 87
FIGURE 16 - ILLUSTRATION OF THE PENTECOST FROM THE HORTUS DELICIARUM OF HERRAD OF LANDSBERG (TWELTH CENTURY) 90
FIGURE 17 – AN ANCIENT RELIEF, PURPORTEDLY OF NEPHILIM 99
FIGURE 18 - STONES FROM THE TEMPLE IN THE TYROPOEON VALLEY IN JERUSALEM 102
FIGURE 19 - KEY CITIES WHERE PAUL FOUNDED CHURCHES 127
FIGURE 20 - THE PAROUSIA OF JESUS CHRIST 133
FIGURE 21 - THE COMMON PRESUMPTION: WE CAN KNOW NOW! 141
FIGURE 22 - THE PARABLE OF THE FIG TREE 144
FIGURE 23 - THE SITE PLAN FOR THE FUTURE TEMPLE OF EZEKIEL (EZEKIEL 40-48) 157
FIGURE 24 – LOT AND HIS FAMILY FLEE SODOM AND GOMORRAH 171
FIGURE 25 - ANTHROPOLOGIST ERNST BECKER, AUTHOR, THE DENIAL OF DEATH 178
FIGURE 26 - THE BAALBEK MEGALITHS 199
FIGURE 27 - THE RUINS OF PUMA PUNKU 200
FIGURE 28 - DRS. STRANGELOVE AND KISSINGER 211
FIGURE 29 – BARAK OBAMA AS MABUS; RAY MABUS, SECRETARY OF THE NAVY 212
FIGURE 30 - THE DESECRATION OF THE TEMPLE BY ANTIOCHUS EPIPHANES IV 217
FIGURE 31 - NIMROD, THE MIGHTY HUNTER 219
FIGURE 32 - THE ALL-SEEING EYE OF OSIRIS 221
FIGURE 33 - THE ALL-TIME GREATEST MOVIE ABOUT THE ANTICHRIST: *THE OMEN* 223
FIGURE 34 - ZEUS TURNING LYCAON INTO A WOLF, ENGRAVING BY HENDRIK GOLTZIUS. 225

FIGURE 35 - THE PRESCIENT SCIENCE FICTION OF H.G. WELLS 227
FIGURE 36 - BONHOEFFER - THE COST OF DISCIPESHIP 258
FIGURE 37 - TRANSFIGURATION OF CHRIST ICON, SINAI 12TH CENTURY 269
FIGURE 38 - THE GNOSTIC GOSPELS 274

DEDICATION

This book is dedicated to my father, William C. Woodward, who remains a steadfast example of true spirituality, unconditional Christian love, and attentive commitment to his family...
all at 95 years young!

ACKNOWLEDGEMENTS

Special thanks to everyone I have solicited to provide comments, raise questions, and gain ideas for titles, cover design, and appropriateness of content. I remain, however, solely responsible for any and all mistakes contained within this work.

I remain always grateful to my friend Bob Ulrich for his input and suggestions to make my books more interesting to readers.

As always, thanks to my wonderful wife Donna, for her enduring love and support during the time I have been missing in action preparing this manuscript for publication.

PART ONE:
SIGNS OF THE COMING APOCALPYSE

1: INTRODUCTION
JESUS: THE APOCALYPTIC RABBI

[Jesus] answered and said unto them, "When it is evening, ye say, 'It will be fair weather: for the sky is red.' And in the morning, 'It will be foul weather today: for the sky is red and lowering.' O ye hypocrites, ye can discern the face of the sky; but can ye not discern the signs of the times?"
(Matthew 16:2-3)

*"Immediately after the tribulation of those days shall the sun be darkened, and the moon shall not give her light, and the stars shall fall from heaven, and the powers of the heavens shall be shaken: And then shall appear the sign of the Son of man in heaven: and then shall all the tribes of the earth mourn, and they shall see the Son of Man
coming in the clouds of heaven
with power and great glory."*
(Matthew 24:29-30)

SIGNALS IN THE SKY

LOOKING FOR SIGNS IN THE SKY SEEMS TO GO HAND IN HAND WITH ANTICIPATING THE RETURN OF JESUS CHRIST—HIS SECOND ADVENT. JESUS HIMSELF TALKED OF HEAVENLY SIGNS which herald the coming of the Son of Man at the end of the age. The citation above used as an epigraph from Matthew 24 makes this perfectly clear—a darkened sun, a hidden moon, falling stars, the shaking of the heavens and the earth. And the greatest sign of all, the Son of Man coming in the clouds of heaven with power and great glory. There is no shortage of heavenly signs when Jesus comes again. But are there signs beforehand, signs that tell us that the last days now stand only a few short months or years away?

There is an old saying that some readers may not recognize:

> RED SKY AT NIGHT—SAILORS DELIGHT.
> RED SKY IN THE MORNING—SAILORS TAKE WARNING!

The weatherman says this rule of thumb applies only to the middle latitudes of our planet. The evening sky of red represents an abundance of tiny particles in the atmosphere, typical of a high pressure system. It yields clear skies overhead. On the other hand, a red sky in the morning bears bad tidings because it implies a storm is approaching, particularly if the sky lowers at that time.

Jesus' adage was the equivalent Hebrew aphorism. The point Jesus made was how paradoxical that the religious leaders of the day *could* tell the weather (not their expertise) while failing to foresee how the religious and political climate would affect their nation—matters about which they were supposed experts. It was more than just mishearing the weather report. To risk mixing a metaphor, it was a giant case of not seeing the forest for the trees. The Jewish leadership should have recognized that cataclysm was inevitable. All the ingredients were there like chemicals ready to combust. A small spark would set off a massive exposition. They were clearly missing the signs that signaled destruction ahead.

HOW JEWISH NATIONALISM KILLED THE MESSIAH

However, the religious leadership of Israel's first-century theocracy, like all other forms of government, had a stake in keeping the status quo. Hoping against hope, the Pharisees and Sadducees compromised aspects of their political control to maintain their tenuous hold on the Jewish people. They tottered on a precarious pivot point, an uneasy separation of church and state, which accepted Rome as the keepers of the order while priests practiced the Mosaic Law mostly unperturbed. Their fatal mistake was assuming that 'church and state' could remain so neatly distinct, that the negotiated peace they managed could last indefinitely. It was Jesus who challenged the legitimacy of the Jewish leaders (while simultaneously representing almost no threat to the Roman State), which upset the balance they had negotiated.

And yet, Jesus was not unaware of the political situation. His was a day when other Jews were consumed with fervent Jewish nationalism that butted up against Roman hegemony. Zealots, the freedom fighters of their day, continued to test the resolve of their Roman occupiers. Insurrection never seemed more than one incident away.

FIGURE 1 - JESUS ENTERS JERUSALEM AND THE CROWDS WELCOME HIM BY PIETRO LORENZETTI, 1320

As we know, Jesus would be a victim of this tense atmosphere. He would be falsely accused by the Jewish leaders of threatening the authority of Caesar. In part, he was crucified to temporarily quench the fire fueling potential Hebrew revolt. Despite the fact that Jesus' solution—inward transformation—could have quieted the tempest fanning these flames of rebellion, both Romans and Jews finally saw fit to crucify Him instead, during the quiet morning hours on the day of Preparation (before Passover)—before the multitude awakened. The leadership of both governing groups feared that the agitated throng—drawn to Jerusalem for the momentous Jewish holy day—would seek to make Him king.

But Jesus would have no part in being made King or in directly challenging the Romans. He encouraged His followers to "render unto Caesar those things that are Caesar's and unto God those things that are God's." He allowed a tax gatherer, a social pariah, to be His disciple suggesting that He would not give in to 'guilt by association' nor would He be interested in winning the approval of the masses. He walked away from crowds that desired to make Him king. As to violence, He preached that "those who live by the sword die by the sword." In his last days, He came into Jerusalem riding on a donkey to underscore His approach was peaceful, without threat to the powers that be.

Still, the implied danger remained—due to His popularity with the common people and His public display of malice toward the religious leadership—both factors which set Him on the path to crucifixion. With religious and civil powers on edge, their selfish agendas at risk, and the momentum of events increasing, His death sentence was a *fait accompli*.

THE UNEXPECTED END TO HIS MINISTRY

And so Jesus was crucified. He had attempted to warn His disciples beforehand that He would die, that His death was necessary. Jesus explained that it was the only way they could receive God's salvation. *"Ye know that after two days is the feast of the Passover, and the Son of man is betrayed to be crucified."* (Matthew 26:2) *"The Son of man must be delivered into the hands of sinful men, and be crucified, and the third day rise again."* (Luke 24:7) But his disciples could not come to terms with the fact that He could die—let alone resolve the meaning of His death. They remained blind, despite His instruction, to the foreshadowing inherent in the Passover, the major feast (the 'holy day' or holiday) transpiring at that very moment when He was put to death. He was the Lamb of God sacrificed to propitiate the 'angel of death' even as the first Passover lamb in the days of Moses had symbolized.

The three days after Jesus' death were dark indeed. No doubt Jesus' followers were replaying His words over and over in their minds, struggling to make sense of what had just happened. When the news came from the women attached to their fledging band of believers—that the Lord's body was missing, their shared tragedy was then made worse like a knife twisted in an open wound. Sorrow seemed turned into spite as they heard of this unthinkable crime. Who could be blamed but those who hated and killed Jesus? After all, The Temple Guard had been present at the tomb. They were the police keepers of the Jewish leaders. Who else could have taken the body?

Quickly, however, a different report came to them that Mary Magdalene had seen Jesus alive and He had even spoken encouraging words to her. John and Peter immediately rushed to the tomb and saw His grave clothes. Soon, the reports of His appearance grew more frequent until finally Jesus appeared to the eleven disciples (minus Thomas) behind closed doors where they were 'holed up' possibly in fear to avoid the fate that had been dealt to their leader. But now they saw Him firsthand with their own eyes: the astonishing reports were true. Jesus had overcome death. Moreover, His body was gleaming and His appearance transformed. He was now difficult to recognize. And yet, there was no mistaking Him. His words burned in their hearts. He called them by name.

The power of the resurrection did more than lift the spirits of the disciples. Seeing the risen Christ demonstrated that what He had told them was true. Their commitments were vindicated. Peter had wondered aloud whether 'having given up everything' (including family and fortune) had been worth it. *"Lo, we have left all, and have followed thee"* (Mark 10:28). They could now see the living proof before them. Who else could come back from the dead? This was Jesus whom they had trusted, He was indeed the Christ promised by the prophets of old.

FIGURE 2 - JESUS' ASCENSION TO HEAVEN DEPICTED BY JOHN SINGLETON COPLEY, 1775

IN THE VERY SAME WAY AS YOU SAW HIM LEAVE

Several weeks followed and then they were gathered together again, no longer confused about the reality of Jesus' resurrection. Thomas too now believed after the Savior showed him the scars in his hands, His feet, and His side. And yet, all the disciples still remained trapped within the same nationalistic framework as the Zealots—they too assumed that redemption was a political revolution rather than personal transformation.

We read in Acts, chapter 1 (verses 6-8):

⁶ When they therefore were come together, they asked of Him, saying, "Lord, wilt thou at this time restore again the kingdom to Israel?"

⁷ And He said unto them, "It is not for you to know the times or the seasons, which the Father hath put in his own power.

⁸ "But ye shall receive power, after that the Holy Ghost is come upon you: and ye shall be witnesses unto me both in Jerusalem, and in all Judaea, and in Samaria, and unto the uttermost part of the earth."

We are taught that "no one shall know the day nor the hour" of the Lord's return. The statement in verse 7 is slightly different but seems to convey the same admonition. Perhaps that is so. Perhaps we should never focus on when the Lord will return. But is this what the passage teaches, that His disciples should abstain from all wonderings about the time of His return? Hardly.

Here Jesus' words imply only a mild rebuke, not for asking when He would return but in hoping for His return for the wrong reason. They remained focused on their 'deliverance' from the enemies of Israel. Therefore, Jesus set them straight. Their mission was not to foment an insurgency against the Romans or to retaliate against the leaders of Israel, despite the loathing which Jesus held for them. They should not see Jesus as the Conquering King—not yet. The agenda for the disciples was *to be witnesses*, first in the city of Jerusalem, then in their province of Judea, and then beyond their homeland. This plan was global in scope. They were not to think in terms of a Kingdom in Israel, but a Kingdom of God across the entire earth. This was their mission statement.

> [9] *And when he had spoken these things, while they beheld, he was taken up; and a cloud received him out of their sight.*
>
> [10] *And while they looked steadfastly toward heaven as he went up, behold, two men stood by them in white apparel;*
>
> [11] *Which also said, "Ye men of Galilee, why stand ye gazing up into heaven? This same Jesus, which is taken up from you into heaven, shall so come in like manner as ye have seen him go into heaven."*

Within this passage, we see a paradox in the meaning of the Kingdom of God: *it was not for them to know the exact time or season.* And yet, time is slipping away. Jesus Christ will be returning—and soon! This is the strategic principle we will examine in this book.

Luke tells us that two men (suddenly) stood by them in white apparel and said, in effect, "There is no time to waste. You must get busy now. This same Jesus, which you have just seen ascend into heaven, will come back to this earth in the very same manner." The implication was that they should assume He would be coming back within their lifetime, maybe within a decade or less! They must be witnesses and yet they must witness with haste, with a sense of urgency. They only thing they were to wait for was the coming of the Spirit, so that their efforts would literally be 'imbued by power from on high.' The mission was so critical that God Himself, in the form of the Spirit of Christ, would come to live in them that He might help them achieve their objective. The Spirit would enable their witness to the works of God, to the salvation Jesus Christ had just won for everyone in the world.

This was also a key aspect to the message: *the emphasis was universal in scope.* They were *not* to 'hang out' in Jerusalem and wait for Jesus to come back to save the Temple. He had already predicted that the Jewish Temple would be destroyed. *"Not one stone will be left upon another.*" (Mark 13:2) As magnificent as the Temple was, it was soon to crumble. The foundation of the new faith was not in a building made with human hands. God had once chosen to live inside the Temple, in the Holy of Holies. Solomon had built a house for Him—one of the Seven Wonders of the ancient world. But no longer would the LORD God dwell there. Now He would live *within them*. As stalwart as the stones were, as solid and indestructible as the Temple appeared, it would not stand the test of time. A different kind of stone would comprise the essence of the true religion from henceforth.

This new faith as exemplified in the affirmation of Peter (Peter, the *petra*, the 'little rock')—a new faith that would become a giant rock (a *petros*) able to withstand all attacks. It would prevail against the very gates of Hell itself (Matthew 16:18). The coming destruction of the Temple stood as a not-so-subtle clue that the Jewish religion should not be their focus. *Their very bodies would become the Temple of the Lord.* (See 1 Corinthians 3:16, 6:19) So they must revamp their way of thinking. They must get out of Jerusalem and go beyond their Jewish homeland. They must take the message to the ends of the earth.

And yet, this same Jesus would return again VERY SOON in like manner. Consequently, there is no time to lose! It was, after all, a very big world, bigger even than the disciples knew.

THE APOCALYPSE, A KEY ELEMENT TO THEIR MESSAGE

And yet, the passage remains puzzling for several reasons. We should not find it challenging because of the miraculous event which took place (Jesus ascending into the clouds) or angels appearing alongside the disciples with a message as firm as it was frantic in content. Many (if not most) who believe in Jesus Christ today believe miracles do happen and that these events as recorded in the Bible and *are just as likely to be literally true* as they are to be spiritual symbols of a living Christ. Jesus' directive, however, seems to be in stark contrast with the statement from the angels. On the one hand, Jesus admonishes His disciples not to ask about whether the Kingdom is coming at this time. On the other, the message from His angelic ambassadors left no room for debate: Jesus will be coming back again, physically and "in the clouds, just as you saw Him leave." His return will be spectacular. And when He returns, it will be too late for those who have not heard of Him, those who have not accepted His message. Otherwise, why would there be such a sense of urgency? Therefore, the gist of their proclamation was obvious: "Get the message out now. Hurry!"

Despite this splendid sense of urgency, here we are 2,000 years later and still Jesus has not returned in the same manner as He left. So we are inclined to wonder whether the message of Jesus' soon return was perhaps a 'bit' overstated. Were the angels sensationalists, motivating the disciples with misleading information? Worse, was Jesus mistaken about a matter so vital to His legacy? I hardly think so.

Modern theologians believe that Jesus was literally a man of his time—and He was flat wrong about the end of the world. While that modernist conclusion is easy to draw, it obviously makes Jesus out to be something of a fool. That perspective may occupy the highest citadels of theological scholars, but it lies at the bottom of a very dark and dank pit of gross error. Jesus was not mistaken about His Second Advent. There was much more to the story than what such conventional wisdom supposed.

Lest we fail to get the point like the disciples failed to understand, let me draw out the point plainly. *The disciples were to be His witnesses throughout the world and for the remainder of the age in light of the very fact that He would come back.* The message was not inaccurate at all—not if we realize that the *coming apocalypse comprises an indispensable element in the Christian gospel just as much today as it did two millennia ago.*

INTRODUCTION

The Lord requires we be forever vigilant about His return. In essence, that is what this book contends. We should be watching—everyday. As my friends at Prophecy in the News have always said in closing their television program, "Keep looking up!" No doubt there are times when such advice could get you into trouble. Goodness knows ranchers here in Oklahoma are careful NOT to look up.

The Apocalypse, however, constitutes the *sine qua non* of the gospel of Jesus Christ. What does that Latin phrase mean? The words literally mean "without which not." But Merriam-Webster tells us that *sine qua non* means something that is absolutely indispensable. It is essential. If you do not have this element then you have nothing at all. In the context of the Apocalypse and the Good News of Jesus Christ—His gospel—there is no gospel if there is no apocalypse. As we will discuss later, Jesus placed the apocalypse at the center of His message. His understanding of the Kingdom of God was not an ethereal spiritual cosmology such as the Gnostics propounded when they twisted the gospel to fit their perennial philosophy already ages old by the time they sought to corrupt Christianity with its arcane assertions. Neither was it a sentimental conception of religious meaning which we encounter in New Age books or lectures. It was not enlightenment granted by the Buddha. It was not empowerment through mastering magical incantations or rituals. No, to Jesus Christ, *the Kingdom of God was a physical, historical, "in your face" turning of the tables on the unrighteous powers that control the world.* As His beatitudes emphasized, the world would soon be turned upside down. Those in power would soon find themselves put out to pasture. Those that were poor in spirit who feel estranged for their inability to manifest what religious leaders lauded as true religion—they would be the role models of the Kingdom of Heaven. Those who were meek and controlled nothing in this present age, would soon inherit (possess) the whole world in the age to come. Those who were in last place will win the blue ribbon and those who were first in line will be made to wait until the very last. The Kingdom of God consists in a monumental *reversal of fortune*. The Kingdom of God envisions this radical change in the way the world will be governed and how its citizens will live their lives. This is the gospel Jesus preached.

KEEPING A KINGDOM MINDSET

Given this paradoxical character of the Kingdom of God—that Jesus' disciples are asked to embrace the paradox of seeking to convert the whole world even while they remain vigilant waiting for His return—perhaps we should stop asking the question of "when will it happen." Perhaps we should only ask, "What must we be doing today since Jesus is coming very soon?" There is little doubt that we should *maintain a Kingdom mindset* in more ways than one. Not only should we realize that the methods and standards of the present age are anathema in the age to come. We should also face the ever-present proximity of His return. We live in a transient time—we are between two ages. We must relinquish the values of the old age. We must embrace the values of the new, even though the new world to come awaits consummation. This contradiction comprises "the already, not yet." It constitutes the tension within which the Church of Jesus Christ must practice its faith—exemplifying the new Kingdom. *We are to model that Kingdom today, even though our lifestyle will not be fully in fashion until the Kingdom comes.*

So does this make the question of when Jesus will return a non-sense question? Should we live like the existentialist who finds meaning by embracing the paradox of meaninglessness? Should we commit ourselves to an existence in which a final resolution never arrives? Given that Jesus demanded His disciples believe in His immediate return, all the while knowing that His Kingdom was at least two millennia away,[1] what manner of man

---

[1] Yes, I believe that Jesus had awareness that His Kingdom was not to come until many centuries in the future.

was this that asked his followers to adopt such an irrational lifestyle, conflicting with the values of the world, and their everyday common sense and better judgment?

If we assume (incorrectly I might emphasize) that there was never to be resolution in the form of a physical, earthly kingdom, then clearly the gospel of Jesus Christ must mean something very different than what the Church has taught its members for most of its 2,000 year history.

No, the intention of this paradox must be that the followers of Jesus Christ ought always to remember that for each of them, the duration of their waiting, their anticipation of the Kingdom, remains bounded by two very real truths: *one—we are all finite and we will die someday; two—that someday may be today.*

We never have that much time left in the bank. At most, we will enjoy no more than 80 years of service, and then we will move on to the next phase of our existence. Likewise, we never know whether the day in which we find ourselves will be our last day. Like Job, we should recognize that our life is but a breath— our existence hangs by a thin thread (Job 7:7). When our number is called and our time is up, we will be with our Lord and the Kingdom of God, for each one of us—separately—begins at that distinctive moment. Either (1) living in light of the imminent time-space return of Christ, or (2) the transition to living consciously in His presence, always stares us squarely in the face, whether we realize that ultimate reality or not.

EVEN MODERN THEOLOGIANS TESTIFY TO THIS TRUTH

For the past one hundred years, most liberal theologians asserted that Jesus Christ looked to a physical Kingdom of God in this world. He believed in the apocalypse. He preached a coming Kingdom in which God would break into the natural order and bring justice to the world. Unfortunately, these teachers believed he was deceived to think that way, being one of many "apocalyptic rabbis" roaming about the countryside in Palestine, expecting the world to end soon in flames of fire. It is important, however, to recognize these 'doubting Thomases,' while not regarding Jesus to be the Son of God in the correct sense, *still asserted Jesus DID believe in a coming Kingdom of God in a real, not 'spiritual' sense.*

Bart D. Ehrman, in his book, *Jesus: Apocalpytic Prophet of the New Millennium* argues a compelling case for this view. Although the most prolific and popular writer on New Testament topics today, ironically Ehrman writes as an agnostic. He investigates and writes as an historian, absent faith that Jesus Christ was anything more than a remarkable personage.

But what does Ehrman assert concerning this principal character of religious history, one Jesus of Nazareth who is worshipped by over a billion people today? Jesus must be understood as a person in the context of his day and age. He must be seen as an *apocalypticist*—a rabbi utterly convinced the world was coming to an end. His entire message—the coming of the Kingdom of God—begins and ends with his radical (and socially 'sideways') perspective. Ehrman states:

> What has struck me over the years, though, is that the view shared probably by the majority of scholars over the course of this century, at least in Germany and America, is equally shocking for most nonspecialist readers. And yet it is scarcely known to the general reading public. This is the view that is embraced in this [Ehrman's] book. In a nutshell, it's a view first advanced most persuasively by none other than the great twentieth-century humanitarian Albert Schweitzer. It claims that Jesus is best understood as a first-century Jewish apocalypticist. This is a shorthand way of saying that Jesus fully expected that the history of the world as we know it (well, as he knew it) was going to come to a screeching halt, that God was soon going to intervene in the affairs of this world, overthrow the forces of evil in a cosmic act of judgment, destroy huge masses of humanity, and abolish existing human political and religious institutions. All this would be a prelude to the arrival of a new order on earth, the Kingdom of God. Moreover, Jesus expected

that this cataclysmic end of history would come in his own generation, at least during the lifetime of his disciples. It's pretty shocking stuff, really. And the evidence that Jesus believed and taught it is fairly impressive.[2]

Such strongly supportive testimony for the assertion that Jesus preached the apocalypse, looked at from the standpoint of evidentiary value, *constitutes a more decisive witness than those who believe in Bible prophecy and the divinity of Jesus Christ.*

Why would I say that? Because Ehrman's view, like most modern theology, rejects Jesus ever claimed to be the Son of God—it expresses doubt that Jesus even claimed to be the fulfillment of the Son of Man referenced in the Book of Daniel and other inter-testament writings (one thinks of the Book of Enoch and other extra-biblical sources discovered in the Dead Sea Scrolls). Nonetheless, liberal scholarship asserts Jesus did believe in the physical manifestation of the Messiah in the realm of space-time. The Kingdom of God would intersect the realm of humankind. It was not to be 'pie in the sky by and by.' Rather, in the same guise as Jesus actions in the Temple when he overturned the tables of the moneychangers, the Kingdom of God would upset the apple cart. It would forever alter the normal ways of the world where the poor are oppressed while the rich run the show.

Thus, modern theologians, no friends of literal biblical interpretation, do *not* deny that Jesus preached the imminent literal apocalypse—*they simply reject that what he preached would ever come to pass*, as such change would require the supernatural intervention of God. From their viewpoint, Jesus may have been mixed up about certain things. But he was never double-minded about the end of the world. He based His whole ministry on that assumption.

---

[2] Ehrman, Bart D. *Jesus: Apocalyptic Prophet of the New Millennium* (p. 2). Oxford University Press. Kindle Edition.

Liberalism, of course, does not leave it there. It goes on to assert that while Jesus believed in apocalypse and the upheaval of the world system, He was just wrong to think that God would stop the injustice and terminate mankind's reproachable reign. Of course, that is where *we that believe Jesus was the Son of God* (and was *not* confused about the meaning and timing of the apocalypse), part company.

Assuming, for the sake of argument that Jesus is who we evangelicals believe He claimed to be—i.e., the Son of Man and the Son of God, of all Christian 'branches' of faith we should be the most eager to understand the essence of His gospel so we remain true to its substance. If His principal teaching consisted of the coming Kingdom, it should be front and center in the pulpits of America. *Even liberal theologians would confirm this very truth.* To be authentic, we had better understand why Jesus was an apocalypticist.

EVANGELICALS DENY THE MESSAGE OF THE KINGDOM

How ironic then that famed evangelical preacher Rick Warren dismisses the apocalypse and coming Kingdom as a matter of no import to Jesus. In his blockbuster book, *The Purpose Driven Life*, Warren makes no bones about it. Prophecy is *not* important.

> When the disciples wanted to talk about prophecy, Jesus quickly switched the conversation to evangelism. He wanted them to concentrate on their mission in the world. He said in essence, "The details of my return are none of your business. What is your business in the mission I have given you. Focus on that!"[3]

What a thorough misrepresentation of the truth! Warren contends 200 years of liberal protestant scholarship, the emphasis of the true church almost 2,000 years in the making, and the 'fundamentals' espoused by evangelicals in this country during the past century have all gotten the gospel wrong. Instead, the essential

---

[3] Pastor Rick Warren, *The Purpose Driven Life,* p. 285.

message should be about the here and now, about finding purpose in life today through this up-to-date 'Jesus.' To Warren, Jesus believed the apocalypse was malarkey and would have nothing to do with it! Furthermore, neither should the disciples.

How tragic that Warren's message is considered an idyllic statement of evangelical belief! It fails even to be a fair portrayal of liberal protestant scholarship. It can only be a statement that has been thoroughly infused with 'positive thinking' if not out-and-out new age mysticism. Furthermore, Warren pulls Jesus completely out of his historical context and puts words into his mouth that reflect the Gospel According to Rick. For these reasons, I choose not to back away from a most critical assessment of Warren's message: Rick Warren preaches another gospel than that which Jesus Christ preached. *His assertion that Jesus possessed a lackadaisical attitude toward Bible prophecy could not be further from the truth*. It ignores scores of Jesus' statements to the contrary. As such the Gospel According to Rick could not be more at odds with the essential message of this book. However, I do not intend to mount a negative polemic against those in evangelicalism such as Rick Warren who dismiss the importance of eschatology, let alone who fail to proclaim the message of the Kingdom of God. The truth will become evident of its own accord as we advance a positive polemic demonstrating why the apocalypse matters not only doctrinally but practically to those who seek to be disciples of Jesus Christ.

To recap: the coming of the Kingdom of God was the heart of Jesus' message. Virtually all respected Bible scholars (liberal or conservative) assert this to be so. The only real issue concerns whether *we should believe Jesus or not* and put into practice the form of spirituality he taught and exemplified, which hung on the promise of His soon return. Additionally, unless we conclude that Jesus intentionally wished to mislead His disciples about His return to this world (to culminate the age in which we now live), it seems most illogical to assume the central teaching of the gospel of Jesus Christ is based upon a non-literal, non-historical, indeed nonsense *non-event*.

The Kingdom of God is coming. It will happen in space-time. The "other side" will break into our experience one day. The curtains will be pulled back. The day of reckoning will come. The time of reward and recompense will be here before we know it.

BLOOD MOONS AND THE SIGNS OF HIS COMING

The recent interest in the so-called blood moons (lunar eclipses) of 2014 and 2015, have brought the question back into the discussion for many—not just those who study Bible prophecy. The very unusual occurrence of four blood moons within a short interval of time (in this case 18 months), with those blood moons falling on certain very important of the Jewish 'feast days,' has given rise to increased speculation about the end of the world. Why is this the case? *Because the blood moon portrays a portent in the heavens that speak of apocalypse.*

For many reasons, the apocalypse appears imminent. But whether it commences soon, several decades from now, or beyond—more than ever before—the only hope for our troubled nation and our world *rests in the truth of the Bible and its prescriptions for our personal lives, our culture, and our nation.*

Many will object to this assertion; their tag-line likely being, 'been there, done that.' However, the unfortunate reality remains that the witness Jesus' followers were ordered to give to the utmost parts of the world and to the very end of the age, often failed to resemble what Jesus truly taught and the authentic spirituality he demands of us. Somewhere along the line, those meant to serve as 'salt' in the world lost their savor. No small part of why this happened owes to the fact that the apocalyptic element of Christianity was downplayed or eliminated altogether. The message "Jesus is coming" was "interpreted right out of existence," being altered to mean something far different than what Jesus instilled in the minds of His closest followers.

In other words, the Christian message appears irrelevant to many members of our society not because it was tried and found wanting; but because many of its teachers today (and during the past two centuries) so rarely represented a most essential element of the gospel of Christ, leading too few converts to commit themselves to its achievement.

Many modern-day preachers ceased the proclamation of an authentic gospel when they jettisoned elements *indispensable* to its meaning, in particular the biblical catchphrase *"The Kingdom of God is at hand!"* Fearing an accusation of preaching 'hell, fire, and brimstone' too few ministers heralded what Jesus proclaimed, "Repent and believe—before it is too late!" For far too long, the gospel has been diluted—its life-changing message watered down. It has failed to affect society because it became a message directed *only* for inward comfort, not outward change.

A 'KINGDOMLESS' GOSPEL HAS HAD LITTLE IMPACT

And yet, Christ's admonition that God's Kingdom comes, remains crucial for this element catalyzes all other aspects of Christ's radical solution for humankind—a solution that has both personal and social implications. When the gospel of Christ does not contain a strong dose of apocalyptic fervor, the audience interprets the offer of salvation *as a 'take it or leave it' proposition*. It is advice only—lacking any mention of repentance from immorality, any mandate to forsake self as priority, any call for justice for those dispossessed. Without the stark reminder that the Kingdom of God is not of this world—not compatible with human government or manmade religious efforts to acquire happiness and purpose—Christianity has nothing different to offer, nothing worth dying for. And once we acknowledge that there is nothing worth a martyr's death, we soon realize that there is nothing worth living for either.

True Christianity and *true spirituality* (what we believe and how we put it into practice) stand upon the premise *our time in this life remains short*—every moment counts. And yet, in the short period we have on this planet, we leave a legacy—good or bad. Each and every day our actions leave an indelible imprint in the fabric of time. Our lives either enhance the design in the tapestry or disfigure the picture it provides. As an old preacher friend of mine used to say, "Every day is a day of judgment."

At the danger of reducing this truism to a sound bite, or worse, an abbreviated limerick, allow me to offer this rhyming proverb: *We spin the weave we wish to leave.* To switch the metaphor: we make our mark indelibly on the paper regardless of whether we lift a pen. The gospel of Jesus Christ teaches *how we should live* and *why this lifestyle provides hope and meaning.* However, the irony is that evangelists diminish the impact of the gospel when they disregard the proximity of the end of days.

The paradox should not be that surprising to those who reflect on the teachings of Jesus. They were full of apparent contradictions: "He who loses his life for my sake shall find it." "He who wishes to be great among you must be servant of all." And many other similarly disconcerting teachings. Should it be shocking that the most effective way to change the world is to predict that its ending has now come into view? Indeed, in the final analysis, the so-called harbingers of doom may be the greatest of optimists for they see a new world coming after the existing order crumbles. They expect that a society now stressed to the breaking point stands at the brink, ready to be overturned. Soon it will be transcended. In short, therein lies the message of the Kingdom of God.

It remains my contention, however ironic it may seem to the reader, that too little optimism exists today because far too few hold fast this conviction that the apocalypse stands ready to break upon us—the Kingdom of God is near to us (Luke 10:9). In fact, it appears in our midst now (Luke 17:21).[4]

To be more emphatic: there remains only one foundation from which to build an enduring hope. It requires believing in a gospel with the conviction that only the Second Advent of Jesus Christ can achieve the radical transformation humanity needs, both individually and corporately. His return culminates history, specifically accomplishing our salvation as expressed through the words of the New Testament. We cannot compromise and say we must only experience inward transformation because we do not know when the Lord will return. That is, as they used to say, a cop out.

In response, atheists or agnostics will complain: "At best this can be no more than a dereliction of duty! At worst it is the greatest of grand delusions!" But the promise of the Second Coming comprises *the gospel truth*. As we will soon show, it conveys what Jesus taught. Likewise, His Apostles institutionalized this expectation at the beginning of His church. Even as the first century came to a close and the Lord had not returned, we saw throughout the 'patristic period' (characterized by early leaders like Polycarp, Irenaeus, Justin Martyr, Origen, Athanasius... leading up to St. Augustine), that the soon coming of the Lord was strenuously upheld. It was essential to the Church's message. The Lord may tarry—but that does not mean He has forever delayed His return.

The dark predictions of what lies ahead—a sun *black* like a sackcloth of hair and a moon turned *blood red*—are merely the most dramatic of many ominous signs depicted for the last days by the Bible. Not long ago, almost everyone agreed these images were no more than imaginative symbols. However, such frightening pictures no longer seem too fantastic to occur in our empirical

---

[4] *"Neither shall they say, Lo here! Or, lo there! For, behold, the kingdom of God is within you." (Luke 17:21)*

reality. Many scenarios suggest how such horrible sights could become the standard way our 'sky lights' appear. In this regard, it now seems easier than ever to be a biblical literalist. The blood moons of 2014 and 2015 remind us of this unimpeachable fact.

EVEN SCIENCE TELLS US THE APOCALYPSE IS NEAR

However, empirical evidence—now more than ever—makes the approaching apocalypse appear much more plausible (if not totally probable). In other words, the argument that we are living in the last days relies not on fanciful interpretation of scripture nor on a consensus of the world's religions that the end is near. Rather 'secular' science, in this context a most surprising partner to the Bible, forecasts impending and insurmountable catastrophes.

Comet collisions could come crashing into our planet, unprecedented solar activity might destroy our electrical grid, increasing stress on Earth's tectonic plates seem likely to generate more and more massive earthquakes, unprecedented climate change threatens to kill off entire species, and biological threats (be they natural or manmade) could destroy human life altogether. Pick your poison: science serves up a surplus of calamities that serve as most proximate perils.

Whether we choose to accept what the Bible predicts, or whether we simply acknowledge what science projects concerning the future, either source tells the same story: we seem ultimately destined for doomsday. It is not a question of if, but how soon. Since this fate has been forced upon us, addressing the apocalypse is no longer merely a matter of 'getting the gospel message right.' It appears to be a question of life and death which we must stare right in the eye.

For this reason, as well as to try to rectify the right meaning of the gospel for the benefit of my readers, the pages ahead underscore that our confidence and hope must come from (1) a better understanding of what the Bible says is soon coming to pass; (2) what we can do to escape the worst of these cataclysms; and

(3) most notably, why we should eagerly look forward to the amazing promises of the coming Kingdom of God.

However, please rest assured, I do not argue we should 'give up' and decide that we ought to resign from all forms of social activism, or pledge our efforts solely to evangelism (to get as many into the life boats as possible since the ship stands destined to sink). *The true gospel insists upon achieving balance.* We must prepare for the worst, but hope for the best. We must provide for our families, but realize that the ultimate provision for those we love amounts to far more than just food and clothing. We must assume the Lord returns today, but plan for tomorrow. We must warn everyone that our out-of-control ship continues full speed ahead heading straight for the rocks. Unless we change course now, we will crash headlong into them. We can change course—but only if enough people convince the captain to turn the rudder.

While hardly comforting, this description of our predicament sums up the tension inherent in the Christian message and in living an authentic Christian life, a manner of living mandated for those who choose to pick up their crosses daily and follow Him. For only in taking up our crosses can we find real peace, enduring meaning, and unassailable hope.

THE PURPOSE OF THIS BOOK

In my others books, I have asserted that authentic Christianity *constitutes an apocalyptic religion*—and should rightly continue to be so even to this day. However, I did not put forth in those books anything more than a cursory argument for why a preoccupation with biblical prophecy was pivotal to our preparedness and effectiveness as believers. It remains my hope that I close this gap thoroughly through this offering. After demonstrating the premise that there are myriad signs of His coming and that Christianity comprises an apocalyptic faith drawing upon the original biblical texts, I turn my focus to the promise of Christ's return and how it provides hope—a hope that makes a difference in our lives now even as we face countless upheavals in the months and years ahead. Furthermore, I will answer the question, "How can we obtain confidence and optimism about the future despite the dismal state of our world and its prospects for substantive change?"

For those who believe in Jesus Christ, we have no excuse if we fail to take Bible prophecy seriously and understand the 'times and seasons.' Our inheritance as the children of God includes His Word in the Bible: we can learn *what happens next* and *what the world to come is like*. Jesus taught His disciples these very truths. Moreover, it should be our priority from a practical standpoint: we learn where we must ground our hope. Once we come to realize the stark contrast between what humanity plans for this world compared to what it means for the Kingdom of God to invade it, we can reorient our viewpoint finding that purpose and hope. We will be empowered afresh to display the love of Christ within our relationships, experience peace in these troubled times, and exude courage to face the challenges ahead.

Moreover, believing in Christ's Second Advent increases the impact Christians make in the world—today. It makes the world a better place. Although opposed to conventional wisdom, historically this has been shown to be true. The first Americans believed they were to be the 'shining city on a hill' paving the way for the millennial reign of the Messiah. When revivals broke out in our country (several times, the so-called *Great Awakenings* of which there were four), many political advances were achieved.[5] Doubtless, the assertion strikes many as ironic. *But believing in the new world soon to come enables greater influence on the world in which we live in—now.* It energizes our commitment. Once we are

---

[5] "Joseph Tracy, the minister and historian who gave this religious phenomenon its name in his influential 1842 book *The Great Awakening*, saw the First Great Awakening as a precursor to the American Revolution. The evangelical movement of the 1740s played a key role in the development of democratic concepts in the period of the American Revolution. This helped create a demand for the separation of church and state." (See en.wikipedia.org/wiki/Great Awakening).

convinced of the coming Kingdom, transformation begins in the *hic et nunc,* the 'here and now.' By knowing the fate of our planet, we prepare ourselves to deal with the pending challenges. Likewise, by providing the Bible's perspective on the 'hope for the hereafter,' *we gain confidence in our ability to withstand current challenges.*

Finally, allow me once more to reiterate the balance I hope to communicate: I applaud and encourage activities that promote peace, social justice, and building stronger relationships among families, groups, diverse cultures, and nations. I say this despite my belief that our most vital hope lies exclusively in the coming *genuine new world order* (not the one which has been called for by the celebrated politicians of our times, which I believe is based on secular humanism and plutocracy), as promulgated by the Judeo-Christian scriptures, implicit in the hopes of our nations' founders, and exemplified through the countless men and women who have supplied this nation such a rich heritage.

Therefore, let us champion once again the original gospel *byword* and the consistent insistence of Jesus' followers through the ages: *the Kingdom of God is at hand!* Will we embrace this remarkable reality or in apathetic doubt dismiss it? That choice remains for each person reading this book, individually, to make in the solemnity of his or her own heart.

2: HEAVENLY PORTENTS OF THE APOCALYPSE

Blow ye the trumpet in Zion, and sound an alarm in my holy mountain: let all the inhabitants of the land tremble: for the day of the LORD cometh, for it is nigh at hand; a day of darkness and of gloominess, a day of clouds and of thick darkness, as the morning spread upon the mountains: a great people and a strong; there hath not been ever the like, neither shall be any more after it, even to the years of many generations... The sun shall be turned into darkness, and **the moon into blood,** *before the great and the terrible day of the LORD come.*
(Joel 2:1-2, 31)

And I beheld when he had opened the sixth seal, and, lo, there was a great earthquake; and the sun became black as sackcloth of hair, and **the moon became as blood**.
(Revelation 6:12)

WHAT THE WORD APOCALYPSE MEANS

THE WORD *APOCALYPSE* CONNOTES FRIGHTENING IMAGES OF DEATH AND FOREBODING. HOWEVER THE LITERAL MEANING OF THE WORD IS FAR MORE BENIGN. TRANSLATED LITERALLY FROM the Greek, apocalypse means a *disclosure of knowledge.* It is connected to the act of revealing. Hence the apocalypse is a revelation or a revealing—an exposé. A better definition might be *a disclosure of information which had not been previously made known.*

This does not keep us from connecting the word with the most awesome of images associated with the end of the world. To picture the meaning of apocalypse, we think of heavenly signs and wonders—of portents that presage calamities coming from the sky. Indeed, the Bible fills our mind's eye with such images. The passage from the Book of Joel, the second of the 12 Minor Prophets, speaks of the *Day of the Lord* which is associated with the apocalypse. Indeed, according to most interpretations, the Day of the Lord is synonymous with the day that the apocalypse will come to pass. [1]

The most talked about portent of the apocalypse in our day is *the blood moon*. The phrase *blood moon* conveys the color of the moon during a lunar eclipse. When the earth passes between the moon and the sun during a full moon it literally casts a giant shadow. It is probably too technical for most readers so I won't try to explain the *umbra* and *penumbra* of the earth's shadow. Suffice it to say these portions of the 'earth's shadow' applies different amounts of lighting to the moon's surface. However, speaking non-technically, the sun's light bleeds around the edges of the earth, this light passes through the earth's atmosphere where it is scattered by the molecules of the earth's atmosphere. This refraction causes the resulting light that passes onto the moon to appear red as it is projected upon the moon's surface. Usually the moon appears as a darkish red-gray—*not blood red.* But of course the phrase 'blood moon' conveys a much more graphic and

FIGURE 3 – THE BLOOD MOON OF APRIL 15, 2014

---

[1] The meaning of the Day of the Lord is complicated because there are so many biblical names for this period. We will study its meaning later in this book.

colorful expression than a 'darkened gray' moon. Thus, the more poignant description has come to be the standard way to refer to the phenomena. The fact the Bible talks in several places about the moon turning to blood no doubt helped the phrase enter our vernacular.

The apocalypse is generally portrayed by signs in the heavens. This signs are seen as portents. Portents are *omens* and this noun comes from the verb *portend* and the Latin verb *portendere* which means 'to foretell.' Portents are signs of impending calamity, usually signs seen in the sky. Historically comets have been regarded as the most visible and powerful portents. When comets appear

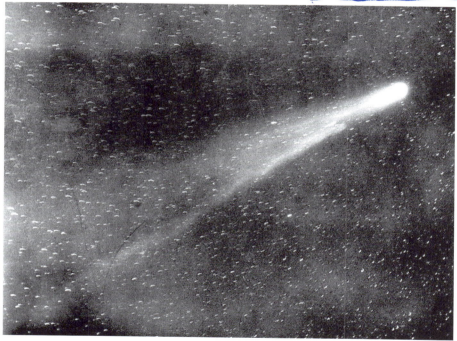

FIGURE 4 – HALLEY'S COMET, 2010, OFTEN SEEN AS A HARBINGER OF DOOM

the rise or fall of empires are often predicted. The most recent comet portending doom was the comet Hale-Bopp in 1997. Of course, the only real doom was for the Heaven's Gate cult, forever remembered as the group of fanatics that committed mass suicide expecting the world to end. They hoped that their deaths would send them straight up to what they believed was a spacecraft trailing the comet, commissioned by aliens to save these cult members from certain death destined for all those who remained on earth.

The planet Mars has been regarded often as a portent especially when it comes nearest to the earth. At its *opposition*, when it orbits on the same side of the sun as the earth, it appears its brightest and its reddest. The distance between Mars and the earth varies dramatically because of Mars' highly elliptical orbit. At aphelion, Mars may be 250 million miles from earth. At perihelion, Mars may be as close as 34 million miles as it was within this decade. Thus, the intensity of its brightest and color widely varies. Like a 'blood moon', the red color of Mars symbolized death and destruction. Indeed, in ancient Rome, the planet Mars symbolized war as its patron god Mars was equated with the god of War.[2] In Rome, the doors to the Temple of Mars would be flung wide open whenever the Roman Empire was at war (which was often!)

TODAY'S MOST POPULAR PORTENT

But those who study biblical prophecy have seen the portent of the blood moon peak their interest due to a fascinating discovery by pastor Mark Biltz, born in Kansas but today a Tacoma native. In 2008, Biltz communicated his astronomical findings to a national audience when he appeared on Prophecy in the News (produced in my home town of Oklahoma City). Co-hosts J.R. Church and Gary Stearman were most intrigued by Biltz's findings. On the program Biltz referenced NASA's web site that maintained a calendar of eclipses, both solar and lunar. NASA referred to a phenomenon as a *tetrad*, or four consecutive total lunar eclipses occurring during a two-year period. What was most peculiar to Biltz was when this

---

[2] Romans considered themselves 'Martians' or children of Mars. Rome was founded by Romulus and Remus, the twins suckled by a she-wolf, but descendants of Aeneas a warrior of the Trojan War, who was purportedly the offspring of Mars himself. The account of his experiences is the subject of Virgil's' *Aeneid*.

series of consecutive lunar eclipses occurred. Tetrads have happened dozens of times during the Christian era. But only eight times have tetrads occurred on Jewish Feast Days (the same two feast days, two years running).

Given that Judaism observes a lunar calendar (our Gregorian calendar is a solar calendar), in which 'new moons' and 'full moons' establish new months and new years; thus, lunar eclipses might seem to be of little consequence.

Still, when correlating the tetrads to events affecting the Jewish peoples, Biltz identified some startling results. He noted that the tetrads might have heralded 'red letter dates' for the Jews. He was particularly sensitive to that possibility since Biltz had previously studied in depth the meaning behind the Jewish Feast Days, the 'holy convocations' given by Moses to the Hebrews as recorded in Leviticus, chapter 23. Learning about the symbolism of these true holidays (aka 'holy days'), energized his newly adopted Christian faith. Biltz knew he had Jewish roots, but the lessons concerning the importance of Hebrew Feasts were electrifying. He describes his discovery with these words:

> One morning, as I was praying, a thought popped into my head: Why don't I compare the dates of the eclipses on the NASA website to the dates on the biblical calendar? When I did, I was shocked to find that all four eclipses— over both years— fell on the biblical holidays of Passover and the Feast of Tabernacles. I just about jumped out of my skin. Immediately I ran to my computer and pulled up NASA's website to look up other times when there have been four consecutive blood moons, which are total lunar eclipses, where the moon appears blood red. NASA calls four total blood moons in a row a *tetrad*, and they list their occurrences. I noticed there weren't any in the 1600s, 1700s, or even the 1800s. The last time there was a tetrad was back in the 1900s, and to my amazement, they also fell on the feasts of Passover and Tabernacles. When I noticed the years these phenomena occurred, my mind began reeling. The last two times there were four blood moons in a row, they happened, first, right after Israel became

a nation in 1948, and then again when Israel retook Jerusalem in 1967. I started doing a Hallelujah dance.[3]

At first blush, these instances of the tetrads did seem to hold special meaning when connected to those years in which the tetrad fell (1949-50 as well as 1967-68), dates associated with key events in the life of Israel, although the tetrads before these two much more recent sets appeared to hold less meaning. Biltz was not ready, however, to dismiss the others as without consequence. They still might be meaningful.

Below are the tetrads that fall on consecutive Jewish holidays:

- 162-163 AD — Passover and Feast of Tabernacles
- 795-796 — Passover and Yom Kippur
- 842-843 — Passover and Yom Kippur
- 860-861 — Passover and Feast of Tabernacles
- 1493-1494 — Passover and Feast of Trumpets
- 1949-1950 — Passover and Feast of Trumpets
- 1967-1968 — Passover and Feast of Trumpets
- 2014-2015 — Passover and Feast of Tabernacles

The 1949-1950 tetrad occurred during the Jewish War of independence. The 1967-1968 tetrad commenced a few months before the June 1967 'Six-day War.' Although not a perfect fit, it seemed to suggest a correlation worthy of making note. Moreover, if one connected the events of those years, seeing in them auspicious dates for Israel in which the respective wars solidified a place in the world for a Jewish homeland (and to reestablish Jerusalem as the capital of Israel), it should logically lead one to wonder if the tetrad of 2014-2015 might also point to a time of war which builds on the territorial gains obtained in the previous two "blood moon wars." Given the current tension between Israel and Iran, the fear that

---

[3] Biltz, Mark (2014-03-18). *Blood Moons: Decoding the Imminent Heavenly Signs* (Kindle Locations 101-109). WND Books. Kindle Edition.

Iran is preparing a nuclear weapon to be directed at the nation of Israel, it would not be an outrageous prediction that war looms.

Still, there are problems drawing this conclusion. There were intervening wars that produced much less propitious results. For one, the Yom Kippur War of 1973 almost destroyed Israel. Many other instances of conflict and war transpired between then and now, none of which were glorious victories.

Secondly, the outcomes cited in the wars of 1949 and 1967 were, for the most part, positive events. The outcome certainly was good. In conflict with this fact, however, Jewish tradition holds that for Israel blood moons portend *bad outcomes* instead of good ones. If true, how do we reconcile these issues?

WHAT DOES THE TETRAD MEAN FOR ISRAEL?

In an article written for *The Truth*, September 2, 2013, Michael Snyder puzzles over the meaning of the current tetrad (underway now as I write these words in late April, 2014):

> Is Israel going to be involved in a war during the blood red moons of 2014 and 2015?
>
> According to ancient Jewish tradition, a lunar eclipse is a harbinger of bad things for Israel. If that eclipse is blood red, that is a sign that war is coming. And blood red moons that happen during Biblical festivals seem to be particularly significant. There was a "tetrad" of blood red moons that fell during Passover 1967, the Feast of Tabernacles 1967, Passover 1968 and the Feast of Tabernacles 1968. And of course the 1967 war during which Israel took full control of Jerusalem took place during that time period. There was also a "tetrad" of blood red moons that fell during Passover 1949, the Feast of Tabernacles 1949, Passover 1950 and the Feast of Tabernacles 1950. If you know your history, you already are aware that the Israeli War of Independence ended on July 20th, 1949. So does the blood red moon tetrad of 2014 and 2015 signal that another season of war is now upon us?

FIGURE 5 – OLD ORTHODOX WALL PAINTING OF THE APOCALIYPSE FROM OSOGOVO MONASTERY, REPUBLIC OF MACEDONIA

Pastor John Hagee has further popularized what is now known as the *Blood Moon Prophecy* as he has a world-wide television audience and boasts of being a New York Times bestselling author. Hagee has stated that this particular sign in the heaven will change the course of human events. Coinciding with the Feast of Tabernacles on September 25, 2014 is the beginning of a final year of a seven-year Jewish calendric cycle known as the *Shemittah*. The overlapping of a heavenly sign with yet another dating factor of significance, Hagee contends, "These occurrences are not coincidental. This is the hand of God orchestrating the signs in the heavens. The final Four Blood Moons are signaling that something big is coming... something that will change the world forever."[4] Apparently, the only thing more compelling than one calendric sign from heaven is another date of religious consequence coming right on its heels.[5]

Oklahoma Pastor Mark Hitchcock questions whether the Blood Moon Prophecy smacks more of *sensationalism* than identification of genuine signs in the last days. In his book, *Blood Moons Rising*, Hitchcock criticizes both Biltz and Hagee as guilty of this excess. On sensationalism, Hitchcock cites author and social commentator Richard Swenson, M.D., who offered this sound bite: "Hysteria brings fire to the eyes and acid to the stomach. Hype brings notoriety. Sensationalism brings a tabloid kind of success."[6] Hitchcock continues:

> For sensationalists, signs are everywhere and almost everything. In some circles, wild speculation is far too common and most often is not based on sound principles of biblical interpretation. While

---

[4] John Hagee, *Four Blood Moons: Something Is about to Change* (Brentwood, TN: Worthy Publishing, 2013) pp. 237.

[5] Of course, if this statement is considered by itself, Pastor Hagee has assumed what he is trying to prove.

[6] Richard Swenson, *Hurtling toward Oblivion*, p. 15-16, cited by Mark Hitchcock, *Blood Moons Rising: Bible Prophecy, Israel, and the Four Blood Moons* (p. 18). Tyndale House Publishers, Inc., Kindle Edition.

there are several problems with a sensational approach to signs of the times, one practical problem is that when almost everything becomes a sign, then nothing is a sign. If everything is a sign, then the entire notion of signs becomes meaningless.[7]

Hitchcock contends that the case for the Blood Moon prophecy leans heavily on what is known as 'special pleadings'—a form of argumentation in which one only considers the evidence that confirms a point of view and dismisses any evidence to the contrary. It is akin to stacking the deck. Hitchcock sees this tactic here in spades. Additionally, Hitchcock dismisses the Blood Moon Prophecy in no small part because he wishes to avoid any appearance of *date-setting*.[8] For Hitchcock, signs should not imply any *setting of dates* but should contribute to *setting the stage*.

> God's people sit in the theater of world events awaiting the curtain call of God's apocalyptic drama. We don't know when the play will begin, but like the drama critic, we know much more about it than most. Many stare at the future as at a huge curtain. For them the future is veiled because they have no idea of the plan of God. And they can't see behind the curtain where act one is being set. For believers, however, we see behind the scenes. While it is true that we don't know the moment when the play will begin, we do know the play itself —the main characters and events —and can sense it beginning as we see the actors starting to take their places...[9]

Now, Hitchcock is no skeptic—he is a noted Bible prophecy preacher, pastor, and author having written many books on the subject matter. But he clearly asserts that the Blood Moon Proph-

---

[7] Hitchcock, op. cit., p. 18.

[8] This pejorative harkens back to the frequent failures of Bible believing groups such as the Millerites of the 1840s or the Jehovah's Witnesses in the 1910s and '20s who claimed the world was coming to an end.

[9] Hitchcock, op. cit., (p. 24).

ecy goes too far and might call down fire from heaven (pun admitted but not intended), upon legitimate heavenly signs which duly testify that the 'end of days' draws near. Like Hitchcock, recently this author also raised some concern whether Biltz and Hagee might be making too much of the tetrad/ Festival correlation.

In an article recently written by me for my friend L.A. Marzulli, and his eZine (*Prophecy, Politics and the Supernatural*, May 2014 edition), I point out another soft spot in the Blood Moon Prophecy:

> One could adduce many other auspicious events which would seem to have greater significance and might deserve to be underscored by providential, heavenly signs. For instance, we could point out the First Zionist Conference in Zurich in 1897; or the 1917 date of the so-called Balfour Declaration (which gave the blessing of the British) to the creation of a homeland in Palestine for the Jews; or especially the capture of Jerusalem by the British General Edmund Allenby that same year; or on the dark side the horror of *Kristallnacht* (November 9, 1938, the 'night of broken glass,' the violent anti-Jewish pogrom which broke out in Germany signaling the ensuing Holocaust). Of course, tetrad lunar eclipses did not coincide with any of these very significant events. If one argues that the tetrads 'red circle' certain key dates, why are some highlighted and not the others? It is a legitimate question.

Despite this concern, I am persuaded that *the there is something to the Blood Moon Prophecy.* So then how do we judge the Blood Moon Prophecy to be legitimate apocalyptic sign in the heavens?

Here is how we can build a case for it: one can argue that until 1948 with the reestablishment of the Jews in their ancient homeland of Israel, any tetrads overlapping with the highest of Jewish Feast Days had little to no prophetic significance. Not until Israel was 'back in the land' did 'red letter' events qualify for prophetic recognition. The Yom Kippur War, the skirmishes in Southern Lebanon and Gaza have all been 'negatives.' Perhaps the Blood

Moon tetrad is meant to herald something positive for the reestablishment of Israel as a nation and as a prediction that soon, "all Israel shall be saved." (Romans 11:26)[10]

This might only seem to be a convenient argument to which panicky advocates resort in order to advance their failing case. And yet, this principle of prophetic interpretation has been invoked by many prophecy scholars for the past 70 years or so. Many *futurists* hold to this principle [those who believe Bible prophecy includes elements not yet fulfilled] as well as dispensational scholars [that school of theologians that has championed eschatology during this same 70-year period]. Therefore, I offer this principle up for how one can reasonably regard the Blood Moon Prophecy to be an authentic heavenly sign purposefully intended by the God of the Bible (that is, signaling that the last days are indeed upon us).

In summary, the argument for the meaningfulness of the twentieth and twenty-first century tetrads builds upon the facts that consecutive occurrence of these lunar eclipses are (1) rare astronomical events which (2) coincide with meaningful Jewish Feast Days and (3) take place within the same timeframe as what biblically oriented Christians see as prophetically important occurrences. Therefore, given this alignment, they may be genuine divine signals. This collection of three tetrads in the twentieth and twenty-first centuries may form a 'gestalt' that is worthy of note.[11] Collectively, they may call attention to the relevance of Bible prophecy at this specific period in history. *Indeed, whether right or wrong, one could argue the Blood Moon Prophecy has already achieved this objective* (although I would insist that if it constitutes a genuine sign, by definition it must be legitimate.)

---

[10] The meaning of 'all Israel shall be saved' stands as the crux of the conflict between dispensational and covenantal schools of theology. This matter requires careful analysis in its own right and it outside the scope of this study.

[11] A psychological term, *gestalt* implies the whole is more than the sum of its parts.

ASCRIBING 'FULFILLED' STATUS TO BIBLE PROPHECIES

Given the nature of proclaiming any biblical prophecy to be fulfilled, we ought to recognize that prophetic fulfillment possesses a subjective element implying a built-in time delay, a period where we observe the outcome to see if what transpired truly constitutes a work of God. To some extent, we must maintain a 'wait and see' attitude, a manner of vigilance in which we keep an eye on what has happened and over the passing of time, determine whether the Bible's prophecies should be declared 'now fulfilled.'

From this perspective, the tetrads of 2014-2015 may have authentic significance. There is nothing misleading by pointing out that like the blood moons of 1949-1950 and 1967-68, the blood moons of 2014 and 2015 may coincide with prophetically significant events. The blood moons could constitute a sign that something will happen (or is happening now) that brings us one giant step closer to the apocalypse. Hitchcock's assertion that the act of connecting events to the tetrads, in the manner that Biltz does, invalidates the Blood Moon Prophecy constitutes a two-edged sword. His criticism actually applies to virtually all prophecies.

Consider messianic prophecies (those Old Testament prophecies concerning the messiah that Christians believe Jesus Christ fulfilled): declaring them *fulfilled in Jesus Christ* requires faith (or more precisely, favorable interpretation) to which we who believe assign such meaning—*while disagreeing parties do not* (even though they may otherwise believe in the veracity of the Old Testament). For instance, Reformed theologians reject the prophecies of the Temple in Ezekiel (see chapters 40-48), considering them null and void (i.e., no longer slated to be fulfilled someday) since the Church has replaced Israel and its sacrificial system has been superseded by the crucifixion of Jesus Christ.

Similarly, Judaism rejects that any messianic prophecies have been fulfilled in Jesus Christ since Jesus claimed to be divine and equivalent to Yahweh. This claim automatically makes him incapable of being the messiah. Why? From their point of view, the Messiah is an important figure, but he is not equal to God. If Jesus claimed to be the equivalent of God (which many Jews acknowledge He did—and of course the Church has argued for 2,000 years the very same thing), certainly he must have been wrong about this most important matter, that being His identity! With that fatal flaw, how could He possibly be the Messiah?

Therefore, assessing any prophecy as 'now fulfilled,' requires connecting specific events to that prophecy and regarding them as *fulfillment*. From the standpoint of canonizing the creeds and beliefs of the Church, it also requires sanctioning through consensus.

Is it not safe to say that we, those who study Bible prophecy, are already on the edge of our seats? We expect major events to take place at any moment. Is it wrong to suggest that the blood moons *may* have meaning? Is it out of bounds to propose that they could constitute a partial fulfillment of Bible prophecy? No. That is the nature of watching and waiting until the Lord returns. *That is how we ascribe meaning to all prophetic fulfillment.*

GOD'S APPOINTMENT OF THE SUN, MOON, AND STARS

We know the Bible states that God *made* (better translated, "appointed") the sun, moon, and stars, for signs and seasons as well as for days and years.[12] The firmament declares the glory of God. Most every biblically-minded Christian agrees with the contention that the paths of the planets and the placement of the stars in the sky testify to the providence of God. As the giant E. W. Bullinger wrote in his classic book *The Witness of the Stars*, the stars and planets play no small part in proclaiming the glory of God, in telling the gospel story, and (I venture) telling the season of the

---

[12] See Finish J. Dake's treatment of the Hebrew words *asah* compared to *bara* (*made* versus *created*) in Genesis, 1, in his book, *Another Time, Another Place, Another Man*.

Second Coming (if we would but know how to read their meaning[13]). Genesis 1:14 relates God's purpose with these words, *"And God said, Let there be lights in the firmament of the heaven to divide the day from the night; and let them be for signs, and for seasons, and for days, and years."* Seeing natural conjunctions of the planets, stars, sun, and moon as potentially meaningful heavenly signs is a biblically sound principle. Each would-be sign, however, has to be judged on its own merits. The blood moons of 2014-2015 are no different.

Mark Hitchcock asserts that all authentic signs in the heavens are *supernatural* (such as the three hours of darkness over the land from the sixth to ninth hours the day Jesus was crucified—an event likely witnessed by the secular world).[14] *But authentic signs and wonders are not always supernatural.* For instance, the rainbow constitutes God's heavenly sign expressing His covenant with mankind never to destroy life on earth again by means of a flood.

---

[13] The words of Revelation 12 that speak of the Woman with the moon and stars under her feet may be pointing to a significant astronomical event at the time of Jesus' return.

[14] Assuming that the event was a solar eclipse, the only eclipse witnessed in Judea in this timeframe would have been in 24 AD, on November 29 (far from Passover), and it would have lasted only 1 and ½ minutes (hardly three hours). From an entry in Wikipedia, we read:

"There are no original references to this darkness outside of the New Testament; the only possible contemporary reference may have existed in a work by the chronicler Thallus. In the ninth century, the Byzantine historian George Syncellus quoted from the third-century Christian historian Sextus Julius Africanus, who remarked that "Thallus dismisses this darkness as a solar eclipse". It is not known when Thallus lived, and it is unclear whether he himself made any reference to the crucifixion. Tertullian, in his *Apologeticus*, told the story of the crucifixion darkness and suggested that the evidence must still be held in the Roman archives.

Until the Enlightenment era, the crucifixion darkness story was often used by Christian apologists, because they believed it was a rare example of the biblical account being supported by non-Christian sources. When the pagan critic Celsus claimed that Jesus could hardly be a God because he had performed no great deeds, the third-century Christian commentator Origen responded, in *Against Celsus*, by recounting the darkness, earthquake and opening of tombs. As proof that the incident had happened, he referred to a description by Phlegon of Tralles of an eclipse accompanied by earthquakes during the reign of Tiberius (probably that of 29 CE)."
See http://en.wikipedia.org/wiki/Crucifixion_darkness.

Another sign to consider: the star of Bethlehem. Hitchcock asserts that the "star" of Bethlehem was supernatural (and he might be correct), but there are strong reasons to believe it may have been the resulting planetary conjunction of Jupiter, Venus, and perhaps inclusive of the star Regulus (one of the brightest stars in the sky, a star whose name means 'prince'), occurring as it did on June 17, 2 BC.[15]

Assuming for the sake of argument that this planetary conjunction comprised the Star of Bethlehem, we should realize that this particular event may not have been at the exact moment that Gabriel announced to Mary that she would give birth to a son whose name should be Jesus. Neither might it have been the moment that Jesus was born. It might have only been a herald of His birth—a sign that the Magi in Persia (and other devoted Jews around the world who watched anxiously for the Messiah) would recognize, signaling that the Messiah was coming—in that 'day.' Thus, the fullness of time for His advent had now come.

Additionally, we should acknowledge that biblical prophecy is *fore-telling* and *forth-telling*. Prophetic events demand preaching as well as predicting. On this point, I would apply the caveat that we *do not know with certitude the lunar eclipses are indicative of any particular event foretold in the Bible*. I do *not* believe, however, that it is off-base to suggest they remind us that the coming of the Lord Jesus is imminent. Their occurrence at this moment in history may be propitious in regards to the return of Jesus Christ. I would even go so far to say (in regards to the Blood Moon Prophecy) that what is transpiring in Israel during this time and for the next year or two, could be VERY significant prophetically. Since the fulfillment of the Lord's plan for Israel and the Church appears to be drawing to a rapid conclusion, it almost has to be meaningful.

---

[15]"Professor D.C. Morton, the Senior Research Astronomer at Princeton University, said this particular fusion of Jupiter and Venus on that day in history was 'a notable astronomical event.'" See http://askelm.com/star/star001.htm.

HEBREW FEASTS AS PROPHECIES

To reiterate, we do not know exactly what will happen. But we do know that, as Mark Biltz points out, the Fall Festivals will most likely *be the precise days when the prophecies to which they bespeak are fulfilled.* That does not mean, however, that the Fall Festivals of 2014 or 2015 will be the very days in which fulfillment occurs, days of which the feast days testify.

That being said, I should point out that, if one believes the rapture of the Church transpires on Rosh Hashanah (the Feast of Trumpets), then yes, one of the two upcoming Jewish new years' Day (Rosh Hashanah is the Jewish New Year), may be the very day *that prophecy* is fulfilled, perhaps even at the "last trumpet" on that day when the shofar blows 100 times (1 Corinthians 15:52, *"In a moment, in the twinkling of an eye,* **at the last trump:** *for the trumpet shall sound, and the dead shall be raised incorruptible, and we shall be changed."*)

Few Christians challenge the assertion that the Spring Festivals were fulfilled by the death and resurrection of Jesus Christ during **Passover** (the death of the lamb signified the death of the Lamb of God that takes away the sin of the world) and **Feast of Firstfruits** (the resurrection of the just, Christ being the first fruits of their resurrection). Furthermore, it is often argued (without much fear of contradiction within Christendom) that the coming of the Holy Spirit on Pentecost 50 days after Passover fulfilled the **Festival of Harvest** inasmuch the waving of the first sheaves of wheat and barley celebrated by the Festival, symbolized the harvest or gathering of believers now indwelled by the Spirit of Christ on the Day of Pentecost whose account we read in Acts, chapter 2.

God demonstrates His sovereignty over the affairs of men by accomplishing these prophetic events on the very springtime holy days which intrinsically symbolized their ultimate consummation in the space-time events which they foreshadowed.

Likewise, I do not hesitate to predict or to preach that the Fall Feast Days will soon be fulfilled in the same manner. That is, Jesus Christ is coming soon. In the years immediately ahead, Rosh **Hashanah**, **Yom Kippur**, and **Sukkoth** will be consummated— that is, will comprise in their respective calendric days, the fulfillment of what they teach (i.e., signify). To be specific, Rosh Hashanah may see the *resurrection* (including the rapture of the living and the resurrection of the dead in Christ),[16] Yom Kippur will be the literal the *day of judgment* for the nations by Jesus Christ at His second coming, and God's *dwelling with humankind* during the millennium will commence at Sukkoth. This is asserted by many teachers, including Mark Biltz (and maybe Mark Hitchcock).

Will those events, however, commence this fall? Will the rapture transpire on September 28, 2015? That is not for me to say. Biltz inferred this years ago, but he has backed away from that pronouncement favoring instead, the possible beginning of the Tribulation period (co-terminus with the Prophet Daniel's so-called Seventieth Week of seven years). Regardless, the meaning of the Blood Moon Prophecy comprises a timely and auspicious reminder, perhaps even an authentic sign through an astronomical phenomenon intended as a wake-up call for our world (and perhaps even more for the lukewarm church represented by the Church at Laodicea in the Book of Revelation), that what is transpiring in the Middle East in the very tense days in which we now live, presages matters which will prove out to be prophetically *most* significant. Humankind's days of rebellion against his creator are numbered. Time grows short. Even the sun, moon, and stars may testify to these things.

---

[16] I believe there is a strong argument the rapture of the Church may occur on a future Pentecost, a day which varies from year to year. On Pentecost, the dispensation of Law was given by Moses and it was the day in which the dispensation of grace was inaugurated by the coming of the Holy Spirit. Could it be the day in which the next dispensation commences as the Church Age concludes? As I suggest, we must "wait and see."

Indeed, the Scripture is rich with similes and metaphors about signs in the heavens that tell us the Day of the Lord has come.

> *"Behold, the day of the Lord cometh, cruel both with wrath and fierce anger, to lay the land desolate: and he shall destroy the sinners thereof out of it. For the stars of heaven and the constellations thereof shall not give their light: the sun shall be darkened in his going forth, and the moon shall not cause her light to shine. I will shake the heavens, and the earth shall remove out of her place, in the wrath of the Lord of hosts and in the day of his fierce anger and Babylon, the glory of kingdoms shall be as when God overthrew Sodom and Gomorrah"* (Isa. 13:9-19).

> *"All the host of heaven shall be dissolved, and the heavens shall be rolled together as a scroll: and all their host shall fall down, as the leaf falleth off from the vine, and as a falling fig from a fig tree. For my sword shall be bathed in heaven: behold, it shall come down upon Idumea [Edom] and upon the people of my curse to judgment"* (Isa. 34:4, 5).

These signs may be either supernatural or natural occurrences, but either way, the source of these events should be obvious to those sensitive to the prophetic context of all creation at this moment in history. When that day finally dawns, the reality of the Lord's coming will be unmistakable. His return will be inexorable.

In the final analysis, it is not wrong-headed to suppose the blood moons tetrads of 2014 and 2015 represent genuine "signs in the heavens" that foreshadow what the prophets John and Joel wrote: the Sun will be darkened and **the moon will be turned to blood** *in the great and terrible Day of the Lord* (Revelation 6:12, Joel 2:31). Many cataclysmic and decisive events are predestined to happen. I believe the blood moons do signify that what is about to occur over the next 18 months constitutes a warning from God Himself: Christ is completing His preparations for His Bride and through this sign (and the discussions surrounding them) He serves notice to the unbelieving world they have one final opportunity, one last and brief season, to recognize that Jesus Christ is the King of Kings and Lord of Lords.

As we will discuss in detail later, Jesus taught on many occasions that we should be on our guard, to be prepared for His coming. In particular, we should recall Mark 13:37, a verse which cites Jesus' stern warning to all His disciples then and now: *"What I say unto you I say unto all, Watch!"*

The blood moons of 2014-2015 should supply a heightened sense of awe at the marvelous creation and the power of God. But they should also provide a particular reminder that the Lord's return grows near. What is happening in the world, especially what is taking place with the nation of Israel in our day, should give us pause. We should be watching carefully now—very carefully indeed.

3: THE QUEST TO DECIPHER THE FUTURE

[It is] the glory of God to conceal a thing: but the honor of kings [is] to search out a matter.
(Proverbs 25:2)

Remember the former things of old: for I am God, and there is none else; I am God, and there is none like me, declaring the end from the beginning, and from ancient times the things that are not yet done, saying, My counsel shall stand, and I will do all my pleasure
(Isaiah 46:9, 10)

HUMANITY EAGERLY SEEKS TO KNOW THE FUTURE

PERHAPS NO SUBJECT CAPTURES THE ATTENTION OF THE MASSES MORE THAN THE POSSIBILITY WE CAN KNOW WHAT LIES IN THE FUTURE. IN MY SECOND BOOK *DECODING DOOMSDAY*, I summarized the many theories regarding what the future holds. I also demonstrated how underlying many efforts of various 'movements' in today's world, lies an attempt to substantiate a pagan, world religion as old as *Sumeria*.[1] Religions and their prophetic assertions are very much connected.

---

[1] Supposedly Sumeria is regarded by historians as humankind's first recorded civilization, appearing in the fourth millennium BC within Mesopotamia. There are reasons to challenge this position, proposing that civilization may have begun within the land of Canaan, at the foot of Mount Herman. See my book, *Lying Wonders of the Red Planet*, for a discussion of civilization's genesis there.

History demonstrates time-after-time that humankind covets *the truth about the end of the world.* At stake stands more than merely discerning how soon the end may be. It involves more than just *curiosity* which drives this obsession. It centers on *certainty.* For many, the study of prophecy remains *the means to determine what worldview is correct.* In other words, prophecy has the power to disclose which religious perspective is right and which others are wrong. Prophecy comprises a litmus test for what we should believe. As such, we do not just hunger to know the future. We seek proof that what we believe is not ludicrous—but truth we can count on. Built into our DNA is the quest for spiritual truth, meaning, *and* certitude. Faith involves all three.

FIGURE 6 - NOSTRADAMUS ON THE HISTORY CHANNEL

The History Channel has often presented documentaries on history's most famous 'seers,' parading prognosticators before its viewers. It has spent a good deal of time on modern day prophets as well as the possibility that *precognition* may be an innate faculty in all humankind. One documentary substantiated how occult practice reached its zenith at the end of the nineteenth century. The extent of belief in the supernatural was widespread. There were millions of subscribers to dozens of journals on spiritualism. Crystal ball gazing, palmistry, and divination of all kinds were frequent 'parlor tricks' which many believed involved more than simple magic. Mediums, palm readers, fortune tellers, and more serious occult practitioners were to be found throughout Europe, England, and America. In this exposé, *the focus was the individual believer and what the future had in store for that specific person*. And yet, the seriousness of the subject underscored there was much more to it than just 'checking out the daily horoscope' to see what the day holds.

State-side, American *Transcendentalism* in the first half the nineteenth century (think Ralph Waldo Emerson, Walt Whitman, and Henry David Thoreau) gave way to *Theosophy* in the 1880s (Henry Steel Olcott and Madame Helena Petrovna Blavatsky). These writers provided a philosophical foundation (and some degree of sophistication) for an otherwise purely occult and fantastic worldview. In the former case mere *intuition* was championed whereas in the latter, *channeling spirits* (who pretentiously commented on history, philosophy, as well as predicted the future), was argued to be a more reliable source of knowledge than pure reason.

THE HISTORICAL BASIS FOR OCCULTISM

As documented in my previous writings, Theosophy in particular demands a careful treatment since its ideology constitutes something much more serious than merely 'mind over matter.' At the end of the nineteenth century, it flowered into a syncretistic religion infecting not only America but Europe in particular, combining Hindu, Buddhist, and pseudo-science into an amalgamation boasting supernatural 'miracles.'

Theosophy prospered from the 1880s until the late 1940s, when it became better known that the Nazi regime based much of its evil upon Theosophy's most extreme doctrines asserting Aryanism, occult practices, and a view of history built upon the lost continent of *Atlantis* (The 'Secret Doctrine').

Despite such remarkable mythical beliefs which included the myths of 'fire and ice,' the 'hollow earth,' and racial origins stemming from seven root races of the Atlantians (spurring the anti-Semitism of Nazism), much of its 'wisdom' was associated with ancient Egyptian mythology. The stories of Isis, Osiris, and Horus would continue to live on in the practice of Freemasonry (and in the more secretive cults of Rosicrucianism and the practice of Alchemy).

Indeed, Freemasonry comprises perhaps the world's most universal religion—a religion which claims to be no such thing. However, as I have documented elsewhere, Freemasonry remains much more than a charitable fraternity. It is built upon a smartly packaged form of paganism, complete with its particular view of God, and especially hope for the afterlife.

FIGURE 7 - FREEMASON INTELLECTUAL MANLY P. HALL

Freemasons have their own predictions about the future too. Masonic prophecies mirror many of what evangelicals hold to be true: they predict a future world leader will arise, declare his authority in a future Jewish Temple (which they, like orthodox Jews, long to see rebuilt), and institute a form of government based upon pure reason AND the wisdom of the ancients.[2] This leader will not

---

[2] This is well-documented by Thomas Horn in his book *Apollyon Rising: 2012*, as well as in my book *Decoding Doomsday*. Manly P. Hall's *Secret Destiny of America*, in particular delivers the smoking gun.

just to be a clever human endowed with the gift of oration, but is in fact, purportedly a divine being intent on ruling humankind.

The books of Freemason intellectuals, Manly P. Hall and Albert Pike, spell out these plans and predictions in plain English and are available at the local bookstore. There should be no reason to doubt what the mission of Freemasonry is. It stands clearly disclosed.[3] No surprise then that evangelicals have long suspected this forecasted fuehrer of the Freemasons to be none other than the Antichrist.

To push down this path a bit further: it captivates how the impact of magicians of the nineteenth century led to many aspects of the most scientific of US governmental projects: the twentieth century space program. In particular, one fascinating person about whom I have spoken much is one Jack Parsons, founder of the Jet Propulsion Laboratory (JPL). He was personally steeped

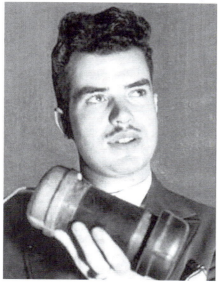

FIGURE 8 - JACK PARSONS AND L. RON HUBBARD OF JPL, CIRCA 1950

---

[3] While most Freemason spokespeople deny they are conspirators or have any such plan for world domination, they never repudiate the writings of Pike or Hall which are unambiguous in this regard.

in *black 'magick.'* Parson was the head of the Pasadena chapter of *Ordo Templi Orientis* (OTO), an order begun by Samuel Mather at the turn of the nineteenth century, alongside the infamous Aleister Crowley. Modeled after Freemasonry (both were 33° Freemasons) the order was based upon what members called the *Thelema Law*: "Do what thou wilt shall be the whole of the law" (i.e., "Do whatever you want is our one and only law—the single law we accept!")

Parsons was a genuine genius in rocket science, developing solid rocket fuel which overcame many of the dangers with liquid fuel (all too often causing rocket explosions on the launch pad!) His inventions and designs for 'booster rockets' remain the basis for NASA's propulsion systems today. Few know that one of his founding colleagues was a suspected NAZI (Theodore von Kármán) and another conspicuous gentlemen, L. Ron Hubbard *founder of Scientology,* likely a Navy spy sent into JPL to keep an eye on these two.

Hubbard eventually ran off to Florida with Parson's wife, Helen, after Helen's sister, Sara had an affair with Parsons owing to the sexual magick of Crowley. Parson was mysteriously killed in 1952 in his personal laboratory, perhaps while attempting to conjure a homunculus. Although declared a suicide, many consider his death an assassination—he was considering taking his know-how to Israel at their behest. Of course, L. Ron Hubbard went on to author notable science fiction works and create the Scientology *cosmology* (to many, another form of science fiction), that several public figures in America continue to support (Tom Cruise and John Travolta being the two most well-known).

FAILURE OF NEW AGE PROPHECY—2012 IS NOW HISTORY

For most of the past decade, popular attention was focused on 2012 and the possibility that the Mayan Calendar (which culminated on December 21, 2012), signified the end of humanity. In reality, there was much more to the whole '2012 thing' than just a dubious prediction that the world was coming to an end. Most of the 'hubbub' about 2012 was actually a loosely formed religion founded on Theosophist roots that took 'new age' affirmations to the next level. Many of the 2012 books promulgated the transformation of humanity which supposedly was to culminate late in 2012 (or immediately thereafter). This purported revolution in consciousness raising linked to a very old world view that human history is comprised of various 'ages' typically characterized as iron, silver, gold, and lastly an age sporting a disparaging label, normally associated with the world in which we now live.[4]

For instance, the Hindu 'Kali Yuga' comprised the current age of depravity to have concluded in or not long after 2012. Likewise, 'The Age of Aquarius'—for those into astrology—was to comprise the next age characterized by *enlightenment*. According to the '2012 religion,' true enlightenment would require the acquisition of a 'higher consciousness'—wherein *we remain in constant contact with the supernatural beings surrounding us*—as well as the inner mindfulness that *we are gods*, capable of infinite possibilities (audacious statements which defy all rational comprehension).

The 2012 'movement' was, until it failed, the most *chic* form of prophecy. In 2012 the transition event was to have occurred—it was our last chance, a time of choice—which would reveal either the moment of redemption for humankind or would become the final straw whose placement on the back of the camel, symbolically, assuredly signaled our doom.

However, despite the fact that we continue to succumb to our natural inclinations—those atavistic, materialistic, and especially capitalistic behaviors—we did not then, nor have we since, slid down the slippery slope to ruin.

---

[4] The Maya and Aztecs labeled the various epochs 'suns' as do today's Hopi Indians. Ominously, we now live at the conclusion of the fifth of five suns. So far, so good?

THE PROOF IS IN THE PROPHECY—IF FULFILLED, THAT IS

When it comes to prophecy in the traditions of major religions, we see a distinct increase in the caliber of prophesied *timespans*. Predictions may cross many centuries if not multiple millenniums. Specific prophecies typically involve nations if not the entire globe. And yet, compared to the Judeo-Christian faith, there lies relatively little emphasis on prophecy. Furthermore, there remains little regard for resting the validity of the religion upon accurate fulfillment of prophecy. In complete contrast, *within the pages of the Bible we read how prophecy matters 'really matter.'*

In the case of evangelicalism, conservative scholars affirm that the authenticity of our faith rests on the spectacular accuracy of what is prophesied in the Bible. In particular, Christianity asserts that Jesus Christ fulfilled scores of prophesies from the Old Testament regarding the nature of the Messiah, His origins, purpose, and destiny. The pinnacle of this 'messianic prophecy' shines in two particular passages spanning entire chapters in the Bible (See Isaiah 53 and Psalm 22 specifically where messianic prophecies abound to the attention of even the casual observer).

Authorities from a conservative vantage point say Jesus fulfilled over 60 specific prophecies related to the Messiah. In particular, the Gospel of Matthew is filled to the brim with instances where the evangelist identified how Jesus fulfilled the predictions of the Hebrew prophets.

PROPHECY MATTERS SINCE IT IMPLIES TRANSCENDENCE

Whether we profess faith in Jesus as Christ or not, except for the few who are hard-core naturalists (believing humans are purely the product of materialistic evolution), *the vast majority of humankind strives to know why we are here*. We attempt to break the doomsday code because we believe someone smart is (or was) out there, who knows (or knew) about end times and is trying to help us to prepare ourselves for it—or to find a means to avoid it altogether. If we find the most reliable source on predicting the future, we likely find the best source to tell us why we are here, or, better yet, in the parlance of our day, 'what life really means.' We look to prophecy as a means to answer life's ultimate questions.

Speaking objectively, there are a number of considered theories concerning where we may find information disclosing doomsday and its implications regarding the identity of our creator. This 'smart someone' could be the God of the Bible speaking through the Scripture; it could be our human ancestors from many millennia ago who left advice embedded in ancient documents or megalithic artifacts; or it could be extraterrestrials who manage our evolution and pass messages to us in unconventional channels.[5] The help we seek lies 'beyond' us: It is from (1) God or (2) enlightened individuals in the past or (3) 'from above' whether it is spiritual beings dwelling in another dimension; or friendly spacemen visiting from a nearby region in outer space. In any event, we assume access to such truth is our heritage—be it out of this world or at least out of the ordinary. Therefore, such wisdom makes a big difference in how we live our lives. Only with help can we reckon (because it is far from obvious) that should such knowledge exist, it is *encoded*, and we must earnestly seek it for it to be deciphered.

Underlying this hypothesis rests a staunch belief in purpose. Humankind's presence is no accident. That is why the spiritually minded eagerly tackle this quest. If we discover such information exists, *we know it sheds a new light on the issue of meaning.*

Consider: What would happen if we uncovered detailed information about Hindu or Muslim prophecies distinctly beyond doubt? What if biblical passages regarding the end time's scenario

---

[5] I mention 'God as an alien astronaut' only as a possibility, not that I give it equal credence to the other alternatives. *Ancient astronaut theory*, made famous by the writings of Erich von Däniken, deserves the state status of a religion. We see Catholic Priests and a few liberal theologians choosing to assert that 'God' constitutes only an extraterrestrial being (s). The Jesuits at the Vatican Observatory are *ready to baptize the aliens*! See Cris Putnam and Tom Horn, *Exo-Vaticana*, Defender Books, 2013.

in fact mirror what happens in the months ahead? What if a spaceship were to land on the White House lawn and its occupants to proclaim that life exists throughout the universe—radiant alien messengers as implicit *living proof*? Furthermore, what if alien life forms informed us (as many 'ancient astronaut theorists' and new age authors have ventured), THEY have been *caretakers of life here on earth*? The most important point becomes exceedingly clear: *once transcendence has been proven* (that is, that something bigger than us exists outside our empirical everyday world); we can surely bet that life as we know it will never be the same. Our meaning takes on a bona fide stamp of legitimacy. *Discovering the source of life provides the means to validate our transcendence.* No doubt, this recognition bequeaths strong motivation to put our hands on a deciphering machine and strive to break the code of such transformative evidence.

This does not mean the hunt exists exclusively as a Christian excursion. Quite to the contrary, the intensely religious from all flavors would be steadfast in their efforts to uncover whether or not this compulsion concerning the future is warranted. And yet, as it now stands, *only Christianity presumes prophecy comprises the litmus test for which religion deserves allegiance.* Discovering who knows the future (who can accurately predict what will in fact happen tomorrow) remains the test God Himself puts forth:

> *Remember the former things of old: for I am God, and there is none else; I am God, and there is none like me, declaring the end from the beginning, and from ancient times the things that are not yet done, saying, My counsel shall stand, and I will do all my pleasure.* (Isaiah 46:9, 10)

That is why God maintained a simple standard for proving the prophet. To speak for Yahweh, he must be 100% right, 100% of the time. There was no room for mistakes. A prophet foretelling something that did not come to be pass should not just have his license revoked, he was to be put to death. Deuteronomy 18:20-22:

> *But the prophet, which shall presume to speak a word in my name, which I have not commanded him to speak, or that shall speak in the name of other gods, even that prophet shall die.*
>
> *And if thou say in thine heart, 'How shall we know the word which the LORD hath not spoken?' When a prophet speaketh in the name of the LORD, if the thing follow not, nor come to pass, that is the thing which the LORD hath not spoken, but the prophet hath spoken it presumptuously: thou shalt not be afraid of him.*

Only after settling the question of which religion truly knows what the future holds, should we then pay attention to whatever else the religion holds to be true.

For believers in the distinctly Judeo-Christian concept of afterlife, we suppose the next life will be much better than our life today. Certainly, *we want our problems and pain eliminated by the coming of Messiah.* While it may be doomsday for the world, because we expect to be saved, we look forward to the Kingdom of God. We see it as *our salvation and our destiny.* Decoding the apocalypse informs us just how soon 'rest from our toils' arrives. Indeed, our assurance relies upon the faith this 'rest' lies ahead.

PROPHECY—FAITH IS MORE THAN WISHFUL THINKING

Taken to the extreme, looking only to the hereafter becomes irresponsible and unbiblical. As we will discuss in more detail later, escaping from this life to the next can be ducking out on responsibilities. It can even prove we lack true faith. But looking forward to the 'City of God'[6] (an historic image representing the New Jerusalem), may reveal our faith. Paul says of Abraham, *"For he looked for a city which hath foundations, whose builder and maker [is] God."* (Hebrews 11:10) And of those who have died in faith looking forward to their future reward:

---

[6] We likely think of St. Augustine's classic work, *The City of God* which actually focuses on the Church as the community of God.

"These all died in faith, not having received the promises, but having seen them afar off, and were persuaded of [them], and embraced [them], and confessed that they were strangers and pilgrims on the earth... But now they desire a better [country], that is, an heavenly: wherefore God is not ashamed to be called their God: for he hath prepared for them a city" (verses 13, 16).

Likewise, those who believe in the rapture of the Church label it 'the Blessed Hope' precisely because it promises believers will avoid

FIGURE 9 – A MEDIEVAL ILLUSTRATION OF AUGUSTINE'S *CITY OF GOD*

some or all of the so-called *Great Tribulation* (usually regarded as the final 3.5 years before Christ physically returns to the Earth. The Bible commends those who look forward to the return of Christ and for those who seek His Kingdom. For instance, is it significant (or not) that only the *Book of Revelation promises a blessing to its readers?*

If we take the Bible to be a sacred book, seeking to know the time and seasons reminds us to prepare for His return. *"Watch for you know not when the Son of Man comes."* Being watchful demands we keep an eye out for the Master. We should do this not just because we are afraid we will get caught in a regrettable action, but because Jesus admonished His disciples to remain alert. Like the wise virgins in one of Jesus' parables, we are to keep our 'lamps trimmed' and buy extra oil in case the groom of the wedding feast tarries and does not show until the wee hours of the morning (Matthew 25:1-12). To do otherwise (as stated in another of Jesus' parables), proves us 'disobedient and foolish servants.' (Matthew 25:14-30).

In summary, prophecy fulfilled confirms our faith. Prophecy validates what we believe and thus, though not necessarily the goal, implies the falsehood of alternative systems of belief.[7] Prophecy fulfilled offers proof that *what we believe* comprises much more than *wishful thinking*.

Christianity may rightly be regarded as the only world religion which welcomes the testing of its validity. Fulfilled prophecy plays a critical role in substantiating the truthfulness of our faith.

---

[7] Proving someone else wrong may not be a desirable aspect of seeking to prove ourselves right. But it's an unavoidable consequence if the basic premise of logic is correct: "A is not non-A." Additionally, anticipating the charge of arrogance, Christianity is not intended at its core to be a 'religion' prescribing repetitive behaviors to make one feel worthy or relieved of guilt. Neither is it meant to teach methods to transcend physical reality, to depart into the realm of the spirit, that we might explore sublime experiences or visions. Instead, it intends first to establish a right relationship between God and humankind, one person at a time. Once through that doorway by receiving Christ, Christianity (and Judaism before it), stresses loving God, "with all our heart, soul, and mind" and "loving our neighbor as ourselves." As Jesus said, these are the greatest commandments (See Mark 12:30, Deuteronomy 11:13; 13:3).

4: CHRISTIANITY—AN APOCALYPTIC FAITH

Watch ye therefore: for ye know not when the master of the house cometh, at even, or at midnight, or at the cockcrowing, or in the morning.
(Mark 13:35)

Watch therefore, for ye know neither the day nor the hour wherein the Son of man cometh.
(Matthew 25:13)

PORTRAYING THE KINGDOM OF GOD IN IMAGES

JESUS CHRIST WAS THE WORLD'S GREATEST TEACHER. WHAT MADE HIM SO EFFECTIVE WAS HIS CLEVER USE OF ILLUSTRATIONS FAMILIAR TO COMMON PEOPLE. HIS MOST POPULAR TEACHING method was the parable. Through His parables, Jesus employed many vivid but quaint images. In one of his fifty-plus parables, he tells us a story of a woman who lost a coin of great value and had to sweep her house carefully to find it. Once uncovered, she called all of her neighbors together to share in her joy. In another parable, Jesus compared the Kingdom of God to an expensive pearl. The Kingdom was like a 'pearl of great price,' so desired by one particular man, he sold everything to purchase it.

Jesus compared God to a judge in some parables and to the master of a vineyard in others; both stories explaining from His perspective what God demands of His servants. Some of these stories were allegories—tales whose characters represented people in real life. Some were no more than simple analogies comprised of a single point to convey an aspect of what God deems important.

One story in particular portrayed 'workers in the vineyard' whose master requested they guard the vineyard while he traveled overseas. Several times the master sent his closest stewards to check up on things. However, in each case the workers killed the servant the master sent. Eventually, the master sent his son, assuming that they would pay attention to him. Instead, the workers elected to kill the son too, thinking by so doing they would inherit the vineyard! Not only does this story illustrate that Jesus knew beforehand He would soon be put to death, but also that it would be the religious leaders (the workers in His 'vineyard') that would commit this improbable act. The 'workers' proved to be the master's mortal enemies.

Jesus employed another simple tool: The comparison between earthly facts and spiritual truths. For instance, *salt* was a powerful commodity in His day. Salt not only enhanced the flavor of food, but preserved it too. In the days long before refrigerators, salt was a miracle compound. Jesus educated His followers to be like salt: "Take responsibility, enhance the world around you, and act as a preservative." If His followers did not function as salt to the circumstances surrounding them, the world would suffer.

In another comparison, Jesus engaged the simile of *light*. His believers were to be *as light* to overcome darkness. To maximize their brightness, they should not be placed on the floor. Rather they should sit on a stand, elevated, to enlighten everyone in the room. We could say Jesus set high expectations for His disciples!

In these plain teachings, Jesus insisted His followers be responsible for preserving and transforming the world in which they lived. If they would not perform this service, they would be considered worthless and risk being thrown into the rubbish heap. And yet, Jesus introduced these admonitions in the context of dramatic changes. Jesus warned of *judgment* (*krisis*, in the Greek from which our word *crisis* is derived). Like John before Him, Jesus proclaimed a radical and imminent alteration to society.

APOCALYPSE IMPLIES GOD'S INTERVENTION

The teaching of Jesus Christ and His Apostles in the New Testament calls for conversion and repentance. Yet, it remains grounded firmly in the conviction that humankind left to its own devices will never achieve a perfect society. Individuals without a spiritual rebirth can never know God. Transforming persons and (perhaps in some cases) human institutions, will eventually demand intervention by God in the space-time world.[1] These 'involvements' may be invisible—like the Holy Spirit (*pneuma* in Greek, aka *the wind* or more precisely, *the breath of God*)—who blows where He wills while remaining invisible. Yet, we do see the Spirit's reality when we witness what it does.

God's actions intersect the human domain. Whether visible or not, when God touches history in this way, like a river, the waters drastically change course. The incarnation comprises God's ultimate *intrusion*. Jesus' presence set this *new course*. The river now flows through different banks and on an alternate riverbed. Jesus' agenda was to radically alter the world. His tagline was the announcement of a new Kingdom. "Behold, the Kingdom of God is here." The message itself is an *apocalypse*—an *unveiling*, which is what the term *apocalypse* means. That is why the final book of the Bible is called both "The Revelation of Jesus Christ" and "The Apocalypse of Jesus Christ." The terms are interchangeable.

In this sense, the arrival of Jesus Christ on the world scene and the 33 years He spent on this earth was *the first apocalypse*—the first unveiling. His incarnation revealed what God is truly like. The return of this same Christ at His *Second Coming* is *the second apocalypse*. It is another revealing. It is safe to assume that we will

---

[1] Many schools of prophetic though teach that the Church will eventually triumph over evil. Amillennial believers (like Roman Catholics and most 'reformed' theologians) teach this. They are historicists or preterists and assert that apocalyptic prophecies harken only to past events. They may believe that Jesus Christ will physically return to earth someday, but virtually all other prophecies are *fait accompli*.

discover much more concerning the nature of God with the second unveiling.

FIGURE 10 - RUSSIAN ORTHODOX ICON, APOCALYPSE

With this recognition, we discover the very 'heart and soul' of the Christian faith is *apocalypse*—it is the revelation of God to His people through the appearances of Jesus Christ. Especially in this regard, we see *the Christian faith is an apocalyptic religion.*

Hence, Christianity is 'apocalyptic' at its very core. If not already plain to the reader, herein lies the book's thesis. Therefore, for added clarity I highlight the inverse statement here as well:

Any Christianity which denies the Second Coming of Jesus Christ to this earth as a 'space-time' reality is inconsistent with the spoken words of Jesus of Nazareth as proclaimed in the four canonical gospels.

There are various arguments, indeed whole schools of thought, concerning exactly *when* Jesus will return and under what circumstances. These are important matters; but none more important than the question of whether or not He will *physically* return. This reappearance is scheduled at the culmination of history. Consequently, any 'gospel'[2] that obscures the apocalyptic message of Jesus Christ and His disciples has no authentic claim to continuity with New Testament teaching.

FIVE THEMES CONFIRMING APOCALYPSE TO BE PRIMARY

The essence of this argument builds upon numerous and plainly stated biblical themes. I cite five of them as follows.

- **The Kingdom is at hand**

First, the vital announcement of Jesus Christ was, *"The time is fulfilled. The Kingdom of God is at hand! Repent ye and believe in the gospel"* (See Mark 1: 15). During the past 200 years, many theologians have turned this proclamation into a mythical mishmash. That might be fine if Jesus did not mention Hebrew Scripture to authenticate His ministry. But he did so repeatedly. Jesus knew why He was here. He clearly regarded Himself as the fulfillment of the messianic prophecies in the Old Testament.

---

[2] Gospel in the Greek is *evangelion*, meaning 'good tidings' or 'good news.' Evangelist and evangelism of course are derived from this word.

After John the Baptist had been imprisoned and became disheartened, John asked his disciples to inquire of Jesus if He was the 'Anointed One' or should they be looking for some other. The account in Luke records the unmistakable answer—Jesus quoted messianic predictions in the book of Isaiah:

> *And John calling unto him two of his disciples sent them to Jesus, saying, "Art thou he that should come or look we for another?" When the men were come unto him, they said, "John [the] Baptist hath sent us unto thee, saying, "Art thou he that should come or look we for another?" And in that same hour He cured many of their infirmities and plagues, and of evil spirits; and unto many that were blind He gave sight. Then Jesus answering said unto them, "Go your way, and tell John what things ye have seen and heard; how that the blind see, the lame walk, the lepers are cleansed, the deaf hear, the dead are raised, to the poor the gospel is preached. And blessed is he, whosoever shall not be offended in Me"* (Luke 7:19-21).

Scores of other passages could be quoted demonstrating that Jesus was crystal clear about His purpose. While the phrase *Kingdom of God* is present in 69 New Testament verses, the earliest gospel, the *Gospel of Mark*, expresses the exact phrase 15 times. Jews understood the Kingdom in the Hebrew context of the *Davidic Kingdom*. While the image of the suffering servant or 'dying Messiah' contradicted the Jewish hope for a conquering Christ, Christianity insists it is through His vicarious sufferings and death the righteous 'enter into this Kingdom.' Christians affirm the Hebrew Scriptures plainly describe both aspects of the Messiah.[3] But it should come as no surprise that the oppressed Jews of Jesus' day much preferred the *Conquering Christ* to the *Suffering Servant*. The Hebrews had been suffering too long already! As noted earlier: after talking with Jesus post-resurrection for 40 days, the Apostles still inquired if He would immediately restore Israel's Kingdom.

---

[3] Read Chapter 53 of Isaiah and Psalm 22 to see this suffering Christ expressed in the Old Testament.

Nevertheless, repentance must come before exaltation. John's ministry of baptism unto repentance for the nation of Israel signaled the priority of cleansing oneself of sins before entering into the Kingdom. Jesus sought the repentance of the Hebrew nation, principally as reflected in the acceptance (or rejection) of its leadership. However, it became clear from the very beginning of His ministry that Jesus of Nazareth would not change the hearts and minds of the ruling class.

Like most political and religious leaders today, the Pharisees, Sadducees, and the royal house of the Herodians had no interest in changing the status quo. While they unanimously hated the occupying Roman forces, when it came time to deal with Jesus—whose message represented a radical modification for their civil society and religious practice—they set aside their differences and banded together. Leveraging their authority with armed guards, they executed Jesus, suppressed His followers, and maintained the existing order. Surely, the Kingdom of Man was not ready for the Kingdom of God.

Of course, thousands of the common folk and a few of the occupying Roman forces embraced Jesus' message.

We remember the words of a particular Roman centurion who had built a synagogue for the Jewish village under his care, asking Jesus just to say the word and his servant would be healed. (See Matthew 8:5-13) Jesus was astonished. He remarked that this Roman, this gentile (a pejorative label for those outside of the salvation of the Hebrew religion), understood the essence of faith better than any Hebrew in the entire country.[4]

The gospel writer tells us that as a result of such great faith, Jesus healed the centurion's servant at that very moment—He 'issued

---

[4] The key to the centurion's faith was his understanding of the linkage between faith and authority; more specifically, Jesus' authority over spirits, sickness, and all the forces repressing humankind. With a single command, Jesus made the servant well.

the order' (just as the Centurion had requested) for the servant to be made well. There was no delay. Nature too was under authority—the authority of Jesus.

- **The Angels Charge: Waste No Time—Witness Now!**

The second factor demanding acceptance of the literal Second Advent of Jesus Christ comes at the Savior's dispatch to Heaven.

At the beginning of the *Book of Acts* we read the dramatic account of His ascension. A cloud approached and took Him away. Then angels appeared, asking His disciples (paraphrasing), "Why are you all standing around, looking up into the sky? This same Jesus will descend, just as you have seen him ascend. It will be in the very same manner." (See Acts, Chapter 1) What did the angels mean? Simply this: "Get busy; there is no time to waste. Stop being awed by what you have just seen—remarkable though it may be. Your mission launches now!" From the very beginning, the growth of the Church of Jesus Christ was predicated upon the imminent return of their Savior. His next advent could not have been more foundational.

However, the disciples were told to wait for the coming of the Holy Spirit before kicking off their efforts. *"And, behold, I send the promise of my Father upon you: but tarry ye in the city of Jerusalem, until ye be endued with power from on high" (Luke 24:49)*. To be effective in their mission, they needed a power boost! We should also make careful note that while this descent of the Spirit of Christ was a 'second coming' of sorts, it was not *in like manner*.

The disciples weren't confused on this matter. It is a mistake to interpret the indwelling of the Holy Spirit as the Second Coming of Christ. That is a popular modern theology misinterpretation. Peter, the early leader, indicated the miraculous signs witnessed in the streets of Jerusalem (the 'unlearned' speaking in tongues they did not know—*real languages*, not gibberish—telling of the wonderful acts of God), revealed to his audience that they lived *in the last days* just as the prophet Joel had predicted

(Acts 2:6-18, Joel 2:28). Having received the Spirit of Christ, Peter preached the need for repentance, particularly since the Son of God had been crucified by the country's leadership (Acts 2:22-23). The Messiah, the one whom they had been awaiting for over 1,000 years, had been murdered as a result of their actions, he failed to live up to their expectations.

Peter pushed his finger directly into the wound. This was an issue of national shame—and his remonstration struck home. The crowd reacted with horror. What should they do? "Repent," he said, "and be baptized for the remission of your sins and ye shall receive the Holy Ghost [Spirit]" (Acts 2:38). Jesus' death was all part of God's preordained plan just as Peter had conveyed. However, he explained this same Messiah would return again—the next time bringing the Kingdom in full force. As a result of his inspired preaching, 3,000 persons were added to their number that very day.

- ***Prepare for the Coming Cataclysms of the Apocalypse***

In addition to the evangelistic directive of Jesus to His disciples, *"Go ye therefore and teach all nations,"* (Matthew 28:19) which as history records resulted in the world being "turned upside down," the gospels weave a prediction throughout their accounts (and later in the epistles of the Apostles): History will culminate in a time of *great tribulation*.[5] There will be distressing realities of earthquakes, plagues, famine, and portents so awesome that *"men's hearts [will] fail them for fear"* of what is soon to come upon the earth (Luke 21:26).

---

[5] Another key point: it was the anticipation of the soon return of Christ which drove the disciples with such fervor. Believing in the Second Coming as an imminent event implied "Time is short. We best get the word out to everyone as quickly as we can." This mind-set inspired and energized the early church.

This is the third major reason for acknowledging the importance of the Second Advent of Jesus Christ: The Apostles message was to warn everyone who followed Jesus. *We must prepare for the coming cataclysms.* Soon God will judge humankind for their wickedness. We must get out of the way of His wrath.

Importantly, it is in this context in which Jesus makes a remarkable commitment to His followers: *"Watch ye therefore, and pray always, that ye may be accounted worthy to escape all these things that shall come to pass, and to stand before the Son of Man"* (Luke 21:36). Jesus tells of a way to escape from these horrors. While there is great debate about the exact timing of His coming for *"those found worthy,"*[6] His promise remains explicit.

Before the worst happens, Jesus has promised to 'catch up' His followers and escort them to heaven. Paul clarifies this method of how Jesus returns for His followers: *"Then we which are alive (and) remain shall be* **caught up** *(harpazo in the Greek and rapturae in Latin) together with them (the dead) in the clouds, to meet the Lord in the air: And so shall we ever be with the Lord"* (I Thessalonians 4:17). The gospel of Christ and its salvation proclaims *deliverance from the wrath of God to come* (I Thessalonians 1:10, Romans 5:9). This is not deliverance from all persecution for we are promised that we will experience ill treatment too for the sake of the gospel. And yet, God's wrath is the 'wrath to come' from which we will be spared. Many see this event—the Rapture—as *"the blessed hope of the Church"* (See Titus 2:13). Even for those who deny that this amazing event could happen at any moment (but steadfastly believe Christ will return to this earth), the Rapture remains a sacred promise of Jesus. Christ's coming for His church stands unquestionably as a major component of His and

---

[6] To be found worthy, we must "receive Him" (John 1:12). We are saved by His grace through faith, a gift of God, not as a result of anything we do (Romans 3:24).

His apostles' teaching. There is little dispute to this fact. [7] *"Therefore you do not lack any spiritual gift as you eagerly wait for our Lord Jesus Christ to be revealed. He will also keep you firm to the end, so that you will be blameless on the day of our Lord Jesus Christ." (I Corinthians 1:7, 8; I John 4:17, NIV)*

- **The Commandment to Watch Always**

So what does Christ command His followers to do in the meantime? This is the issue of "until." *This comprises the fourth key reason to believe in His imminent return.* Jesus commands us "to watch." *Being watchful is not optional.* Time and again in His teaching, Jesus warned His followers to stay alert:

- **Watch** *ye therefore: for ye know not when the master of the house cometh, at even, or at midnight, or at the cockcrowing, or in the morning (Mark 13:35)*

- **Watch** *therefore: for ye know not what hour your Lord doth come (Matthew 24:42)*

- **Watch** *therefore, for ye know neither the day nor the hour wherein the Son of man cometh. (Matthew 25:13)*

As Jesus taught, when the watchful see, *"these things begin to come to pass, then [they will] look up for [their] redemption draweth nigh."* (Luke 21:28) For those who are *"children of the day"* (according to Paul), what happens should be no surprise. They understand the *signs of His soon coming* (I Thessalonians 5:5). Paul emphatically delivered this message to his churches. He instructs his disciples not to falter in upholding its truthfulness and integrity: *"Whereunto he called you by our gospel, to the obtaining*

---

[7] Many committed believers in Christ believe the Rapture happens immediately before Jesus physically comes back to the earth, specifically at the Battle of Armageddon. Most believers today, however, believe His return is at some event well before Armageddon, from a few months to a few years. Indeed, the traditional view known as the Pre-Tribulation position adheres to the belief Jesus returns for His bride at least seven years prior to this prophesied battle.

of the glory of our Lord Jesus Christ. Therefore, brethren, stand fast, and **hold the traditions** which ye have been taught, whether by word, or our epistle." (2 Thessalonians 2:14, 15).

- *Anticipate Salvation's Completion: Our Glorification*

Finally (and fifthly), Christ's return completes *a most vital and essential aspect of the salvation Christians are to receive.* Salvation commences with the resurrection from the dead, but concludes with the *glorification of the body* in the very same manner and form as the body of the ascended Christ:

- *Beloved, now are we the sons of God, and it doth not yet appear what we shall be: but we know that, when He shall appear,* **we shall be like Him**; *for we shall see Him as He is (1 John 3:2)*

- *For whom He did foreknow, He also did predestinate [to be]* **conformed to the image of His Son**, *that He might be the firstborn among many brethren (Romans 8:29)*

- *Whereunto he called you by our gospel, to the obtaining of the* **glory of our Lord Jesus Christ**. *(2 Thessalonians 2:14)*

Until the bodies of those who believe are made like His, their experience of salvation in the here and now is but a taste of the life to come. Much more exists to discover and experience. Christ's gospel expressly promises this to all who trust in Him.

When we explore the many lessons inherent in the New Testament—those doctrines which comprise its teaching—it becomes apparent how most of its promises are staked upon the coming Kingdom to achieve their final fulfillment. Today, as Paul says, *"We see as in a mirror darkly, but then face-to-face"* (I Corinthians 13:12). What we observe are mere shadows of what is to come.

Moreover, should we finally see things as they actually are (in the world to come), Christians will learn what our former, 'clandestine' mission meant. By shining as 'lights in the world' and ' being salt in their circumstances' they sought *to embody the vision of this new world coming*—the Kingdom promised by Jesus

Christ—who guaranteed its realization "in the fullness of time" (Ephesians 1:10; Galatians 4:4). Today, we watch God's stopwatch ticking toward its apex. Time has all but run its course.

FIGURE 11 - FOUR HORSEMEN OF APOCALYPSE, BY VIKTOR VASNETSOV. PAINTED IN 1887

Therefore, we should all prayerfully ask ourselves these questions: "How does the nearness of the apocalypse alter our path?" "Are we seeking to be worthy of escape, to stand before the Son of Man?" We should not get hung up on whether or not the words of Jesus promise a pre-tribulation rapture (although I happen to believe they do). The plain meaning of His statement remains clear: some aspect of the horror of this future time, some facet of the greatest time of tribulation to be experienced by humankind, indeed, most certainly the specific wrath of God which awaits an unbelieving world—can be escaped for those found worthy. We are instructed to earnestly desire to avoid the worst of times in those last days that we might stand before the Son of Man.

5: SIGNS AND WONDERS

*And I will harden Pharaoh's heart, and multiply **my signs and my wonders** in the land of Egypt.*
(Exodus 7:3)
*How great are his **signs**! And how mighty are his **wonders**! His kingdom is an everlasting kingdom, and his dominion is from generation to generation.*
(Daniel 4:3)

SIGNS THAT CONFIRM THE COVENANTS

SIGNS AND WONDERS ARE A COMMON MOTIF IN THE BIBLE. THERE ARE MANY INSTANCES WHERE THE TWO WORDS ARE USED TOGETHER AS A PHRASE, IN FACT A BIBLICAL CATCHPHRASE,[1] TO express the spectacular actions of God.

We take up the phrase *signs and wonders* as used in both the Old and New Testament because the apocalypse is typified by amazing sights and sounds, usually coming forth from the sky or from 'on high' like Mount Sinai (be it in Egypt or Arabia[2]), or from

---

[1] The dictionary in Microsoft Word defines a *catchphrase* as follows: "A group of words, often originating in popular culture that is spontaneously popularized after widespread repeated use." Phrases like "down and out," "tired and hungry," and "waxed and waned" are familiar catchphrases today. "Signs and wonders" was a catchphrase in both the Hebrew Old Testament and in the Greek New Testament.

[2] For an outstanding article on this debate, see Lambert Dolphin's treatment of the issue at http://ldolphin.org/sinai.html.

the Throne of God in heaven. As the reader will see, not to minimize the possible pertinence of the Blood Moon Prophecy, but these signs are a good deal more spectacular than the appearances of solar and lunar eclipses.

The word **sign** (transliterated from the Hebrew *owth,* pronounced 'oath') appears 79 times within 77 verses of the King James Version Old Testament. According to Strong's Concordance, it is used as "a distinguishing mark, banner, military ensign, remembrance, miraculous sign, omen, and warning." And as we will see, it comprises an indispensable element to confirm a covenant between God and humankind.

The first instance of the use of this word in the Bible (as we have already mentioned), appears in Genesis 1:14*: "And God said, Let there be lights in the firmament of the heaven to divide the day from the night; and let them be **for signs**, and for seasons, and for days, and years."*

The second usage stands out too. It deals with the infamous mark upon Cain, a mark meant to warn everyone not to harm Cain in any way, lest God Himself take vengeance upon the one who did. The word translated **mark** is the same as **sign**—*owth*. We read: *"And the LORD said unto him, 'Therefore whosoever slayeth Cain, vengeance shall be taken on him sevenfold.' And the LORD set a **mark** (owth) upon Cain, lest any finding him should kill him."*

THE NOAHIC COVENANT

The third instance of the use of this word regards a heavenly sign—the **rainbow**. Three times the word *owth* is used in the passage below. Clearly, the placement of this sign in the clouds of earth was important to remind humankind that God had covenanted with humankind—he would never again destroy the earth with water. The passage indicates that the sign was to serve as a reminder to God; but, in reality (given we believe God has a very good memory!) this sign was *our* reminder that God would surely keep His covenant.

> *And I will establish my covenant with you; neither shall all flesh be cut off any more by the waters of a flood; neither shall there any more be a flood to destroy the earth. And God said, This is the **token** of the covenant which I make between me and you and every living creature that is with you, for perpetual generations: I **do set my bow in the cloud,** and it shall be for a **token** of a covenant between me and the earth. And it shall come to pass, when I bring a cloud over the earth, that the bow shall be seen in the cloud: And I will remember my covenant, which is between me and you and every living creature of all flesh; and the waters shall no more become a flood to destroy all flesh. And the **bow shall be in the cloud**; and I will look upon it, that I may remember the everlasting covenant between God and every living creature of all flesh that is upon the earth. And God said unto Noah, This is the **token** of the covenant, which I have established between me and all flesh that is upon the earth.* (Genesis 9:11-17)

A classic writer from the first portion of the twentieth century, Arthur W. Pink, provides an overview of the *Noahic Covenant*:

> The facts briefly stated above require to be carefully kept in mind, for they throw not a little light upon the covenant which the Lord God made with Noah. They explain the reason for the transaction itself, and impart at least some aid toward a right conception of the

FIGURE 12 - NOAH'S SACRIFICE BY DANIEL MACLISE

particular form it took. The background of that covenant was divine judgment: drastic, unsparing, [and] effectual. Every individual of the ungodly race perished: the great Deluge completely relieved the earth of their presence and crimes. In due time the water subsided, and Noah and his family came from their place of refuge to people the earth afresh. It is scarcely possible for us to form any adequate conception of the feelings of Noah on this occasion. The terrible and destructive visitation, in which the hand of God was so manifest, must have given him an impression of the exceeding sinfulness of sin and of the ineffable holiness and righteousness of God such as he had not previously entertained.[3]

Thus, the Noahic Covenant came upon the heels of judgment; and its *token*, the *sign* of the rainbow was associated with that judgment, specifically, the promise never to inflict the same judgment upon the world again. As with signs and covenants, we also often see *signs and judgments* linked in the Bible.

THE SIGN AS A TOKEN OF THE ABRAHAMIC COVENANT

Just as the *Noahic Covenant* was commemorated with a sign, an *owth*, so was the *Abrahamic Covenant*. What specific sign? **Circumcision**: *"And ye shall circumcise the flesh of your foreskin, and it shall be a token of the covenant betwixt me and you."* (Genesis 17:11) The sign of circumcision could hardly be more memorable for the Judeo-Christian world. It stands a "sign in the flesh" as the covenant between God and the Hebrew people. (Many Americans born after World War II, whether Gentile or Jew, were typically circumcised "in due course" as a matter of hygiene).

The Apostle Paul discusses circumcision prominently in his letters. Some of his most important arguments use this *sign* to distinguish the *principle of faith* from the *principle of law*. In Romans 2, we read Paul's signature statement on the topic of circumcision:

---

[3] See http://www.pbministries.org/books/pink/Divine_Covenants/divine_covenants_03.htm.

²⁵ For circumcision verily profiteth, if thou keep the law: but if thou be a breaker of the law, thy circumcision is made uncircumcision.

²⁶ Therefore if the uncircumcision keep the righteousness of the law, shall not his uncircumcision be counted for circumcision?

²⁷ And shall not uncircumcision which is by nature, if it fulfil the law, judge thee, who by the letter and circumcision dost transgress the law?

²⁸ For he is not a Jew, which is one outwardly; neither is that circumcision, which is outward in the flesh:

²⁹ But he is a Jew, which is one inwardly; and circumcision is that of the heart, in the spirit, and not in the letter; whose praise is not of men, but of God.

Circumcision was meant to be only a *token of the covenant*. Paul indicates the *keeping* of the law was preeminent. If you failed to keep the law perfectly, then circumcision was invalidated. If you kept the law and yet were not circumcised, the act of keeping the law would make you 'circumcised' in the eyes of God. Circumcision in and of itself was not the crucial act. It was a mere *token* (in the way we use the word in today's vernacular—a 'small symbol of little consequence'). What was crucial was the promise of God to keep His word as well as the faith of Abraham to believe God at His word. From the Christian perspective, circumcision stands as a matter of the heart (the spirit) and not essence of the law.

THE NAME, THE PRESENCE, AND VOICE OF GOD AS A SIGN

We see the next use of the word *owth* in the Bible within the Book of Exodus, in the context of Moses' first visit to the Mountain of God, known as Mount Sinai. Here the *sign* appears to be *knowing the name of God*—I AM THAT I AM (YHWH) and *the experience of God Himself* as the Hebrews would soon encounter Him in "the holy mountain."

*"And he said, 'Certainly I will be with thee; and this shall be a **token** unto thee, that I have sent thee: When thou hast brought*

forth the people out of Egypt, ye shall serve God upon this mountain'... And God said unto Moses, I AM THAT I AM: and he said, Thus shalt thou say unto the children of Israel, I AM hath sent me unto you.'" (Exodus 3:12).

Eventually, the people would hear the voice of God, a voice so loud, so fearful, and heard for such an extended time that the Israelites pleaded with Moses to make His voice stop. It is no small thing that the *voice sounded like a trumpet*. The voice of God appears always to sound like a thunderous, if not also shrill trumpet.

- Isaiah 58:1, *"Cry aloud, spare not, lift up thy voice **like a trumpet**, and shew my people their transgression, and the house of Jacob their sins."*

- Revelation 1:10-11, *"I was in the Spirit on the Lord's day, and heard behind me a great voice, **as of a trumpet**, Saying, I am Alpha and Omega, the first and the last."*

- Revelation 4:1, *"After this I looked, and, behold, a door was opened in heaven: and **the first voice which I heard was as it were of a trumpet talking with me**; which said, Come up hither, and I will shew thee things which must be hereafter."*

FIGURE 13 - MOUNT SINAI ON THE SINAI PENINSULA IN EGYPT (TRADITIONAL SITE)

This sign of a voice emanating from the mountain, from on high, was a most fearful sign.

> *And it came to pass on the third day in the morning, that there were thunders and lightnings, and a thick cloud upon the mount, and **the voice of the trumpet exceeding loud**; so that all the people that was in the camp trembled... And when the voice of the trumpet sounded long, and waxed louder and louder, Moses spake, and God answered him by a voice. And the LORD came down upon Mount Sinai, on the top of the mount.* (Exodus 19:19-20)

The Apostle Paul (traditionally thought to be the writer of the Book of Hebrews) provides commentary on this event in the New Testament. Paul illustrates that the old covenant involved fear and trembling on the holy mountain outside of Egypt—Mount Sinai.

> [19] *And the **sound of a trumpet, and the voice of words;** which voice they that heard intreated [entreated] that the word should not be spoken to them any more:*
>
> [20] *(For they could not endure that which was commanded, 'And if so much as a beast touch the mountain, it shall be stoned, or thrust through with a dart:*
>
> [21] *And so terrible was the sight, that Moses said, "I exceedingly fear and quake"')* (Hebrews 12:19-21)

No doubt the sights and sounds were frightening. Living in Oklahoma, I can relate to such an awesome sight. When we see what meteorologists call a 'wall cloud,' we know a Tornado likely lurks within. The wall cloud is massive and sometimes appears as a giant spiral reaching high into the atmosphere. The sight can be enough to buckle the knees.

As articulated by Paul, however, the New Covenant takes us to an even higher and better place, where the sight looms awesome but the fearsomeness less palpable. It comprises a place where we enjoy a more excellent company of angels, perfected human beings, and Jesus our mediator—*Mount Sion* (aka Zion, in Heaven)—the Mount Zion of which the earthly Zion resembles only a facsimile.

> *22 But ye are come unto Mount Sion, and unto the city of the living God, the heavenly Jerusalem, and to an innumerable company of angels,*
>
> *23 To the general assembly and church of the firstborn, which are written in heaven, and to God the Judge of all, and to the spirits of just men made perfect,*
>
> *24 And to Jesus the mediator of the new covenant* (Hebrews 12:22-24).

FIGURE 14 - THE PILLAR OF FIRE IN THE MIDST OF THE HEBREW CAMP

THE MEANING OF OWTH OFTEN EQUATES TO OATH

Given the history of the use of the word *owth*, is it not likely that the etymology of the English word *oath* connects to the Hebrew word owth (two words pronounced the same and denoting virtually the same concept)? I venture it is although I have not yet been able to verify it in several resources recently referenced.[4] Thus, the conclusion appears rather obvious: tokens and covenants have a very strong affinity for one another. It is safe to say the meaning of the notions of *oaths* and *signs* go together like hand and glove, or smoke and fire (two modern catchphrases by the way, to clarify *ad nauseam* the meaning of *catchphrase*).

SIGNS AND WONDERS

The second word of our catchphrase, *wonder*, is the Hebrew word *mowpheth* (as transliterated from the Hebrew alphabet).[5] Nehemiah 9:9-12 contains an important instance in which we see the catchphrase "signs and wonders" used (by Nehemiah) as he prays to the God of Israel.

> [9] *And (thou--YHWH) didst see the affliction of our fathers in Egypt, and heardest their cry by the Red sea;*
>
> [10] *And shewedst* **signs and wonders** *upon Pharaoh, and on all his servants, and on all the people of his land: for thou knewest that they dealt proudly against them. So didst thou get thee a name, as it is this day.*
>
> [11] *And thou didst divide the sea before them, so that they went through the midst of the sea on the dry land; and their persecutors thou threwest into the deeps, as a stone into the mighty waters.*
>
> [12] *Moreover thou leddest them in the day* **by a cloudy pillar***; and in the night* **by a pillar of fire***, to give them light in the way wherein they should go.*

---

[4] "Old English *að* "oath, judicial swearing, solemn appeal to deity in witness of truth or a promise," from Proto-Germanic **aithaz* (cognates: Old Norse *eiðr*, Swedish *ed*, Old Saxon, Old Frisian *eth*, Middle Dutch *eet*, Dutch *eed*, German *eid*, Gothic *aiþs* "oath"), from PIE **oi-to-* "an oath" (cognates: Old Irish *oeth* "oath"). See http://etymonline.com/index.php?allowed_in_frame=0&search=oath&searchmode=none.

[5] Pronounced mo-fãth, as in "Give me mo' faith Lord." No doubt biblical wonders did give their observers much more faith. But to be precise, I do not propose any etymology to this colloquial phrase!

Nehemiah emphasizes the issue of signs and wonders to remind his colleagues of the faithfulness of God toward the Hebrews. He highlights two of the most dramatic signs and wonders: *the pillar of smoke* by day and *the pillar of fire* by night. These were fearful signs and wonders indeed, connecting Heaven and Earth, demonstrating the miraculous power of God and the practical value of His actions on their behalf (that is, *a guiding light*).

Jeremiah echoes the exact same sentiment as he exults in the power of the Lord God of Israel. In a magnificent passage in Jeremiah, chapter 32, Jeremiah testifies to the greatest of God with these words:

17 Ah Lord God! behold, thou hast made the heaven and the earth by thy great power and stretched out arm, and there is nothing too hard for thee:

18 Thou shewest lovingkindness unto thousands, and recompensest the iniquity of the fathers into the bosom of their children after them: the Great, the Mighty God, the Lord of hosts, is his name,

19 Great in counsel, and mighty in work: for thine eyes are open upon all the ways of the sons of men: to give every one according to his ways, and according to the fruit of his doings:

20 Which hast set **signs and wonders** *in the land of Egypt, even unto this day, and in Israel, and among other men; and hast made thee a name, as at this day;*

21 And hast brought forth thy people Israel out of the land of Egypt **with signs, and with wonders,** *and with a strong hand, and with a stretched out arm, and with great terror;*

22 And hast given them this land, which thou didst swear to their fathers to give them, a land flowing with milk and honey.

THE TESTIMONY OF DANIEL'S GENTILE KINGS

Even King Nebuchadnezzar of Babylon extols the power of the God of Israel within the Book of Daniel. In a section written in Aramaic (the language of Babylon), we see the phrase **signs and wonders** employed here as well. In Aramaic, the word for signs is transliterated *āth (compared to owth—the sound of a long 'a' instead of a long 'o')*. Wonders is transliterated *tĕmahh*. The catchphrase **signs and wonders** was so catchy even the gentiles utilized it to express supernatural sights and sounds.

FIGURE 15 - DANIEL IN THE LIONS' DEN

In context, we learn Nebuchadnezzar had just come through a bout of *lycanthropy*—thinking and acting like a beast (a wolf to be specific). Daniel interpreted the King's horrific dream, warning him that unless he practiced righteousness and showed justice to the poor, he would find his sanity departing him for a period of seven years.⁶ One year after the dream had been interpreted thus by Daniel, the King waxed lyrical concerning his own might and power, and how he himself was responsible for his privileged position rather than giving thanks to the King of Heaven. Instantly, judgment fell. The king was driven mad and into the forests where he eat grass like a beast and was covered with the nightly dew.

But God was faithful to His word. After seven years had passed, God restored the King's sanity and his kingdom. Therefore, Nebuchadnezzar praises the God of Daniel, the King of Heaven. *"I thought it good to shew **the signs and wonders** that the high God hath wrought toward me. How great are **His signs**! And how mighty are **His wonders**! His kingdom is an everlasting kingdom, and His dominion is from generation to generation."* (Daniel 4:2-3)

Apparently, Daniel had a way with the kings he served. Later, King Darius was persuaded that Daniel had a wonderful spirit within him and therefore, Darius entrusted Daniel with great authority. This caused envy among Daniel's enemies leading to his being thrown into the famous lion's den.

After Daniel was spared *death by dinner* (his being the lion's dinner that is), Darius the king was exultant. Despite Darius' law being the cause for Daniel's unexpected night's stay amongst the surprisingly hospitable lions, Darius did not want Daniel to become lion's food. Darius feared Daniel's God. When Darius saw Daniel alive and well in the morning—like Nebuchadnezzar—Darius praised the God of Heaven with these enthusiastic words:

> ₂₅*Then king Darius wrote unto all people, nations, and languages, that dwell in all the earth: "Peace be multiplied unto you.*

---

⁶ In this experience, most scholars see Nebuchadnezzar exhibiting the traits of the Antichrist and the seven years, the seven years of tribulation. As I have discussed elsewhere, there exists an intriguing connection between the wolf and the antichrist. Lycos was associated with Apollo. Hitler was known as Grey Wolf.

> *²⁶I make a decree, That in every dominion of my kingdom men tremble and fear before the God of Daniel: for he is the living God, and stedfast for ever, and his kingdom that which shall not be destroyed, and his dominion shall be even unto the end.*
>
> *²⁷He delivereth and rescueth, and he worketh **signs and wonders** in heaven and in earth, who hath delivered Daniel from the power of the lions."* (Daniel 6:25-27)

In this case, the sign was quite another matter—supernaturally satiating the appetite of lions so they would not eat God's prophet.

THE DISCIPLES WERE PROVEN BY SIGNS AND WONDERS

Just as the prophets (especially Moses, Elijah and Elisha) proved themselves by working signs and wonders in the name of the God of Israel, the disciples of Jesus Christ were accredited by also demonstrating similar signs and wonders. In the Greek language of the New Testament, **signs and wonders** was expressed with the words (transliterated) *sēmeion kai teras*. It appears as a frequent phrase employed by Luke in the Book of Acts. We read of four primary instances. The first instance: just after the Holy Spirit has fallen upon all those gathered together at the time of Passover (when there appeared as it were "tongues of fire"), Peter began preaching to the crowds and quoted the Old Testament prophet Joel:

> *¹⁹And I will shew **wonders** in heaven above, and **signs** in the earth beneath; blood, and fire, and vapour of smoke:*
>
> *²⁰The sun shall be turned into darkness, and the moon into blood, before the great and notable day of the Lord come:*
>
> *²¹And it shall come to pass, that whosoever shall call on the name of the Lord shall be saved.*
>
> *²²Ye men of Israel, hear these words; Jesus of Nazareth, a man approved of God among you by **miracles and wonders and signs**, which God did by him in the midst of you, as ye yourselves also know* (Acts 2:19-22)

Next, we see how after Peter and John had been threatened to speak no more in the name of Jesus (having spoken in front of Annas and Caiaphas the High Priests, being filled with the Holy Spirit and speaking eloquently of the works of Jesus), the new community of faith came together and Peter led them in prayer, reminding everyone of the powerful works of Jesus, God's Holy child: *"By stretching forth thine hand to heal; and that **signs and wonders** may be done by the name of thy holy child Jesus."* (Acts 4:30)

FIGURE 16 - ILLUSTRATION OF THE PENTECOST FROM THE HORTUS DELICIARUM OF HERRAD OF LANDSBERG (TWELTH CENTURY)

The third instance follows shortly thereafter: Peter had rebuked two members of the young Church, Ananias and Sapphira, condemning them for lying to the Apostle (and the Holy Spirit) about the price they received for the property they sold on behalf of the community (at which time they immediately dropped dead from his pronouncement). We learn of the fear and amazement of the Church. Luke tells us, *"And by the hands of the apostles were many **signs and wonders** wrought among the people; (and they were all with one accord in Solomon's porch)."* (Acts 5:12)

Then we shift to the acts of Paul. In Iconium, Paul and Barnabas were the subject of controversy between the Jews and Gentiles there. Luke tells us that they were accomplishing great things despite the disputes that had arisen.

> *Long time therefore abode they, speaking boldly in the Lord, which gave testimony unto the word of his grace, and granted **signs and wonders** to be done by their hands.* (Acts 14:3)

In the same manner, Paul references signs and wonders he performed which attested to his credentials as an Apostle. In Romans 15:19, Paul relates that, *"Through mighty **signs and wonders**, by the power of the Spirit of God; so that from Jerusalem, and round about unto Illyricum, I have fully preached the gospel of Christ."* Likewise, in 2 Corinthians 12:12, *"Truly the signs of an apostle were wrought among you in all patience, in **signs, and wonders**, and mighty deeds."*

The writer to the Hebrews speaks of the importance of the Gospel, made surer by the teachings of those that heard Jesus. He says:

> *"How shall we escape, if we neglect so great salvation; which at the first began to be spoken by the Lord, and was confirmed unto us by them that heard him; God also bearing them witness, both with **signs and wonders**, and with **divers miracles**, and gifts of the Holy Ghost, according to his own will?* (Hebrews 2:3-4)

SUMMARY: THE VARIOUS TYPES OF SIGNS AND WONDERS

The Bible employs the catchphrase *signs and wonders* in three different languages and in several different contexts, meaning many distinctive things. In some cases, natural phenomenon comprise examples of signs and wonders, the rainbow being the most noteworthy mentioned, which also served as a sign of a covenant. In other cases, a covenant sign consisted in the human act of *circumcision*. Both are seen as *tokens*, or *owths* in the Hebrew.

In stark contrast, there are many other cases of signs and wonders that testify to *supernatural actions* performed by God. In Egypt the signs and wonders were intended to make Pharaoh 'awestruck'—so much so that Pharaoh would *let the Hebrew people go*, initially to worship Yahweh in the wilderness, but eventually to let them go entirely back to their land in Canaan. However, just as Donald Rumsfeld's bombing program (which he termed 'shock and awe') failed to frighten Saddam Hussein in Iraq in the decade now past, shock and awe failed to achieve the desired outcome in ancient Egypt. Pharaoh simply hardened his heart. No doubt Saddam did the very same thing.

Signs and wonders certainly included Moses' parting of the Red Sea (although that miracle has been explained away by naturalists for at least two centuries), and the subsequent drowning of the armies of Pharaoh when the waters that had been held back to allow the Hebrews to pass through, were released by Yahweh. Then the waves came crashing down on the Egyptian Chariots and their most unfortunate drivers, ensuring the 'resurrection' of the Hebrew people who had walked through the dry land of the Red Sea (also a mighty miracle, as not only did the waves part, but the *seabed was turned into a dry road* for the Hebrews to follow).

Then the Hebrew people were guided by the mighty pillars of smoke and fire. It was certainly hard to miss those constant companions. Of course, we recall that Moses had witnessed the burning bush much earlier. That too was a sign and wonder although, like the writing of the Ten Commandments by the finger of God, it was not something that anyone other than Moses experienced firsthand.

However, the entire throng, several million strong, were held in shock and awe by the voice of God, sounding as a trumpet, when his voice shook the earth from the Holy Mount, Mount Sinai. We learn in the story how God descended like a burning cloud upon the mountaintop. God told Moses to set markers around the mountain to keep the people back lest they should come upon the mountain and be killed. Many other signs would Moses work as he brought the people through their 40 year wilderness journey, whether it was the provision of manna, the 'gift' of the quail to provide a bit of variety to their diet (and to soften their complaints), or the sudden gushing of water provided by God when Moses struck the rock with his famous rod (or his brother Aaron's—the rod that budded and was placed in the Ark of the Covenant).

Jeremiah and Isaiah recounted these great signs and wonders. Then as well as now for orthodox Jews, these actions on the part of Yahweh demonstrated the covenant between Him and His people. Daniel the Beloved (as he is known among orthodox Jews—they do not consider him a prophet—intriguing since Jesus said he was the greatest prophet!) caused kings whom he served to recognize the many signs and wonders of the Hebrew God. Nebuchadnezzar's 'instant insanity' was a sign (his lycanthropy) and that he was delivered just as Daniel had prophesied after precisely seven years. The fact that Daniel predicted exactly what would happen and events came to pass exactly as he had said, was proof enough to Nebuchadnezzar that he had most certainly better 'straighten up and fly right' (another modern catchphrase made famous by singer Nat King Cole of course!) Likewise, when Darius learned that God had miraculously spoiled the lion's appetite to feast on Hebrew prophets (apparently, they much preferred despicable Medes and Persians), he was genuinely awestruck and sent a letter worldwide (at least to the ends of his empire), testifying to the greatness of Daniel's God.

As we move to the New Testament, of course Jesus performed many signs and wonders that the Apostles recounted (and as recorded in the Book of Acts). These signs could be healings, raising the dead back to life), demonstrating his mastery over nature (good examples would be stretching just how far a few loaves and fishes could be made to go; and of course there was that walking on water). John in his gospel uses the word 'signs' and points out that even the skeptical among the Hebrews were impressed by the amazing works that Jesus did. As Nicodemus said, perhaps not being entirely sincere: *"Rabbi, we know that thou art a teacher come from God: for no man can do these miracles (sēmeion) that thou doest, except God be with him."* (John 3:2) And of course, as will discuss in the next chapter, signs by themselves are not always convincing, specifically to those that demand a sign before they are willing to believe.

Finally, the Apostles worked signs and wonders too, testifying to the power of God, and confirming their credentials as those 'sent' by God (which is what the word *apostle* conveys). The signs and wonders attested to the message of the gospel and played no small part in convincing the world that Jesus Christ (and His mighty apostles) were the 'real deal.'

Signs and wonders seem to do that—at least for those whose hearts have been prepared by His Spirit to see them in all their splendor.

6: SIGNS OF THE TIMES

The Pharisees and Sadducees came to put Jesus to the test. They asked him to show them a miraculous sign from heaven. He replied, "In the evening you look at the sky. You say, 'It will be good weather. The sky is red.' And in the morning you say, 'Today it will be stormy. The sky is red and cloudy.' You know the meaning of what you see in the sky. But you can't understand the signs of what is happening right now. **An evil and unfaithful people look for a miraculous sign***. But none will be given to them except the sign of Jonah."*
(Matthew 16:1-4, New International Readers Version - NIRV)

"No one knows about that day or hour. Not even the angels in heaven know. The Son does not know. Only the Father knows. Remember how it was in the days of Noah. It will be the same when the Son of Man comes. In the days before the flood, people were eating and drinking. They were getting married. They were giving their daughters to be married. They did all those things right up to the day Noah entered the ark. **They knew nothing about what would happen until the flood came** *and took them all away. That is how it will be when the Son of Man comes."*
(Matthew 24:36-39, NIRV)

MANY EXPECT THE APOCALYPSE DRAWS NEAR

ONE OF MY FAVORITE MOVIES OF ALL TIME IS JAMES CAMERON'S *TERMINATOR 2: JUDGMENT DAY (1991)*. THE MOVIE INTRODUCED SOME OF THE GREATEST SPECIAL EFFECTS EVER SEEN AT the cinema. Most readers remember the story: Sarah Connor strives to save her son John who represents the one chance humanity has AFTER the world as we know it is destroyed by *Sky Net* and the Terminator machines. The movie portrays a vivid nightmare scenario of a nuclear holocaust producing doomsday. When we think about 'the end of the world,' we cannot help but contemplate horrible images such as we see in Cameron's vision of what may be our fate if the machines ever take over.

We know the climax of history by many names, some biblical and some not: Judgment Day, the Day of the Lord, the Time of Jacob's trouble, Doomsday, the End of Days, the End of Time, the Apocalypse, and of course, Armageddon. Humanity seems to have a deeply rooted sense that the outcome of our story is not a *happy ending*. Surveys today tells us a majority of Americans believe the world is coming to an end. Something terrible will happen. We learn this in a recent poll conducted by the Barna Group:

> PITTSBURGH, PA, Sept 11 — According to its summer 2013 OmniPoll[SM], a well-respected faith and culture research company in Ventura, CA, found that 41% of all U.S. adults, 54% of Protestants and 77% of Evangelicals believe the world is now living in the biblical end times. When asked: "do you, personally, believe that the world is currently living in the 'end times' as described by prophecies in the Bible, or not?", a startling 41% of all participants said yes. The number was even higher for Protestants with a figure representing just over one in two protestant adults. The highest number registered was by Evangelicals with three out of four evangelical Christians in America believing the world is living in the end times. Catholics were at the other end of the spectrum, however, with 73% saying no; though practicing Catholics registered quite a bit higher at nearly 45% saying yes to now living in the end times.
>
> To reach their surprising findings, the Barna Group conducted 1,000 online surveys among a representative sample of adults, ages 18 and older in the United States from July 29, 2013 through August 1, 2013. The margin of error was +/-3.2 percentage points, at the 95% confidence level. The unusual OmniPoll question was commissioned by James F. Fitzgerald, producer of The WatchWORD Bible® New Testament, in concert with the release of his new book, *The 9/11 Prophecy—Startling Evidence the Endtimes have Begun* (WND Books), for the 12th anniversary of the attacks on September 11, 2001.

> Fitzgerald said to his knowledge there had not been a poll like it before on the question of the end times. [1]

Whether we turn to the Bible or to science, it seems that disaster and cataclysm awaits. Today, many books speculate that both natural and mad-made disasters loom. The authors of these books awaken some to disasters that we can avert. But others lay out catastrophes we cannot avoid. All reinforce an existential sense of foreboding.[2] Ray Kurzweil's *singularity* predicts a dizzying future in which 'change goes exponential' likely making humanity unable to cope with an increasing rate of radical transformation in our world. Drinkable water will soon be in short supply. Hunger will reach new highs—even in the United States. True artificial intelligence will finally be achieved within the next decade producing computers that not only 'out-compute' us (which they have done for years), but outthink us in decision making. The machine will be smarter than us. The only cataclysm which seems avoidable now: running out of energy. A slew of new ideas promise cheaper fuel. The ongoing 'oil crisis' that plagued the world since the 1970s and made the politics of the Middle East front page news worldwide will soon give way to an energy surplus that—like the price of telephone service and 'internet connect'—will go down instead of up in the years just ahead.

But other forms of disaster threaten. The history channel in February of 2009 spent an entire week chronicling the many ways catastrophes could destroy humankind. Throughout the last three months of 2008 and all of 2009 the collapse of the world economy

---

[1] See http://pressreleases.religionnews.com/2013/09/11/shock-poll-startling-numbers-of-americans-believe-world-now-in-the-end-times/

[2] The natural disasters that could wreak havoc upon us include sun storms pummeling the earth and thereby generating monster hurricanes; comets striking us with deadly force; or massive cauldrons (like Yellowstone Park) exploding and sending mountains of volcanic ash into the atmosphere creating a 'nuclear winter effect' destroying most animal and plant life on earth. Moreover, these are only a few of the not-so-pleasant possibilities.

seemed more probable than not. In many ways, the economy did collapse and a number of nations did not recover, essentially going bankrupt (Iceland, Greece, to name but two). From 2010 to 2013, it was two steps forward and one step back. Economic recovery was never judged immune to a full retreat into a 'double dip recession.' In 2014, not a day goes by without some expert (and many without any credentials) laying claim to a sure sign of our undoing. We are told why economic collapse remains inevitable. Few fiscal prophets see improvement ahead. References to economic collapse are legion. I cite a typical comment below:

> Despite the US stock markets doing relatively well at the moment, some financial experts have made economic predictions for 2014 that claim a stock market crash in January is possible. Further, the out of control US debt will cause the US dollar to be removed as the reserve currency and trigger an economic collapse:
>
> *"The central issue is confidence in America, and the world is losing confidence quickly. At a certain point, soon, the United States will reach a level of deficit spending and debt at which the countries of the world will lose faith in America and begin to withdraw their investments. Many leading economists and bankers think another trillion dollars or so may do it. A run on the bank will start suddenly, build quickly and snowball."*[3]

Whether we are talking economics or politics, if someone predicts an awful event lies just around the corner, we no longer call such a person an *alarmist*; they are a *realist*.

FOR UNBELIVERS, NO SIGN OF DISASTER MAY BE COMING

Jesus chided the religious leaders of his day—the intelligentsia of his time—for their failure to understand what was happening to them and their nation. He also warned the common person to be cautious about the future—do not assume life will continue in a

---

[3] See http://www.prepperfortress.com/predictions-for-2014-end-of-the-world-world-war-3-us-economic-collapse/

state of 'normalcy' (as we might label it today, the 'status quo'). Changes happen, whether desired or not. There is no one, no life-force, not even God Himself who guarantees *life as we know it* will continue 'as is.' To paraphrase Jesus' words: "It is just like in the days of Noah... everyone was drinking and eating, marrying and giving in marriage (life as usual), and then *BAM!*—the flood came and destroyed everyone and stopped everything they

FIGURE 17 – AN ANCIENT RELIEF, PURPORTEDLY OF NEPHILIM

were doing." In this instance, Jesus' point was almost a contradiction to His earlier rebuke to the Jewish leaders for their failure to read the signs of the times when he pointed out they could interpret the meaning of red skies but not the political implications of what was happening in their nation. However, in contrast to His earlier rebuff, in the reference to the days of Noah, Jesus predicted that most will not be able to discern what was about to happen. "Don't expect any sign of disaster before disaster strikes. It will be like the people in Noah's day who never saw it coming! The everyday events of life just kept right on taking place until the end came. And then, it was too late."

Recently, there have been a surfeit of books on the amazing story of the Nephilim of Genesis 6:4. *"There were giants in the earth in those days; and also after that, when the sons of God came in unto the daughters of men, and they bare children to them, the same became mighty men which were of old, men of renown."* The phrase "as in the days of Noah" has led to the speculation that what took place during Noah's time, the corruption of humanity by the interbreeding (apparently) of angels with 'the daughters of men', will occur again.

In several of my other books, I have also written about this possibility and cited examples where what is happening today concerning the strange goings on of alien abduction, may be nothing less than exactly that, an unbelievable as it would be.

However, we should not fail to consider the explicit point Jesus was making in this passage. If we look carefully at the context, Jesus was speaking specifically about whether or not there would be a sign of the apocalypse that would wake the world up and cause them to realize that judgment was coming. His primary point *about the lack of warning*—the absence of a sign—was the characteristic of Noah's day. It will be exactly the same at the time of His return. Everyone will assume 'life goes on' just as it has since the beginning of time. Certainly, this is the very same point which Peter makes in the controversial book we know as 2 Peter:

> *2 That ye may be mindful of the words which were spoken before by the holy prophets, and of the commandment of us the apostles of the Lord and Saviour:*
>
> *3 Knowing this first, that there shall come in the last days scoffers, walking after their own lusts,*
>
> *4 And saying, Where is the promise of his coming? for since the fathers fell asleep,* **all things continue as they were from the beginning of the creation**.
>
> *5 For this they willingly are ignorant of, that by the word of God the heavens were of old, and the earth standing out of the water and in the water:*

⁶Whereby the world that then was, being overflowed with water, perished.

For almost everyone, as Paul teaches, will not be looking for the signs of Jesus' coming. They will be blind to the warnings because they are *children of the night*, and not of the day. In stark contrast, all those who are watching will detect the signs of His coming. Those who are not watching will be caught unawares.

²For yourselves know perfectly that the day of the Lord so cometh as a thief in the night.

³For when they shall say, Peace and safety; then sudden destruction cometh upon them, as travail upon a woman with child; and they shall not escape.

⁴But ye, brethren, are not in darkness, that that day should overtake you as a thief.

⁵Ye are all the children of light, and the children of the day: we are not of the night, nor of darkness.

⁶Therefore let us not sleep, as do others; but let us watch and be sober.

⁷For they that sleep sleep in the night; and they that be drunken are drunken in the night. (1 Thessalonians 5:2-7)

THERE ARE ALSO SIGNS THAT GO UNDETECTED

Sometimes change is so significant it can be labeled *epochal*.[4] Jesus saw the political conditions of his day and could see the inevitable clash between Jewish nationalism and Roman authority. He understood that the status quo was about to change forever for the Jewish people. He warned the politicians and the people to wake up and realize disaster was pending. His prophecies were very specific: The heart and soul of the Jewish identity, their temple, would soon be destroyed. He told His disciples *"Not one stone will be left upon another"* (Matthew 24: 2). His retort

---

[4] An *epoch* is the beginning of a period in history that authorities consider significant. An epochal event changes the course of history.

struck down their cherished belief that the nation of Judea and the Hebrew religion was as solid as the stones of the Temple. Looking at them, how could anyone think differently? The stones were massive. The Temple complex was bigger than three football stadiums. It seemed immovable. Like these stones, the disciples assumed that nothing could shake the religion of Yahweh.

FIGURE 18 - STONES FROM THE TEMPLE IN THE TYROPOEON VALLEY IN JERUSALEM

In response to their assumption about the unshakable quality of their Hebrew heritage, to the core beliefs that had been instilled by years of teaching and the inundation of 'conventional wisdom' that ignored the signs of the times, Jesus warned them not to be fooled by the seemingly indestructible building within which God had even once chosen to live. Despite all of this sacred history, the Temple could be shaken. In fact, Jerusalem would be razed and the Temple would be utterly destroyed. The generation that He was speaking to would witness all of these events. (Matthew 24:34)

Moses predicted fifteen centuries earlier that one day the Jews would be dispersed throughout the world and no longer enjoy the comfort or familiarity of their homeland or their way of life. As a nation, they would be homeless. The people of Judea must have assumed that the diaspora was already a completed fact, the worst was behind them. No doubt it was considered a *fait accompli* that with the former destruction of the Temple by Nebuchadnezzar and the removal of all of Judea to Babylon six centuries earlier, that what Moses once predicted had already come to pass. The Northern Kingdom of Israel had been destroyed and its people carted off to destinations unknown. They were dispersed throughout many lands. While it may be true that these ten tribes were not really 'lost'—nevertheless, these ancient Hebrews would be very hard to find! Was this not the dispersion Moses described?

When the Hebrews of Judea (the Jews) returned to Jerusalem led by Zerubbabel to rebuild the Temple, and later when Nehemiah led others to rebuild the walls of Jerusalem, no doubt the Jewish leaders taught the people that the Kingdom of the Jews would thenceforth weather any storm. The then current occupation of Rome would not last forever. Soon God would act on their behalf. The Romans would be expelled. The worship of Jehovah would be undaunted once more. The massive stones set beautifully in place was proof enough. Their Temple was the symbol of that inevitability. And yet, Jesus spurned that common notion. The Kingdom of Judea was to crumble within a generation. When this 'natural' sign came of the city of Jerusalem being surrounded by armies, it would be time to drop everything and flee. Jesus had given them a sign: "*And when ye shall see Jerusalem compassed with armies, then know that the desolation thereof is nigh. Then let them which are in Judaea flee to the mountains; and let them which are in the midst of it depart out; and let not them that are in the countries enter thereinto.*" (Luke 21:20-21) The surrounding armies of Rome were a *visible and unmistakable sign* to the people of Jerusalem: "Get out while the gettin' is good!"

In 67 AD, the Roman general Titus and his army surrounded Jerusalem. Titus, the son of Vespasian (and soon to be Caesar himself), gave the inhabitants of Jerusalem a chance to escape the siege. Christian Jews, heeding the warning of Jesus from 35 years previous, left the city and fled to other Christian communities in neighboring lands. However, both the fervent nationalists as well as the piously religious could not conceive of how God would allow His eternal City to be destroyed. So they stayed. And Jesus' prediction of the destruction of Jerusalem came to pass exactly as he said. Titus burned the temple to the ground. The Roman armies lifted and separated the stones to find the temple gold which had melted during the fire and seeped between the cracks.[5] As Jesus said, *not one stone was left upon another*. Within a few more years, the nation of Israel was doused and the land desolate. Their world ended. Before this occurred, to the Jews their temple seemed the stoutest of symbols that their religion and existence was indestructible. It had withstood the threats by Alexander the Great in the third century BC, Antiochus Epiphanes IV of the Syrians in the second century BC, and the Roman emperor Pompey 60 years before the birth of Jesus Christ. Prior to the act of the Roman Titus, predicting the temple's doom was like predicting, well, the Second Coming of Christ today. Like the Jews, we assume it inconceivable that our world could come to a screeching halt.

JESUS CITES THE BIBLE'S BIGGEST WHOPPERS

It is particularly noteworthy that Jesus uses two stories both involving 'signs of the times', that of Jonah and Noah, to point out how history will soon make a dramatic turn. Generally, theologians want to label Jonah (the prophet swallowed by that big fish) and Noah (who built what appeared an impossibly big boat) as

---

[5] Recently, it has been authenticated that the gold of the Jewish Temple was actually the financial means by which the Roman Coliseum was built. Outside the Coliseum a placard has been found that declares the Coliseum a gift from Titus, the General of the Army destroying Jerusalem, to his Father, *Vespasianus* (aka, Vespasian), the Caesar until Titus himself became Caesar in 79 A.D. The placard ties the gold of the Jewish Temple to the completion of the Coliseum.

obvious 'mythical' figures, supplying such colorful object lessons. It is most interesting since it suggests Jesus made a big mistake in his quarrel with his opposition. Since Jesus emphasized to the Pharisees the 'stark reality' of the situation, picking these particular stories to reinforce His point should be laughable. It would be like predicting on the front page of the *Wall Street Journal* the US economy is set to crash because Charlie Brown carelessly lost his lunch money in that morning's *Peanuts*. As the logicians say, it is *a non sequitur*.

Nevertheless, Jesus uses some of the biggest 'whoppers' of all Bible stories to make His point. In so doing, we should make special note of what this implies about His high regard for the Scripture. If Jesus did not believe that Jonah and Noah were real historical characters, if He regarded these accounts as mere 'Bible Stories' to tell the kids (but discounted their historicity), it would weaken His most important prediction that a national catastrophe was soon to occur. *His polemic speaks volumes.* However, beyond Jesus' testimony that these two colorful figures were real life persons just as the Bible teaches, He confirms an age-old heuristic: *past events teach us what the future holds.* We sense through His words (with my modern paraphrase applied) the contempt He felt for the 'blind guides' of the Temple religion: "Just like the flood of Noah, another judgment looms and you religious leaders are too caught up in your self-seeking politics to realize what is about to happen. Read the signs of the time. A change is inevitable. The 'establishment' will soon come tumbling down. 'A change is gonna come!' The world you live in will be turned upside down."

Of course, this is not to ignore the fact that apocalypses come in various shapes and sizes. When the Spanish came to the New World in the fifteenth and sixteenth centuries, their disembarking spawned an apocalypse for Native Americans. Within a short span of years, the majority of natives died. Worlds collided. American Indians had no immunity against European diseases. This unfortunate fact does not stand alone. We can uncover many such devastating events throughout human history and draw the same conclusion. Massive change happens. The status quo changes. When these alterations come to pass, when the unthinkable breaks upon us, we are uprooted and we must adjust to living life totally differently. Despite the turmoil we face in making such changes, we find we have little to no choice but to do so.

DENYING THE INEVITABLE APOCALYPSE WE SEE COMING

The *apocalypse*, in one sense, means much more than a one-time event. Whenever massive change impacts a whole group of people, when their lives are turned upside down, what they experience can be likened to *the end of the world*—certainly, the end of *their world as they have known it*.

This type of radical shift in fortunes was the story leading up to World War II. Throughout Europe, the signs were undeniable that Germany would soon launch another war. The vitriol Hitler spewed against the Jews should have been taken seriously by everyone, especially those with any trace of Jewish ancestry. But so many Jews living in Germany, in Poland, in Belarus, indeed throughout all of Europe, were too 'connected' into the economy to give up everything and leave their lives behind—even though it meant the difference between life and death. The signs were inevitable. But the coming of the apocalypse was so radical in its implications, the 'new normal' could not be believed. Millions chose to stay put and by so doing, sealed their horrific fate.

In the final analysis, what seems to be the lesson in these selected passages drawn from the Gospel of Matthew boils down to this colloquial saying: "They should have seen it coming." *Recognizing the signs of the times was in fact the best means to avoid the impending disaster*. Being watchful, being aware of what would soon happen, would have allowed many to escape the impending doom. Since they chose to remain oblivious to reality, however, their world eventually came crashing down. Without preparation, the destruction would be more devastating than anyone could fathom.

LIVING AS IF THE END IS SOON—BECAUSE IT MAY BE

Is not this often the case in our personal lives? We hear tell of accounts where lives that should have been lost, *are miraculously spared*. Death is averted. Afterwards, the usual sentiment is "I will never live my life the same way again... I will appreciate each day because it could be my last." Those who have had the so-called 'near-death experience' know just how precarious life is. They are the first to point out how we must relish each day as a gift.

Will we experience the 'end of the world' in our lifetime? Many evangelical scholars confidently predict we will witness the events associated with the Second Coming of Christ within the next two to three decades if not sooner. What is irrefutable even by those who doubt the validity of the Bible's teaching concerning the Apocalypse and the foreboding signs of the end: Many groups of our human brothers or sisters (numbering in the tens of thousands or in the tens of millions), will experience a cataclysm that changes their world forever. An apocalypse is inevitable.

Where will we be when that happens? We may hear of such occurrences on the news or we may observe it much more closely. Living in Oklahoma and experiencing the threat of EF5 Tornadoes —witnessing the death and devastation they cause—it is an ever-present reality during the spring and late summer. Therefore, the lessons we must learn are clear: we dare not think, "What happened to them cannot happen to us." To be sure, our greatest safeguard remains to remember that what happened to them *can happen to us*. An uncertain destiny awaits all of us.

Christianity is not intended to be a religion characterized by fear. Indeed, quite the opposite is true. It stands as a religion of hope. However, there remains a certain 'reality check' we must embrace if we wish to be authentically Christian.

As stated at the outset, we are encouraged to be 'watchful' and on our guard. *"Keep watch! Be careful that no one fools you."* (Matthew 24:4) Christian truth teaches many things, but its lesson of 'Judgment Day' serves as a lasting reminder we must not be lulled into a belief that safety and security stands as an entitlement.

Historians generally agree that if the German church had been on its guard, Hitler would likely never have come to power. Their failure constitutes our warning: we must be constantly vigilant and read the signs of the times lest something similar happen in our land. *Tomorrow could be different than today.* It could be very different indeed.

We should consider how *today begets the offspring we know as tomorrow.* What we do or do not do, will have lasting repercussions from this point forward.

7: KNOWING THE END AT THE BEGINNING

> *The word of the blessing of Enoch, with which he blessed the elect and righteous, who will be living in the day of tribulation, when all the wicked and godless are to be removed... Concerning the elect I said, as I began my story concerning them: The Holy Great One will come out from His dwelling, and the eternal God will tread on the earth, [even] on Mount Sinai, and appear in the strength of His might from heaven... And the earth shall be wholly torn apart, and all that is on the earth shall be destroyed, and there shall be a judgment on all... And behold! He comes with ten thousand of His Holy ones [saints] to execute judgment on all, and to destroy all the ungodly [wicked]; and to convict all flesh of all the works of their ungodliness which they have ungodly committed, and of all the hard things which ungodly sinners have spoken against Him.*
> (Enoch 1:1, 3, 4, 7, 9)

FORESHADOWING: A TECHNIQUE IN TELLING A STORY

ONE OF THE GREAT PLOYS FOR MYSTERY MOVIE PLOTS IS FORESHADOWING *THE END AT THE BEGINNING*, WHEN THE VIEWER CANNOT POSSIBLY KNOW HOW THE FORESHADOWING RELATES to the story as a whole. After this 'reveal' is complete (but without explanation to its meaning), the movie then 'goes back in time' to where the story really begins. At this point, the viewer becomes engrossed in the story (if it is a good one!).

For the next two hours or so, the movie director does his or her best to make the viewer completely forget about what happened at the movie's outset. Once the finale arrives, the foreshadowing event appears unexpectedly. The viewer is shocked how the conclusion was clearly shown at the beginning; yet, the viewer did not remember or relate what they saw 'early on' in the story as it unfolded. When the Director twists this ploy just right, the viewer may be dumbfounded as to just how he or she was tricked by the director's story-telling genius. Being misled in this way makes for a great tale and a satisfying mystery movie experience. Believe me, I have been fooled more times than not!

THE BOOK OF ENOCH—AN EARLY BOOK OF PROPHECY?

One of the great mysteries in biblical studies is the place and value of the *Book of Enoch*. Like a good mystery plot, Enoch comprises a very old book (between 2,200 to 5,000 years old) which begins by providing information directed far into the future concerning *the end of the world*. The author addresses himself to 'the elect'—a rare phrase in the canonical Hebrew Bible as we will see. Moreover, what remains so intriguing (if not ironic), is that Enoch speaks to those *living at the end of history* although Enoch lived *at history's beginning.* How could someone living 'at the very beginning' of time know how 'the end' would turn out?

The Book of Enoch has become a very popular book over the past 100 years. It is even referenced indirectly by Freemasons. Sometimes we hear tell of a special type of magic: *Enochian magic*[1]—which, as we will see, refers to the god Hermes and the ancient magical system known as *Hermeticism*. Both systems of magic connect humankind to the religion of Egypt. Enoch, like Melchizedek (described as the Priest and King of Salem in Genesis and the Book of Hebrews) is indeed a mysterious character.[2]

---

[1] "Enochian magic is a system of ceremonial magic based on the evocation and commanding of various spirits. It is based on the 16th-century writings of Dr. John Dee and Edward Kelley, who claimed that their information was delivered to them directly by various angels. Dee's journals contained the Enochian script, and the table of correspondences that goes with it. It claims to embrace secrets contained within the apocryphal Book of Enoch" *See Wikipedia, Enochian Magic.*

[2] For inquiring minds, ancient Jewish wisdom, according to 'my' Rabbi, Daniel Lapin, asserts Shem, the son of Noah, was this preist.

The story and traditions surrounding Enoch are considerable. Some mythologies see Enoch as the planner and originator of the *Great Pyramids of Egypt*. This theory suggests that since the pyramids were undeniably built before the Flood, the people who built the pyramids were not Egyptian. These traditions suggest the pyramids were known as the *Pillars of Enoch*. Additionally, Enoch may have been the real person behind the god *Thoth*, the Egyptian version of the Greek god *Hermes*. Since Enoch was thought to be the originator of writing, this mythical god Thoth inherited this attribute supposedly creating written communication. With but a small leap in logic, the ancients came to regard him as heaven's *messenger*.

Many interpret Isaiah 19:19 in connection with Enoch. Their contention is the Giza pyramids were originally monuments to Enoch's God (and the God of Adam and Noah): *"In that day shall there be an altar to the LORD in the midst of the land of Egypt, and a pillar at the border thereof to the LORD."* The Pyramids lie upon the border which exists between Upper and Lower Egypt. Additionally, since they contain no hieroglyphics anywhere on their many vast inner or outer walls, some speculate their purpose was not to entomb mummies of the Kings. Instead they appear to 'encase' *ancient wisdom*—as their extraordinary dimensions incorporate mathematical knowledge about the world's geography—knowledge vastly beyond the grasp of early humankind.[3] Even the notion of 'pi' (π—3.14159...) appears intentionally constructed within the ratios of these megalithic buildings dating almost 3,000 years before Christ walked the earth.[4]

---

[3] See my discussion on the pyramids in my previous book, *Decoding Doomsday*, for specific information about this ancient knowledge.

[4] My friend and co-author Douglas W. Krieger argues that Shem was the builder of the pyramids subsequent to the Flood through which he and his family had just passed. The sacred cubic which appears to be equal to 25.20 British inches (2.1 feet) enables all sorts of fascinating calculations when applied to the pyramids of Giza. See his book, *Signs in the Heavens and in the Earth: Man's Days are Numbered*.

However, connecting Isaiah's statement to the Egyptian pyramids may be a stretch given that the Giza pyramids existed at least 2,000 years before Isaiah, and since the context of Isaiah 19 infers a time far into the future when the Egyptians speak the language of Canaan (perhaps Arabic? 5), are judged by God, but then healed by Him. Along with Assyria, at this future time Egypt is under the authority of Israel (which has never transpired before). God speaks of all three peoples representing one-third of His entire earthbound family—reflecting upon the unity of all Semitic peoples, specifically Abrahams' offspring, all of which were to be blessed by God.

PATRISTIC REFERENCES TO THE BOOK OF ENOCH

Likewise, in today's discussions of prophecy, the *Book of Enoch* often pops up. As we will see, there are many absorbing themes in the book. We know it is quoted in the New Testament by both Jude and Peter. Yet, it is not a part of the Protestant or Catholic Holy Bible. The early church was clearly split on its authenticity and its position in the canon. Those who comment on it in our time suggest the book is much like Daniel and Revelation; that is, it is 'apocalyptic' in nature. It speaks about the horrible judgments which will come to humanity at world's end. Many of the so-called 'Church Fathers' treated the book as sacred; like Peter and Jude, they quoted the book in their writings. We find this true of Justin Martyr, Irenaeus, Origin and Clement of Alexandria. Tertullian (160—230 AD) especially considered the book to be Holy Scripture. Indeed, to this day the Ethiopian Coptic Church preserves and upholds the book as part of its official canon.

---

[5] Arabic developed from ancient Aramaic (the language of Jesus and the language of 'Canaan'). Today, it is a melting pot of language spoken throughout most of the Middle East bequeathing many words to Spanish, Portuguese, and other European languages. As Alexander the Great enforced the Greek language upon most of the known world in the fourth century BC, Mohammed and his followers imposed this language across the Islamic nations in the eighth century AD and forward.

On the other hand, the early 'fathers' Hilary, Jerome, and Augustine challenged its authenticity. As a result, for almost 1,400 years the book was 'lost' to Western Christianity. It was not found again until a Scottish explorer, James Bruce, went to Ethiopia at the end of the eighteenth century upon hearing rumors of its existence there. Bruce brought back three copies of the book written in the Ethiopian language. Scholars suggest that the text was originally Aramaic and may have been translated into Greek before being rendered into the Ethiopian language.

The first English translation was published by Richard Laurence in 1821. Another edition, more famous than Laurence's, was printed by R. H. Charles in 1912. Thereafter, a Greek text surfaced followed by an Aramaic version discovered in cave 4 at Qumran as part of the Dead Sea Scrolls in 1947.[6]

The book is traced to at least the second century BC and may have been written much earlier. In fact, there are suggestions by some, perhaps 'romantically,' that the book (or the first portion of it) was written by Enoch himself prior to the time of the flood. Some authorities considered Enoch to have been the first human to have developed the language known as 'proto-Hebrew.' As noted before, tradition indicates that he was the originator of written language altogether. We do know that the Proto-Hebrew alphabet was similar to early forms of Greek and Phoenician alphabets. Indeed, these three very ancient non-pictorial languages show many similarities (all three are based on symbols representing *sounds* rather than *pictures* as in hieroglyphics—although Hebrew seems to contain both characteristics). These languages appear to date to at least 1650 BC. It seems likely that *commerce* between the Greeks,

---

[6] This recap is taken from Joseph B. Lumpkin's 'intro' to his version of *The Book of Enoch, a Transliteration*, and published May 2004.

Phoenicians, and Hebrews was the catalyst for the 'growth and development' of these alphabets, aka writing systems, during the centuries before King Solomon (who lived circa 1,000 BC).

If Enoch wrote the original (or portions thereof), this fact would push the dating back to at least 3,000 BC. As I have noted earlier, Biblical genealogy suggests the Flood of Noah occurred approximately 2,350 BC. If the Book of Enoch was taken aboard Noah's boat, logically it would have been penned before that date.

THE BOOKS' EARLY HISTORY

So when was Enoch born and how long did he live? Jewish authorities suggest that Enoch was born in the Jewish year 622.[7] Moses indicates that Enoch lived for 365 years, and then 'God took him' (a mystery about which we will talk more in a moment). This would place Enoch's disappearance from the earth at about 988 in the Jewish calendar (around 3,000 BC).[8] The Flood was about 650+ years later. Just for context, Abraham lived about 1,000 years after Enoch (around 2000 BC) and 1,000 years before Solomon. A simple ('rounded') timeline may help frame the chronology:

Adam's Creation	Enoch Translated	Flood of Noah	Abraham	Solomon's Temple	Jesus' Birth
4000 BC	3000 BC	2350 BC	2000 BC	1000 BC	1 BC

---

[7] Jewish dates begin with the birth of Adam in year one, which works out to our 4004 BC, according to a number of sources.

[8] See *Dating Discrepancies in the Hebrew Calendar*, Sheldon Epstein, Bernard Dickman and Yonah Wilamowsky. This trio is composed of educators whose joint works on Biblical and Talmudic topics appear in *Tradition*, *Higayon*, and *Location Sciences*.

On the other hand, given the Christian New Testament quotes Enoch toward the end of the first century (probably around the time Jerusalem was destroyed in 70 AD), the book would have been known and revered well before that time, as inclusion in the Essenes' community confirms.[9]

Therefore, while admitting it to be a quixotic notion that the book was written by the actual Enoch, nevertheless it was certainly written well before the time of Jesus. Surprisingly, although written at least 200 years before the Christian New Testament, it foreshadowed the beliefs of the Christian community regarding events such as the Rapture, the return of Messiah with His saints, and the Great Tribulation at the end of time. In and of itself, these factors are all highly significant as the same points are reflected in the actual writings of the New Testament.

Was the book shared by Christians and Jews? Yes, but only for a time. Merely to speak of God *literally* 'walking on the earth', would disqualify the Book of Enoch from consideration by the Jewish Rabbis as they finalized their canon (in the second century AD, about 100 years following the destruction of the Essene community). To be more specific, the book smacks of a belief in 'incarnational theology' (that God could become man—something orthodox Jewish theology rejects) even though the author placed his setting in the antediluvian (pre-Flood) age. After Jesus and the rise of Christianity, Jewish scholars dismissed any notion that the Messiah could be divine. As stated previously, the Messiah was 'anointed' by God, but his essence was human and never divine.

ENOCH AND THE ELECT

Enoch's vision of 'the end times' is remarkable in that it confirms many of the main contentions Christians make about events we label the Great Tribulation—and how this final act of human

---

[9] The Jewish sect that assembled the Dead Sea Scrolls circa 40 AD.

history plays out. How fascinating that the author addresses the *elect of God* who are living in the 'end-time tribulation' when the world will experience great devastation. This word has a special meaning and was used sparingly (13 times) in the Old Testament. Strong's transliterates the Hebrew word בָּחִיר *bachiyr* (and pronounced bachk-hē-ear) and means *to be chosen, to be selected*. The King James translates *bachiyr* as **elect** four times, **chosen** eight times and **choose** once in reference to Saul. (2 Samuel 21:6)

The children of Jacob are his chosen ones (1 Chronicles 16:13, Psalm 105:6). Psalm 89:3 references David as his chosen one to whom God swore with a covenant (that David would have a descendant to sit upon the throne, namely, the Messiah). If not for Moses, his chosen, God would have destroyed the people (Psalm 106:23). Otherwise, the KJV refers to God's servant, "mine elect" as *either Israel* or *His servant the Messiah* in Isaiah 42:1, 43:20, 45:4, 65:9, 65:15, and 65:22). Make note of these four uses of elect:

1. *"Behold my servant, whom I uphold; **mine elect**, [in whom] my soul delighteth; I have put my spirit **upon him**: he shall bring forth judgment to the Gentiles." (Isaiah 42:1)*

2. *"For Jacob my servant's sake and **Israel mine elect**, I have even called thee by thy name: I have surnamed thee, though thou hast not known me" (Isaiah 45:4).*

3. *"And I will bring forth a seed out of Jacob, and out of Judah an inheritor of my mountains: and **mine elect** shall inherit it, and my servants shall dwell there. (Isaiah 65:9).*

4. Likewise, another verse from Isaiah seems to refer to the Jewish people but at a very special point in time. *"They shall not build, and another inhabit; they shall not plant, and another eat: for as the days of a tree [are] the days of my people, and **mine elect** shall long enjoy the work of their hands" (Isaiah 65:22)*.

In every instance where we see the term *elect*, it refers to the Messiah or Israel during the Messianic Kingdom. The elect are a select group (literally). In all instances where we see the word *bachiyr* translated *chosen*, it refers to Moses, David, the Messiah, or the 'chosen people.' Since Enoch dedicates his book 'to the elect,' he connects with a special audience linked to the Kingdom of God, but specifically at the time of Earth's *Great Tribulation*.

Enoch promises *the elect* that the ungodly will be eliminated altogether from the world. So stand strong! At this same time, God will walk upon the earth. Ten thousand saints (no doubt a number signifying a 'countless' contingent) will come with the Lord to execute judgment. In Jude, we read the Enoch reference:

> *"And Enoch also, the seventh from Adam, prophesied of these, saying, 'Behold, the Lord cometh with ten thousands of his saints, to execute judgment upon all, and to convince all that are ungodly among them of all their ungodly deeds which they have ungodly committed, and of all their hard [speeches] which ungodly sinners have spoken against him'"* [10] (Verses 14, 15).

This passage implies the division of humanity into three distinct groups: (1) The Saints that come with the Lord; (2) the believing who will inherit the Kingdom; and (3) the unbelievers who will be taken out of the earth and cast into 'outer darkness' or into 'the lake of fire.' As such, the verse implies a particular cosmology at the end of the age. Some of the elect have been transformed into 'Saints' and are capable of moving between heaven and earth. Some of the *elect* still live on the earth with 'standard equipment on board'—they have not been transformed into immortal persons and are 'earth-bound.' Lastly, at the beginning of the Kingdom, anyone who does not belong to this exclusive club—the *elect*—will be eliminated. The ungodly will *not* inherit the Messiah's Kingdom.

My wife frequently reminds friends that if they ever 'go to the mill, go with a *really bad person!*' What is her point? It refers to Jesus' teaching in Matthew 24:40-42: *"Then shall two be in the*

---

[10] Not surprisingly, taking the Lord's name in vain and doing evil in the name of God are extremely bad things to have on your record.

field; the one shall be taken, and the other left. Two women shall be grinding at the mill; the one shall be taken, and the other left. Watch therefore: for ye know not what hour your Lord doth come." The moral of the story: Better to be the one the Lord selects to enter into the Kingdom! Be one of the elect. It is not a good time to be 'outstanding in your field'—you may be left standing alone!

ENOCH THE REPRESENTATIVE OF THE RAPTURE

The passage in Enoch predicts that the '*Lord will come with 10,000 of His saints to execute judgment.*' This pronouncement repeats the same concept from the Hebrew prophets (remember Enoch was not a Hebrew—he came before Jacob/Israel), who also lived hundreds of years before the time of Christ. Several examples follow:

- *I have commanded my sanctified ones, I have also called my mighty ones for mine anger, [even] them that rejoice in my highness.* (Isaiah 13:3)
- *Assemble yourselves, and come, all ye heathen, and gather yourselves together round about: thither cause thy mighty ones to come down, O LORD.* (Joel 3:11)
- *I saw in the night visions, and, behold, [one] like the Son of man came with the clouds of heaven, and came to the Ancient of days, and they brought him near before him.* (Daniel 7:13)
- *And then shall appear the sign of the Son of man in heaven: and then shall all the tribes of the earth mourn, and they shall see the Son of man coming in the clouds of heaven with power and great glory.* (Matthew 24:30)

Important also: we must learn the meaning of Enoch's 'mysterious vanishing.' While Enoch's book discusses many topics which we do not have time to cover here (such as the 'Watchers' and the 'Nephilim'), we must make mention of *his disappearing act.*

Consider Enoch's fascinating account of his 'whirl wind tour' of the earth aboard a flying vehicle. Enoch describes angels which escort him to heaven and guide him on this tour. Not only did Enoch travel around the world, we learn he also moved 'to and fro' between heaven and earth. Significantly, one of his rides was a one-way ticket to heaven. Only Elijah the prophet experienced the same type of trip—and his journey 'upstairs' was precisely in the form of a real *whirlwind ride* (II Kings 2:11). Do not be distressed, however; neither Enoch nor Elijah experienced death to make the trip!

We learn from both Moses and the writer to the Hebrews (recall tradition states the author was Paul), that Enoch was a righteous man who walked with God. Because of this righteousness, God 'took him.' Paul says it this way: *"By faith Enoch was translated that he should not see death; and was not found, because God had translated him: for before his translation he had this testimony, that he pleased God."* (Hebrews 11:5) Just as the rapture is described as 'snatching up' or 'catching up' in the twinkling of an eye, so God's grab of Enoch seems to be an event that happened in a split-second. Here we have a real case of Enochian magic!

M.R. De Haan (1891—1965) was a great 'old-time' evangelical preacher, founder of the Radio Bible Class, and scholar who wrote many pamphlets as well as a 'mere' 25 books, many of which focused on the Second Coming of Christ. It was De Haan's view that Enoch embodied a foreshadowing of what happens to the Church (true believers) before the time of tribulation (aka, the *Great Tribulation*). Just as 'in the days of Noah,' there will be three groups of people: (1) *God's people* which pass through the judgment (Noah and his family represent the Jewish people); (2) *unbelievers* who perish during the judgment (those who scoffed in Noah's time like those who scoff before the future Great Tribulation—who will be removed from the earth in a most undesirable manner!); and (3) *believers* (the saints) who please God (as did Enoch) and are translated *before the judgment commences.* Being righteous in God's eyes (since they embraced the salvation Jesus Christ offers by His substitutionary atonement), they are been removed from the earth *before* the Great Tribulation—the time of judgment—which is equivalent to Enoch being 'taken' before the Great Flood in De Haan's view of an authentic and intentional biblical analogy. The strategic principle: God removes His righteous elect before He executes His wrath. The Lord preserves His chosen ones.

Few prophecies are the subject of as much derision as the concept of the *rapture of Christians*. But the story of Enoch points out several interesting concepts that substantiate why the rapture is no pipe dream:

- The rapture is not without precedent. Enoch was 'taken' by God and did not experience death just as Elijah was taken up by the whirlwind. It has happened before. It can and will happen again.

- The translation of Enoch is connected to the Flood of Noah and should be included in the epoch Jesus implied when He speaks of *"As in the days of Noah, so shall it be in the days of the Son of Man..."* Both of these experiences are unique times of judgment. God is directly intervening in the affairs of men. There are many attributes that these epochs share, but a *rapture of the righteous* appears most certainly to be one of them.

- Enoch prophesies the coming of God, the Mighty One from Heaven, who comes to earth with ten thousand of His saints. It is intriguing and no small coincidence that *the first prophet to predict the rapture was the first person to experience it*. Since coincidence is a word that does not exist in the Hebrew Bible, we can assume this connection is no coincidence either.

GOD'S FOREKNOWLEDGE OF HIS ELECT

One of the Bible's most amazing psalms is *Psalm 139*. The psalm speaks of God's foreknowledge, His 'knowing beforehand,' about every aspect of our lives. God knows where we are all the time. We cannot escape His presence no matter where we go in the world. Before we speak, God knows what we are going to say.

Additionally, the Psalmist relates how God thinks about the Psalmist (King David in this case) far more than the Psalmist thinks about God! We read: *"How precious also are thy thoughts unto me, O God! How great is the sum of them! If I should count them, they are more in number than the sand: when I awake, I am still with thee"* (verses 17, 18). We learn our very form and features are all part of God's plan for us. Perhaps the most staggering thought: to learn God picked out a specific time in the history of the world for our life to be lived. The fact that we live during the twenty-first century comprises no accident. *"And in your book were all written the days that were ordained for me, when as yet there was not one of them"* (verse 16). God knows the 'book of our lives' from cover to cover. He knows how our story concludes before the moment we are born. Nothing is left to chance! And yet, we are free to choose (and be held responsible for those decisions).

As we approach what appears to be the culmination of this present age, especially as the times grow tougher and the ominous portents signaling the end come to pass, it is crucial we remember this amazing truth. Days gone by, whether easy or hard, are in God's pre-written biography authored by Him for each of us. Today's experience, although difficult, are contained within the plan of God. The days which lie ahead are as 'foreordained' as the moments already passed, moments we know testify to God's providence. Whenever despair or fear grips us, we should recall God has brought us each step of the way so far and will carry us the rest of the way home. God never deserts His saints in mid-stream!

The Book of Jeremiah discloses one of the most comforting verses in the Bible. This book tells the story of a greatly revered prophet living just prior to the captivity of the whole Hebrew nation of Judah in the sixth century BC. Nebuchadnezzar, the King of Babylon, busied himself carting off the Jews to Babylon. This was not a highlight in Jewish history—it was the very worst of times. Yet, there was hope. The New American Standard Version translates Jeremiah 29:11 with these words: *"For I know the plans that I have for you, says the Lord, plans for welfare and not for calamity to give you a future and a hope!"* The King James Version brings a different sense to the meaning of Jeremiah: *"For I know the thoughts that I think toward you, saith the LORD, thoughts of peace, and not of evil, to give you an expected end."* However Bible translators choose to express it, the message remains clear: God thinks about us constantly. God remembers His Plan. He continuously thinks good thoughts toward us, assuring us that our 'end' happens just as expected. God remains our Father—to the very end of the age, until we are called and caught up into His presence to be forever with Him.

AND GOD REMEMBERED NOAH

Perhaps the most powerful statement in the entire Bible illustrating that God's providence constitutes a 'personal matter' concerns Noah's time spent in the ark. When Noah was tossed to and fro by the greatest storm in the history of the world, he might have been puzzling over whether the ark was sufficiently 'waterproof' and stout enough to withstand the raging tempest. He could have assumed the worst: Sure, God carefully oversaw the ark's loading but will He still look after all the inhabitants during this treacherous voyage? Will He forget us? After all, how could God's plan include the horrifically frightening sounds, the creaking, and the threat that this ark would be torn apart? If Noah only considered his circumstances solely relying upon 'sense data,' it would have been logical to figure his family would face the same fate as the rest of humanity now destroyed in the devastating flood, their screams drowned out by the waters beating up against his giant boat. And yet, the Bible calmly asserts the basis for Noah's assurance: **"And God remembered Noah**, *and every living thing, and all the cattle that was with him in the ark..."* (Genesis 8:1).

"And God remembered Noah." The LORD was thinking about every creature, big or small, whether superbly human or a mere creepy crawler. He kept watch—making sure that each and every

one was safe and dry. Jesus said "every hair on your head is numbered" (Matthew 10:30). God's providence is personal! Noah knew that God remembered. Noah realized despite the fright the animals and his family experienced, they all remained safe, being held firmly in the arms of the Almighty God. Noah knew God's plan would not be thwarted.

God knows the end at the beginning. He sees the day we will join Him even if we cannot see such a time in the midst of today's troubles. And God is fully capable of assuring, no matter what end He has in mind, it will come to pass exactly, in every detail, just the way He planned. That is why we must remember, despite the worst things we can imagine, nothing confronts us that first God has not first filtered it through His fingers.

Paul reminds us in Romans 8:35-39,

Who shall separate us from the love of Christ? Shall tribulation, or distress, or persecution, or famine, or nakedness, or peril, or sword? As it is written, 'For thy sake we are killed all the day long; we are accounted as sheep for the slaughter.' Nay, in all these things we are more than conquerors through him that loved us. For I am persuaded, that neither death, nor life, nor angels, nor principalities, nor powers, nor things present, nor things to come, nor height, nor depth, nor any other creature, shall be able to separate us from the love of God, which is in Christ Jesus our Lord.

To paraphrase Paul's admonition: whatever we experience at this time or anytime in the future remains *powerless to separate us from the love of God*. We have that promise. As the days progress, we will be challenged to remember this promise even as God remembers each one of us. Likewise, we will not lack our daily bread, the provision He refreshes every day pledging to meet our most urgent needs. God stands always attentive to His children.

He knows the end from the beginning.

Remember the former things of old: for I am God, and there is none else; I am God, and there is none like me, **declaring the**

end from the beginning, and from ancient times the things that are not yet done, *saying, My counsel shall stand, and I will do all my pleasure* (Isaiah 46:9, 10)

God's plan 'will out'—whether we are talking the whole world—or just one small solitary life of His elect. God has a plan for each of us. And He continues to monitor that plan every moment of every day.

8: *PAROUSIA*—JESUS' COMING AND ABIDING

*Now we beseech you, brethren, by the **coming** (parousia) of our lord Jesus Christ, and by our gathering together unto him, that ye be not soon shaken in mind, or be troubled, neither by spirit, nor by word, nor by letter as from us, as that the Day of Christ is at hand. Let no man deceive you by any means: for that day shall not come, except there **come** (erchomai) a **falling away** (apostasia) first, and that man of sin **be revealed** (apokalyptō), the son of perdition; who opposeth and exalteth himself above all that is called god, or that is worshipped; so that he as god sitteth in the temple of god, shewing himself that he is god.*

*Remember ye not, that, when I was yet with you, I told you these things? And now ye know what withholdeth that he might **be revealed** (apokalyptō) in his time. For the mystery of iniquity doth already work: only he who now letteth will let, until he be taken out of the way. And then shall that wicked **be revealed** (apokalyptō) whom the lord shall consume with the spirit of his mouth, and shall destroy with the*
***brightness of his coming** (parousia).*
(2 Thessalonians 2:1-10)

THE GOOD GHOSTS OF CHRISTMASES PAST

CHRISTMAS IS A FAVORITE TIME OF YEAR FOR MANY OF US. AS AN ADULT I HAVE THE ADVANTAGE OF MANY YEARS OF EXPERIENCE THAT ENABLE ME TO ANALYZE THE PAST AND INTERPRET NOT only its societal meaning, but in particular what certain events meant to me. Christmas stands as a time to reflect on the past in order to recreate the best of the past in the present. We see this in Dickens' *Christmas Carol*. Dickens placed far more emphasis on

'Christmas past' than on the present or even the future. There are many lessons to be learned from Christmases long, long ago.

Growing up, I was the youngest of four boys. My mother was the youngest of eleven children while my father was the youngest of four brothers. Having so many Uncles and Aunts, I had 23 first cousins. We had a big family. With so many uncles, aunts, cousins, and in some cases, second cousins, our Christmases were raucous events indeed. We opened most all of our gifts on Christmas Eve and for some crazy reason we had to watch each person open his or her gifts one person at a time. It would lead to a five-hour long exposition of beautifully wrapped packages torn asunder throughout the evening (and into the wee hours of the morning). The youngest went first, the oldest last. Thank goodness for that. At least the kids did not have to sit through the entire session. For the adults, it was a test of loving endurance to be sure!

Someone has said, "Families are like fudge. They are mostly sweet, but still there are a few nuts." My family, probably like yours, fits this description perfectly. But in the innocence of youth, I did not realize my relatives had any oddities at all. They were family. And when we gathered together, I was surrounded by people that for the most part loved one another and genuinely valued family as perhaps the most important element of their lives. The partaking of gifts, good food, candy, cakes, and all that goes with the American Christmas, made an indelible impression upon me. In looking back, I realize that our surroundings were actually very modest. We weren't well-to-do. But we were warm, well clothed, and had plenty to eat. As such, my memories are chock full of genuine experiences of joy.

ANTICIPATION—KNOWING IT IS WORTH THE WAIT

For children, so much that pertains to Christmas involves anticipation. We had to wait (it seemed like forever) to open gifts on Christmas morning. We had to stand out in the cold waiting for the parade to pass by to get to see Santa Claus. We had to wade through crowds of shoppers at the department store, and to stand in line to make purchases. Given that these events were all tied to the gathering of the family, much of my anticipation was directed to those last couple of days before Christmas when we and my many relatives would travel from across Texas and Oklahoma to one of my aunt's houses (or in some seasons to our house!). When the family arrived, all heaven was ready to break loose! It was not about the moment of their arrival. That was usually the most awful of times. I had to kiss my aunts. And they insisted we kiss them on the lips (and some of them had mustaches too!) No, it was about the good times after they arrived.

Everyone was together. Candy and cakes came out from the back seat of over a dozen cars. They were stacked high on kitchen counters for easy access. Savory food was put on the stove and the house smelled like a restaurant all afternoon and night. Being surrounded by people, laughter, food, music, and perhaps football on

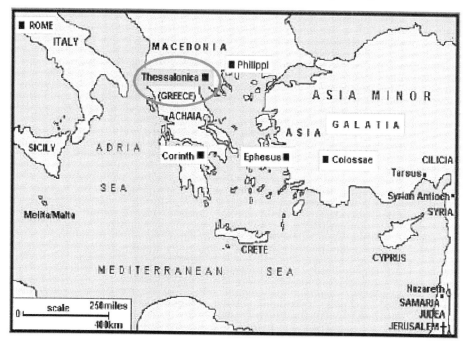

FIGURE 19 - KEY CITIES WHERE PAUL FOUNDED CHURCHES

the television, I was ecstatic. There might even be wrestling matches with my older cousins right in the middle of our big living room next to a magnificently decorated Christmas tree half covered by a mountain of presents. It was an intense experience of contentment and good times.

So what does all of this have to do with the passage at the outset? Actually, quite a lot. Christians have been taught to anticipate the *coming* of Jesus Christ, a second time. We talk about the *Second Coming*, Christ's *Second Advent*, and we connect this phrase to those cataclysmic events that transpire just before and during His arrival. But what comes to my mind most regarding the different expressions for 'coming' and the peculiar one that best describes Christ's arrival. This passage comprises a cornucopia of verbs and nouns all conveying various means of 'coming.' It constitutes a study of contrasts, a section of sacred scripture chock full of lessons regarding the Second Coming that all revolve around the precise meaning of 'coming.'

WHY PAUL WROTE THESSALONICA A SECOND TIME

Paul wrote his second letter to the saints at Thessalonica to clarify the time of the Lord's 'coming.' We deduce from the words of Paul that the Thessalonians believed they were already living in the Day of Christ (also known as The Day of the Lord), a time of wrath immediately preceding the physical coming of Jesus Christ at the Battle of Armageddon. Apparently, someone had written a letter purportedly from Paul telling the church that they were now living in the great time of tribulation also known as *The Day of the Lord*. He speaks to them like a father consoling his son, *"Now we beseech you, brethren, by the coming of our Lord Jesus Christ, and by our gathering together unto him, that ye be not soon shaken in mind, or be troubled, neither by spirit, nor by word, nor by letter as from us, as that the day of Christ is at hand."* (2 Thessalonians 2:1-2). At the end of the letter, he points out his unique 'mark' that verifies the letter originates with Paul and not from the fraud who sought to confuse and confound them. *"The salutation of Paul with mine own hand, which is the token in every epistle: so I write."* (2 Thessalonians 3:17)

To counteract their consternation, he first reminds them that there will be a specific sequence of events that leads up to the Day of the Lord. *"Let no man deceive you by any means: for that day shall not **come**, except there **come** a falling away first, and that man of sin be **revealed**, the son of perdition"* (verse 3). His rebuttal builds upon the timing of the coming Antichrist. The 'man of sin' or 'man of lawlessness' precedes the coming of Jesus Christ. Moreover, his coming happens *before* the Day of the Lord. Paul is saying to his church, "Stop worrying. We cannot yet be living in the time we call 'the Day of the Lord' because the Antichrist has not yet come." Jesus can only come at the end of that period known as *The Day of the Lord*. But He will not come *until the Antichrist comes first*.

To follow his argument more closely, Paul states that the Antichrist, the son of perdition, can only **come** (*erchomai*) after a "falling away" (*apostasia* - apostasy) comes first. The verb translated **come**, *erchomai*, is frequently used in the New Testament and it has a simple meaning: to "come or go" or "make an appearance." It also has a temporal sense, such as, "one event comes right after another." For instance, the Three Kings *erchomai* (are come now) to worship the Christ child (Matthew 2:2). They **had come at that time** from the east (probably Babylon) to Jerusalem. They arrived at a specific point in time.

Likewise, the *apostasia* comes about at a specific moment. What is *apostasia*? In Greek the word implies "a rebellion, a revolt, a falling away" such as in a state of lawlessness representing a departure from 'law and order' or from orthodoxy in belief. The English word apostasy surely comes to mind. The message is thus, "the Antichrist can only make his appearance at a moment in time in the future after first there *comes to pass* a rebellion or time of lawlessness or a time of great apostasy." (We will discuss in an appendix whether *apostasia* can instead mean "a departure" rather than a falling away. For clarity's sake, we will delay discussing that debate until later.)

ERCHOMAI CONTRASTED WITH *APOCALYPTŌ*

Furthermore, Paul expresses the distinction between the coming of the Antichrist and Second Coming of Christ by using two different Greek words to signify the nature of their respective 'comings.' These two words are quite different from one another. The Antichrist's actual 'coming' Paul expresses as an *apocalyptō*. Three times he refers to the Antichrist's coming with this term. This 'coming' is much more involved than merely 'showing up' as is expressed in *erchomai*. *Erchomai* involves 'coming onto the scene without a fuss.' On the other hand, *apocalyptō* implies 'coming into view with a fanfare.' *Erchomai* is mundane. *Apocalyptō* is dramatic.

One cannot help but notice *apocalyptō* stems from the same root word as the word *apocalypsis*, from which we translate, **apocalypse**. We see John's Revelation as an *apocalypsis*. It is a noun representing 'the full story' of Jesus Christ's manifestation.

But Antichrist's revealing constitutes an *apocalyptō*. "That man of sin (can only) <u>be revealed</u>" (*apocalyptō*) after the apostasy (*apostasia*) has first come to pass.

Furthermore, this apostasy is so significant and so unique it can only happen after something (or someone) else *completely leaves the scene*. Something (or someone) must first *be taken out of the way*.

Paul says, *"And now ye know* **what** *withholdeth that he (Antichrist) might* **be revealed** *(apokalyptō) in his time."* Unfortunately for us, the context is not so obvious here. We do not know with certainty to *what* or to *whom* Paul was referring. Is the "what" that withholdeth or restraineth the son of perdition (1) "the law," (2) "the government that maintains order," or as many evangelicals believe (3) *the Holy Spirit*, who indwells believers?" The implication would be that the Church *is the restrainer* because the Holy Spirit dwells within each believer, each member of the church.[1] Until the Church is taken out of the way the Antichrist cannot make his presence known. The Church must go away before the Antichrist can *apocalyptō*–that is, be revealed.

Paul goes on to reinforce his assertion: *"For the mystery of iniquity doth already work: only he who now letteth will let, until he be taken out of the way."* Paul acknowledges that the 'spirit' of Antichrist, the son of perdition, the man of lawlessness "doth already work." This mystery exists and is here now. However, the full revelation of Antichrist cannot come about, cannot apocalyptō, until the spirit that restraineth stop doing the restraining!

Who is this *"he"* that must first "be taken out of the way?" As many students of biblical prophecy recall, this verse deserves its own careful examination because the doctrine of the rapture of the Church closely connects to it. It is my position that "he" is Christ through the agency of His Holy Spirit as infused in the spirits of believers worldwide. It is the Lord who will ultimately destroy him. The 'spirit' of His mouth consumes him. We read: *"And then shall that wicked (one)* **be revealed** *(apokalyptō) whom the Lord shall consume with the spirit of his mouth."* (2 Thessalonians 2:8) For the third time, Paul uses this word, *apokalyptō*. In each usage, Paul communicates that the revealing compares to an 'unveiling.' Something heretofore has remained hidden and unidentified. It lies 'behind the curtains.' But there will be a moment when Antichrist 'comes.' His coming constitutes a revelation, a surprise, something unexpected. When it happens, the curtains will suddenly be pulled back. It will be like the climax of a makeover when the 'reveal' finally transpires. It can be compared also

---

[1] Some have even suggested that the 'someone' is the archangel Michael although I have not come across a particularly cogent rationale for why this would be so.

to a magic trick whose conclusion causes a double-take or the audience gasping for breath. We know that with any surprise or trick, once the surprise comes (is revealed), it no longer constitutes a surprise. Whatever the 'shock value' was, it wears off rather quickly.

This conveys in part the nature of the coming Antichrist. It is sudden, it is shocking, and it is unexpected. But, the coming of the Antichrist does not go on forever. Antichrist's existence lasts but a moment. True. The Bible teaches he will cause unparalleled trouble for three and one-half years. But it is only for a short while. John says as much in Revelation 17:10, "And there are seven kings: five are fallen, and one is, *and* the other is not yet come; and when he cometh (erchomai), *he must continue a short space*." In this verse, Antichrist coming is minimized because he 'cometh' and stays only a short space.

PAROUSIA—A FORM OF COMING THAT CONTINUES

Paul uses a very different word to express the coming of Jesus Christ. He uses the word *parousia* (pronounced, par-row-see-a). 24 times the New Testament employs it to express a very different type of 'coming.' Unlike *apocalyptō*, it comprises a 'kind of coming' that does not happen in a single moment and then it is over. It stands out as the word which refers to the Second Coming or Advent of Jesus Christ. When Jesus *comes, he stays, he abides. His presence persists*. He sets up His Kingdom and continues on from that moment in time forward.

The word *parousia* consists of a type of *coming* that once completed, it never ends. The word connotes that "when the Lord comes He will never go away again." Furthermore, when He is present, there is no mistaking him. When He arrives on the scene, His presence will be felt from that moment forward.

Moreover, it is not just about His presence. *"Now we beseech you, brethren, by the **coming** (parousia) of our lord Jesus Christ,* *and by our gathering together unto him...*" From its first usage, the reason for the coming of the Lord is to form a community. We are to be "gathered together until Him." Once united, we will not be separated ever again.

FIGURE 20 - THE PAROUSIA OF JESUS CHRIST

Vine's New Testament Dictionary explains *parousia* as a noun composed of two words, literally a presence—"*para*" (with) "*ousia*" (being) (from *eimi*, the verb, "to be"), that: "...denotes both an 'arrival' and a consequent 'presence with.'" For instance, in a papyrus letter, a lady speaks of the necessity of her *parousia* in a place in order to attend to matters relating to her property there. Paul speaks of his *parousia* in Philippi, (see Philippians 2:12, in contrast to his *apousia*, "his absence...")...

Parousia describes the presence of Christ with His disciples on the Mount of Transfiguration, (2 Peter 1:16). When used of the return of Christ, at the rapture of the Church, it signifies more than His momentary 'coming' for His saints, but His **presence** with them from that moment forward until He completes His revelation and manifestation to the world. Parousia constitutes 'being with' someone. When Jesus Christ comes, the inference is plain: He comes to be with us *personally*, and to abide with us from thenceforth *forever*.

AND SO SHALL WE BE TOGETHER FOREVER

For me, it was like this when my relatives were *to come* to our house for Christmas. This was the anticipation so deeply felt when I was wishing for Christmas. It meant 'being together' and being surrounded by the ones you love and that love you.

Looking for the Second Coming of Christ should demand at least the same anticipation as we have for Christmas. Christmas time comprises the season of Advent. Advent is a noun derived from the Latin verb *advenio*, **to come** or **to arrive.** During the season of Christmas, the *coming of Christ* constitutes what we anticipate and celebrate.

Perhaps the oldest Christmas hymn, from the eighth century, is *"O come, O come, Emmanuel."* The hymn constitutes not only a prayer of anticipation, but a song of rejoicing. Emmanuel has come. "Rejoice! Rejoice!" The song tells us that Emmanuel (which just so happens to mean, *"God with us"*) has paid the ransom for captive Israel (and for you and me). Advent stands not just as a reminder that Christ came, but *that Christ will come again.* And when He comes again, *He will be with us forever.* He will never again leave us. *"Now our Lord Jesus Christ himself, and God, even our Father, which hath loved us, and hath given us everlasting consolation and good hope through grace."* (2 Thessalonians 2:16)

Likewise, we will be gathered together with Him and with one another. That is why the coming of Christ and the rapture of the Church are to be great words of comfort that we are to express to one another frequently and to remind one another that when He comes again, it will be like Christmas every day of the year, for time and for eternity!

9: DECODING SIGNS AND SETTING DATES

And he spake to them a parable: "Behold the fig tree, and all the trees; When they now shoot forth, ye see and know of your own selves that summer is now nigh at hand. So likewise ye, when ye see these things come to pass, know ye that the kingdom of God is nigh at hand. Verily I say unto you, this generation shall not pass away, till all be fulfilled. Heaven and earth shall pass away: but my words shall not pass away."
(Luke 21:29-33)

But of that day and hour knoweth no man, no, not the angels of heaven, but my Father only.
(Matthew 24:36)

CODE BREAKING AND CIPHER SOLVING

W E HUMAN BEINGS ARE ALL ALIKE IN AT LEAST ONE WAY. WE LOVE DETECTIVE STORIES, MYSTERIES, PUZZLES, AND EXPOSING SECRETS. IT LIES BURIED DEEP IN OUR DNA.

The books and movies of Dan Brown demonstrate how much we enjoy the intrigue of secret societies and uncovering the hidden facts of history. His novels, *Angels and Demons*, *The Da Vinci Code*, and *The Lost Symbol* effectively employ this powerful hook. Likewise, Brad Meltzer has written a number of mystery books on similar topics; it led to his hosting an entertaining program on the History Channel: *Brad Meltzer Decoded*. Deciphering hidden symbols, cabals, even buried treasure are all subjects Meltzer covered in these documentaries. Plus, they served as perfect examples of phenomenon which reaches out and grabs our attention.

It should surprise no one that those of us who are fascinated by prophecy are also chumps for stories based on such conspiracies. To prophecy buffs, foretelling the future has this same appeal, but *taken up another level*. Prophecy combines all of the aforementioned elements, plus it manifests the *supernatural*. Indeed, detecting the extraordinary enthralls us even more than plain ol' decoding secret messages. Additionally, when "we the faithful" personally witness prophecies we believe have been fulfilled, it reinforces our faith and reminds us how our God works in the space-time world. *Seeing means believing.* We conclude, rightly I might add, that history happens *now*—right in front of our eyes, whenever we observe events we view as prophecies come true. How can we avoid excitement when we witness it first-hand?

Those of us engaged in the study of Bible prophecy for several decades often recite numerous 'predictions' which have come to pass[1] (or are happening as we watch). Allow me to enumerate some of the most prominent ones:

- Respect for the American dollar stands diminished in the world.
- Tens of thousands of Jews returned to the Jewish homeland, precipitated by the fall of the Berlin wall and the dissolution of the Soviet Union.
- Nations move toward a one-world government and single unified currency; thereafter, a charismatic world leader seems destined to step to the foreground to take its reins.
- The 'peace process' for Jerusalem and its neighbors grows increasingly tense. Israel's surrounding neighbors seem ready to instigate a decisive battle in which they seek to destroy Israel and take its land.

---

[1] These predictions are really interpretations of Bible prophecy as expounded by popular prophecy authors like Hal Lindsey, Tim LaHaye, Chuck Missler, Jack Van Impe, and Grant Jeffries. For the most part, however, these authors agreed with the interpretations offered here, forming a compelling consensus.

- A Russian-Iranian alliance, without prior historical precedent, continues to blossom threatening Israel's survival.
- (Future) The one-world government will transact some form of treaty ensuring Israel's peace and security—a commitment for seven years. Mid-way through this period, a leader arises who confirms the treaty then breaks it.

SETTING A TIME LIMIT FOR WHEN IT ALL MUST HAPPEN

Of course, prophecy students single out that the most impressive historic sign of all lies with the formation of Israel in 1948. It was this event, formalized by the United Nations, which proved the predictions of several Bible scholars from a century beforehand that the return of Israel to its native land was no metaphor.[2] The primary prediction in Ezekiel 35-37, highlighted by the classic passage known as "Ezekiel's dry bones" was fulfilled in space-time. For evangelical scholars who believed in a physical return of Jesus Christ, this event moved the prophecy countdown clock irreversibly to the *'full-on'* position. From this moment forward, there would be no turning back. Henceforth, all experts espousing the then dominant Pre-millennial point of view, consistently proclaimed the return of Jesus Christ must come to pass *within this generation*. After all, did not Jesus say that those who see these signs will witness His Kingdom come? "*So likewise ye, when ye see these things come to pass, know ye that the kingdom of God is nigh at hand*" *(Luke 21:28)*. If the countdown began in 1948, then the length of a generation, biblically speaking, should disclose to us, vis-à-vis the 'outside (latest) date,' when Christ's return must occur. And yet, one essential question remains: "Does the Bible plainly

---

[2] I cited in my book *Decoding Doomsday* how Professor George Bush, a first cousin of the two Presidents (six times removed), predicted this in 1843, approximately 100 years before it came to pass. But J.N. Darby, the founder of Dispensational Theology originating around 1825-35, constituted the most influential scholar and predictor of the literal return of Israel to its native land of Palestine. Bush may have followed Darby's lead. Not surprisingly, this view led many English Christians to support Zionism at the end of the nineteenth century.

identify such a specified length of time?" Many authors seem to think so.

THE LENGTH OF A BIBLICAL GENERATION

A widely held view by prophecy pundits from the 1960s through 1980s rested upon the Bible's use of the term *generation*. *The definition most adopted* for a biblical generation included a *time span of 40 years*. Initially, this timing seemed certain. There were two reasons for such unassailable confidence:

1. First, Jesus predicted that within *one generation* of his death the Temple in Jerusalem would be destroyed (See Matthew 24 and Luke 21). This came to pass right on schedule. Pontius Pilate crucified Jesus circa 30-33 AD. In 70 AD, the soon-to-be-Caesar Titus conquered Jerusalem and set fire to its temple. The Roman soldiers literally left no stone unturned as they eagerly sought the melted Temple gold which had seeped between the cracks of the massive stones.

2. Likewise, God judged the Hebrew generation escaping from Egypt (despite the faithful leadership of Moses) for failing to heed His commandment to go forth immediately to conquer the Promised Land. As punishment, this generation of Jews wandered in the Wilderness after the Exodus for 40 years, until *everyone in that generation had passed away*. Only those under 20 years of age could march into the Promised Land along with Joshua and Caleb. Even Moses was prohibited from entering due to one moment of indiscretion.[3]

Consequently, with two such notable examples as precedent, most prophecy authors in the 1970s and '80s contended 40 years was the unimpeachable span of a biblical generation and a clear rule of thumb to establish how much time we have left before Jesus

---

[3] Moses, out of frustration, struck the rock with his rod which God identified as the location of water from which He would supply the Hebrews. God asked Moses only to 'touch' the rock.

comes. Furthermore, assuming as most everyone did that the official formation of Israel in 1948 began the countdown to Armageddon; Jesus Christ's return in 1988 should have been a slam dunk.

Despite a quiet consensus among many evangelical authors, much criticism was leveled at outspoken Bible scholars who took this position. Most notably, many chided Hal Lindsey for arguing

FIGURE 21 - THE COMMON PRESUMPTION: WE CAN KNOW NOW!

forcefully in the 1970's that *1988* was *the* date of Christ's return. By tying these two calculations together, he concluded biblical principles established 1988 as the *time limit* for all the prophesied events to transpire. However, Lindsey was hardly the lone voice in the wilderness making this particular prediction. A book released early in the 1980s entitled: *88 Reasons Why the Rapture Must Happen in 1988*, stirred the kettle as well. Soon, other Premillennial scholars jumped on the bandwagon. But 1988 came and went. The Second Coming did not happen. What was wrong with the logic? After all, was it not derived from sensible biblical interpretation? Probably not.

If good scholarship had overcome the prophetic enthusiasm as it should have, authors would have discerned the Biblical generation can be *one of several lengths.* 40 years does not comprise the only biblical guideline. For instance, Psalm 90:10 indicates a human lifespan should not exceed 70 years, unless by the strength of the life (or by God's grace) it extends to 80 years. *"The days of our years [are] threescore years and ten; and if by reason of strength [they be] fourscore years."* And yet, this constitutes merely one more example. The "biblical lifespan standard" does not establish the length of a "biblical generation" either. We must examine the Bible more closely to draw a reasonable and biblical conclusion.

Identifying the fault in the traditional logic begins by understanding the meaning behind the *two* biblical words translated *generation*. As you might guess, there is a Hebrew word in the Old Testament and a Greek word in the New. We know Jesus used the word "generation" many times in His teachings and proclamations. This word is written in the Greek New Testament as *genea* (pronounced, 'jay-nay-ah'[4]). It generally conveys "a whole multitude of men [humans], with the same characteristics, living at the same time." Jesus invoked this term a dozen times in the Synoptic gospels (Matthew, Mark and Luke). A few familiar examples:

- *"A wicked and adulterous generation (**genea**) seeketh a sign."* (Matthew 12:39)

- *"But whereunto shall I liken this generation (**genea**)? It is like unto children sitting in the markets and calling unto their fellows and saying 'We have piped unto you and ye have not danced and we have mourned unto you and ye have not lamented."* (Matthew 11:16, 17).

- *"The queen of the south shall rise up in judgment with this generation (**genea**) and condemn it."* (Matthew 12:42)

Furthermore, if we consider Old Testament uses of the Hebrew word for generation, *towlĕdah (pronounced, toe-lay-doth)*, the variability of the concept increases. Easton's Bible Dictionary

---

[4] Of course, our word ***genea****logy* comes from this root word. In English, it literally means the 'study of generations.'

recounts several examples of how "generation" is put to work in key passages of the Old Testament:

- Genesis 2:4, "These are the *generations*," means the "history."
- Genesis 5:1, "The book of the *generations*," means a family register, or history of Adam.
- Genesis 37:2, "The *generations* of Jacob" = the history of Jacob and his descendants.
- Genesis 7:1, "In this *generation*" = in this age.
- In Deuteronomy 1:35 and Deuteronomy 2:14 a *generation* is a period of thirty-eight years.[5]
- Psalm 49:19, "The *generation* of his fathers" = the dwelling of his fathers, i.e., the grave.
- Psalm 73:15, "The *generation* of thy children" = the contemporary race.
- Isaiah 53:8, "Who shall declare his *generation*?" = His manner of life who shall declare? Or rather = His race, posterity, shall be so numerous that no one shall be able to declare it...

Thus, Easton concludes the Hebrews "reckoned time by the *generation*. In the time of Abraham a *generation* was an hundred years, thus: Genesis 15:16, 'In the fourth *generation*' = in four hundred years (see Exodus 12:40)."

Therefore, the first and one of the biggest mistakes eager prophecy advocates made during the past few decades rests in their becoming dogmatic about a particular length of time, i.e., identifying the Bible's generation as a timespan implying a specific length of years. We observed how examples exist for the timespan of a generation being 33 years, 40 years, 70 years, 80 years, and even 100

---

[5] Easton, M. G. "Generation", *Easton's Bible Dictionary*, from *The Blue Letter Bible*. 1897. 24 June, 1996 31 Jan 2011. Note: Sir Isaac Newton's study of ancient history suggested that classical Greek studies would show a generation being 33 years.

years. So to suppose that 40 years stands as the exact length of a biblical generation was certainly very bad timing indeed.

Consequently, on the point of the length of a biblical generation, we could surmise that Jesus indicates a finite period of time bounded between 33 and 100 years. It constitutes probably well less than a century but much more than three decades. Frankly,

FIGURE 22 - THE PARABLE OF THE FIG TREE

striving for more precision than this appears to be most unbiblical. Consequently, the gist of Jesus' message can only be summarized as a "timespan less than 100 years."

THE BUDDING FIG TREE—A COUNTDOWN TO HIS COMING?

When we come to the parable spoken within this Bible passage, Jesus makes this point powerfully. And yet, His parable is another example where frequent 'date setting' logic runs afoul, as we shall see next.

Jesus delivered a parable known as *The Parable of the Fig Tree,* to warn us (or better yet, *encourage* us) that we should recognize *when* the time of His return draws very near, even "at the doors." *"When they now shoot forth* (the leaves of the *Fig Tree* or **any tree** in Luke's version*), ye see and know of your own selves that summer is now nigh at hand."* Some authors suggest this parable may actually be an *allegory,* in which distinct elements of the story represent something "in real life." In such a characterization, the *Fig Tree* represents Israel. Its budding represents its return to life as a nation—but more specifically, its resurrection during the last days.

Not that long ago, on his web site the late Grant Jeffrey referred to an apocryphal story from the Gospel of Peter (written in the second century) arguing the *Fig Tree* refers to Israel. While he is correct that the selection from this apocryphal account expressly confirms the common Pre-millennial viewpoint, from an interpretive standpoint (that is, from a *hermeneutical* perspective), we must ask, "Is that therefore what the canonical gospels teach?"

Historic orthodox Christian tradition conveys that any and all allegorical interpretation remains highly suspect. It may be proper to apply allegory to illustrate a truth, but not to determine its essential meaning. In other words, if you build doctrine on an allegorical interpretation you may wind up with egg on your face. Instead, a proper interpretative method usually avoids the allegory and sticks with the more modest concept of *analogy.*

While the fig tree appears to be one genuine analogy for Israel, it does not stand as the only tree. The prophets of the Old Testament compare Israel to an *olive tree* (See Isaiah 17:6, Jeremiah 11:16, Hosea 14:6). Even Paul's analogy comparing Israel to the Church, employs the *olive tree for the comparison, not the fig tree* (See Romans 11:17, 24). Hence, the point of the Jesus' parable appears less definite than Lindsey, Jeffrey and others have proposed. In other words, treating the parable as an allegory and connecting the "budding of the fig tree" with the birth of the political nation of Israel in 1948 seems possible but not obvious. This may be "reading too much into" what Jesus was asserting.

DOES ISRAEL'S RETURN FULFILL END DAYS' PROPHECY?

Consequently, am I contending that the birth of modern day Israel in 1948 lacks importance? Not at all—it was a monumental date. But we would be smarter to think in terms of a progressive fulfillment of the Bible's prophecy of Israel returning to its land and reclaiming its heritage rather than identifying just one date. Indeed, if you recount the historical milestones, the resulting momentum seems most compelling:

- In 1896-99, the Zionist movement called for the nation of Israel to be reborn in the land of Palestine.
- In 1917, England conquered Jerusalem, winning it away from the Ottoman Turks.
- In 1917, Lord Balfour signed the so-called Balfour Declaration stating that the British Empire looked favorably on establishing a homeland for the Jewish people in the Middle East.
- In 1948, the UN partitioned Trans-Jordan to create Israel with specified borders.
- In 1967, the Six-Day War broadened those borders and included the retaking of Jerusalem by the nation state of Israel.
- In 1973, Israel ultimately won the Yom-Kippur War, which led eventually to peace with Egypt, and later Jordon.
- Since that time, Israel fought many other battles to solidify its land holdings and its security in southern Lebanon and Gaza.

In conclusion: By seeking to identify the precise date (so we can start a 'count-down clock'), we depart from what the Bible plainly states and enter the realm of speculation. Speculation is okay. Goodness knows I engage in it too. But it should be so labeled. Based solely on historical events of the twentieth century, we cannot be certain that any one date comprises the 'kick-off event.'

HAS THE TIME OF THE GENTILES COME TO AN END?

In Luke 21:24, we encounter yet another key expression often connected with setting a boundary around the timing of Christ's return—*the time of the Gentiles*. "*And they shall fall by the edge of the sword, and shall be led away captive into all nations: and Jerusalem shall be trodden down of the Gentiles,* **until the times of the Gentiles be fulfilled**." What is the time of the Gentiles? Hal Lindsey asserted that this era ended when Moshe Dayan and the Israel Defense Force took the Temple Mount in 1967. The Gentiles no longer trod Jerusalem underfoot. Nevertheless, fearing a negative reaction from Muslims and other political groups around the world, Dayan elected to turn over the control of the Temple Mount back to the Palestinians and the authority known as the WAQF. If control of the Temple Mount constitutes the continuance of the time of the Gentiles, then that era has not yet concluded.

A scholar of the caliber of the late John Walvoord (1910–2002), former President of Dallas Theological Seminary and a strong voice in Pre-millennialism, believed the *time of the Gentiles* does not end until Jesus physically returns to earth and permanently restores Jerusalem to the Jews. If so, then it is disqualified as any sort of a forewarning that Jesus will soon return. If comes 'after the fact.'

Nevertheless, Jesus' analogy remains meaningful even *if* Israel was not the exact analogue to the fig tree. Indeed, His parable still makes a powerful point: *once the signs commence, once there are blooms or buds, expect the leaves to come next. It is inevitable.*

Thus, what Jesus actually conveys comprises two distinct factors influencing how we understand the timing of His return:

1. First, the signs will move forth with the same certainty as *buds lead to leaves*. That is nature's irrepressible pattern. It happens every year. There has never been a time when the summer leaves failed to come forth after the trees bloom—we can count on it. In this instance, we are being told, "Know this fact remains as certain as facts can possibly be."

2. Secondly, Jesus is saying, "Once this happens, there will be not be another autumn" (staying with His analogy). "Spring will be followed by summer. But this summer *will not give way to autumn*. The leaves will not turn from green to fall colors. The summer following this *budding* comprises the final season. "

So then, what exactly does the *budding* entail? It seems not to be only Israel becoming a nation state per se. In context, the 'budding' consists of those signs which Jesus recounts come together *within one generation*. *"So likewise ye, when ye see these things come to pass, know ye that the kingdom of God is nigh at hand."*

At stake, then, are two things: (1) "Have we properly interpreted the signs per the Bible's prophecies, signs for which we should be watching?" and (2) *if* we have rightly interpreted the signs, we must ask the hypothetical question, "Would God confuse us, allowing events not to run their course to the conclusion?"

WAS JESUS CONFUSED REGARDING WHEN HE RETURNS?

Just to be crystal clear, Jesus seems very sure regarding the timing of His return. Granted, we could adopt the liberal point of view. We could presume that Jesus was a man of His time, purely human, without a clue as to what would really happen in the last days. However, if we affirm our faith in His divinity, it is not as easy to dismiss His assertions regarding what will happen in the Day of the Lord. Listen to His words carefully. Jesus' most affirmative statement given in the Gospels rules out any such possibility. *"Verily I say unto you, this generation shall not pass away, till all be fulfilled. Heaven and earth shall pass away: but my words shall not pass away."* How could Jesus be more emphatic?

Would He intentionally mislead us? Hardly. He would never 'lead us down the primrose path' as my mom used to say (quoting Shakespeare from *Ophelia*). We will not see the clouds gather and then, before the storm clouds burst, see them dissipate and clear skies return. Once the signs coalesce, once the clouds gather, the storm commences. Jesus exclaims with extraordinary emphasis, *He will not fool those who are watching!*

That leaves us with only the first issue: *Have we accurately interpreted the signs of His return?* Since many have been fooled in times past, we must conclude the fault lies not in God's faithfulness but in our ability to interpret His Word.

So the question we should ask is, "Have the predicted signs all come to pass within "this generation" as the Bible intends for us to understand that term? The answer is a resounding "Yes!" We should remember Jesus criticized the Pharisees for their failure to detect the signs of the times. If His point to them was that 'interpreting the times in which they lived' should be obvious (and they failed to 'get it'), is it any less obvious for us? Would Christ's statement infer that knowing the signs of the times remains confusing and complex so we should avoid discussing it? No. The opposite would seem to be the case. The signs unmistakably spell it out.

I believe our generation is *the* generation which will witness the return of Christ Jesus. Can I predict it will happen in this decade? No. But is it not absolutely mandatory it happen within the next few decades if Jesus words are to be vindicated? I believe the answer is even more emphatically "Yes!" Such an affirmation places proper emphasis on Jesus' words in Luke 21. Indeed, if we soft peddle the words and only casually affirm His soon return in the years ahead, we close our ears to the proclamation Jesus so forcibly uttered when concluding His message:

> *"So likewise ye, when ye see these things come to pass, know ye that the kingdom of God is nigh at hand. Verily I say unto you, this generation shall not pass away, till* **all be fulfilled.** *Heaven and earth shall pass away: but my words shall not pass away" (Luke 21:32, 33).*

His affirmation could not be more powerfully set forth. He challenges us to accept that His spoken words are so inexorable, so impossible to stop, we would more likely witness the entire universe collapse into nothingness than His words failing to come true. This is precisely what he means when he says, *"Heaven and earth shall pass away: but my words shall not pass away."* Jesus is adamant. His coming inevitably follows these signs—just as the leaves surely follow once trees break forth in buds.

AFFIRMING THE INEVITABLE WITHOUT SETTING A DATE

Nevertheless, because we humans cannot help but seek to know "the day and the hour"—insisting there must be a code that can be broken specifying the very day He is to return—we drift unavoidably *toward setting the date*. The positive motivation behind our doing this derives from our faith in what we term *the providence of God*. God has established the very stars in the sky and even the timing of when the moon passes in Earth's shadow!

Certainly, when that day comes, when we are in the presence of the saints, we will learn directly from the LORD why that particular date was chosen and exactly how He foreshadowed it. We will experience awe at all the signs given showing the world the days of humankind (left to its own devices) had come to an end.

Nonetheless, in the final analysis, setting a date denies the key principle upon which our lives are based—*faith*. *"The just shall live by faith."* (Romans 1:17) We seek to set dates in part because we lack faith. The tension between knowledge and faith constitutes something of a dilemma for the people of God. We know Jesus Christ will come soon, but we cannot know exactly what day that will be. And yet, if we believe the signs have coalesced, we must insist Jesus comes in our generation, despite our lack of knowing exactly how long such a generation is. To say less than this contradicts Jesus' very words.

Striving to determine the exact date constitutes a vain effort to set faith aside. For once we know the date—if that were possible—we would no longer require faith to believe in His coming. While ironic, it nevertheless remains so. By assuming we can decode the date of Christ's return, we deny the principle to live by faith. We deny the faith we seek so earnestly to demonstrate.

It is at the heart of what Jesus meant when He said *"A wicked and adulterous generation seeketh after a sign."* (Matthew 16:4).

Along with the fact that setting a date (wrongly) brings discredit to the gospel as well as ourselves, we must resist the temptation. We know He comes soon—but we cannot know exactly when. We must steadfastly affirm the return of Christ, all the while decrying any attempt to decode the date.

PART TWO:
KEEPING WATCH UNTIL JESUS COMES

10: AFTER THE APOCALYPSE

Yet have I set my king upon my holy hill of Zion. I will declare the decree: the LORD hath said unto me, Thou art my Son; this day have I begotten thee. Ask of me, and I shall give thee the heathen for thine inheritance, and the uttermost parts of the earth for thy possession. Thou shalt break them with a rod of iron; thou shalt dash them in pieces like a potter's vessel.
(Psalm 2:6-9)

Behold the man whose name is The BRANCH; and he shall grow up out of his place, and he shall build the temple of the LORD: Even he shall build the temple of the LORD; and he shall bear the glory, and shall sit and rule upon his throne; and he shall be a priest upon his throne: and the counsel of peace shall be between them both.
(Zechariah 6:12-13)

And the glory of the LORD came into the house by the way of the gate whose prospect is toward the east. And he said unto me, Son of man, the place of my throne, and the place of the soles of my feet, where I will dwell in the midst of the children of Israel for ever, and my holy name, shall the house of Israel no more defile...
(Ezekiel 43:4, 7)

PARDON ME FOR REPEATING MYSELF

MY FATHER HAS A HABIT OF REPEATING HIMSELF. THIS IS NOT DUE TO HIS AGE. EVEN AT 95 HE IS LUCID AND A GOOD CONVERSATIONALIST. TRUE, HIS HEARING COULD BE BETTER. But he is still a very smart man and comes across that way to those that are fortunate enough to engage him in dialogue.

I am sorry to report that as of this writing, my father now lives in a nursing home. I spend my Sunday afternoons enjoying his company however. We watch movies or television series and discuss them. Due to the magnitude of his age, we know that our time together may be short. We stay calm about that fact, knowing nothing remains that we need say to one another which has not already been said. I remind him that it is not a foregone conclusion he will get to heaven before I do. He has outlived everyone in our family in 'his generation.' And we may be privileged to experience the rapture of the Church together—being a member of the generation that bypasses death and goes straight to 'go' to collect our reward. However, I must not get ahead of myself by launching into that subject. It will come later in this chapter.

He has repeated himself for as long as I remember. Most of us have a fear of repeating ourselves to the boredom of our friends and family. We may say, "I have probably told you this before." Or if it is a joke we will say, "Stop me if you've heard this one." This is not my father's fear. I cannot recall him fearing saying the same thing twice (or countless times). Why this behavior? What comprises his motivation for repetition *ad nauseum*? It appears to be his desire to reflect on his favorite subjects and especially contemplate those insights into life that he most cherishes.

One of his favorites comprises his proclamation that we could enjoy heaven on earth if evil people were simply banished and Mother Nature would be a bit better-behaved. "You know," he would counsel me, "if this world were just free of bad people doing bad things, this world would be a great place. It is a beautiful world. It would be heaven enough if it were only this world without the evil that we too often see." My father would then get a distant look in his eyes as if he could visualize such a world and dream of himself living in its midst. It was as if he was hearing *Satchmo*[1] singing, "And I say to myself, it is a wonderful world."

---

[1] This nickname belongs to Louis Armstrong, for those who are among the musically challenged.

THE MILLENNIAL REIGN—A WORLD REFRESHED

There was a time when I tried to tell him that according to my interpretation of the Bible, he should feel assured such an earth was exactly what 'the Good Lord' (his favorite appellation for our

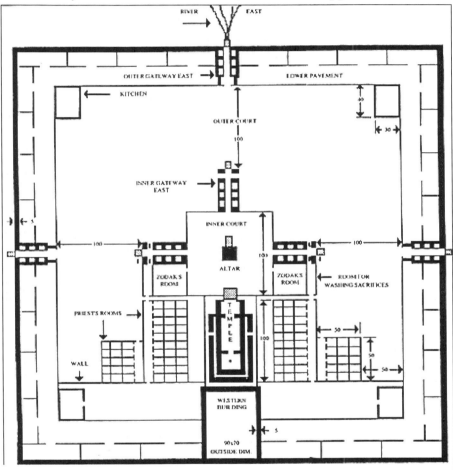

FIGURE 23 - THE SITE PLAN FOR THE FUTURE TEMPLE OF EZEKIEL (EZEKIEL 40-48)

Drawn by Bob Hall, from *The Secrets of Ezekiel's Temple*.

Father in Heaven) has in store for us when Jesus returns. I would attempt to explain that most evangelicals nowadays are 'Pre-Millennialists' and we believe exactly what he wishes for. Jesus Christ will return to this earth to save it from destruction and then begin a restoration of its beauty. Those who have believed in Him over the past 2,000 years will return too atop white horses (now that will be a 'ride!') After Jesus Christ dispenses with the archenemy of the Bible, *the Antichrist*, He will turn His attention to establishing His capital in Jerusalem and will literally reign on an earthly throne in Israel for 1,000 years (why we call this epoch the *Millennium*). Then Messiah Jesus will rebuild the Temple and reign on His throne in that very place.

When responding to my dad, I would try to explain that *'heaven' will come to earth*, metaphorically speaking. Earth becomes 'paradise restored' (as John Milton might say). When Jesus returns, the earth will be made right. The creation will be refreshed. We will live in peace on this planet. The troubles of the past will be no more. As Isaiah said, *"He shall wipe away every tear"* (Isaiah 25:8 paraphrased). The verses at the beginning of this chapter affirm this fact. The Messiah will reign *on this earth*.

As a bonus, those of us that return with Christ will be transformed into new creatures, no longer mortal but immortal. We will be co-regents with Him and will serve Him every day in this wonderfully renewed world. We will not fear death or illness. We will be empowered in more ways than we know to handle our new responsibilities of reigning with Christ in His Kingdom.

Now, understand, my father was not guilty of ignoring me. Nevertheless, about once a year, starting about 30 years ago, he would find an occasion to remind me of his dream and hope for our world. I would once again try to explain that his insight was right on target and articulate in detail why good, biblical interpretation confirms his highest hopes. I thought it would add to his delight if he understood his perspective could be backed up by the Bible. I had that wrong.

THE AFTERLIFE AS A MOTIVE TO ENDURE

Eventually I came to realize that my father did not really want a biblical justification for his dream. He did not want me to explain the difference between Pre-millennialism and Post-millennialism. Such technical distinctions (important though they be!) were lost on him. My sense was that Dad just wanted to ponder such sweet images and enjoy thinking about the future in such a world. This prospect was enough for him. Perhaps the point is my father could visualize 'heaven on earth' and he found in that concept comfort to dissuade doubts about the future and overcome the many daily images of deplorable acts. Thinking about how earth could be transformed into heaven was a powerful coping mechanism. Marx may have thought that believing in heaven was an opiate for the people (to keep them happy despite being *alienated* from their work). However, my dad would tell Marx he was clueless about the satisfaction and confidence believers in Jesus Christ enjoy when they possess unswerving faith in a future life.

My father conjectured about the afterlife just as we all do. We wonder about the afterlife and its characteristics. Our minds are naturally flooded with unbiblical concepts about heaven and life after death thanks to false religions, classical mythology, and television programs that have mediums and ghosts becoming normal characters without any shock value. Indeed, ghosts have become a supernatural means to console us. Furthermore, mediums now solve crimes and whisper so-called truths about life's meaning to their companions. The supernatural is now commonplace.

So what constitutes the truth about the nature of the afterlife? What might the afterlife be like? What does biblical prophecy teach us about the future heaven and earth?

For Christians, there is a lot more to it than we generally suppose. Granted, the reader may be like my father and find the details unnecessary. Just to know that Jesus promises eternal life to those that trust in Him stands sufficient. Perhaps all that you require is the promise that death does not mean 'the end.' If that is sufficient, you are privileged. For me, perhaps unfortunately, I remain insatiably curious concerning what comes next. I want to know about it in detail. The more I can learn, the better!

THE FOUR PHASES OF THE AFTERLIFE

When we study the Bible, it becomes clear that there are four 'phases' of the afterlife. I will not get into the differences between 'Old Testament saints' and 'New Testament saints' although the Bible has something to say about those distinctions too. Instead, my comments are directed toward those who are believers today (although the same applies for all who believed in Jesus Christ since the time of His death and resurrection, which are now 'asleep' as Paul terms it). Here is how I distinguish end explain these four phases of the afterlife:

1. After we die, we are ushered into another dimension Jesus called *paradise*. Summing up this state (from considerable research I have done through the years), it appears we will recognize and encounter others. Our experience there will be vibrant and wonderful, substantive *but not physical*. We will be conscious, but our perception will be quite different than how we experience reality today. Descriptions from many accounts are consistent about hearing singing, seeing beautiful sites, talking with loved ones, and feeling that the experience is superlative to our best times on earth. We will communicate. But we will not be 'physical creatures.' This step into eternity is frequently the subject of books and movies. Testimonies abound of the dying departing with smiles on their faces from what they perceive 'in their mind's eye' just in front of them. Whether or not we traverse a dark tunnel and see a light at the end as many secular stories depict, is not crystal clear. But what Paul teaches is *"to be absent from the body is to be present with the Lord."* (2 Corinthians 5:8) Paul relates we will not experience a moment of loneliness or a sense of separation from God. If we believe in Jesus Christ and the Holy Spirit dwells in us, the Spirit of Christ is with us from the first moment our body turns off the switches until we are resident in God's reassuring presence. The Bible teaches that it is not angels who escort us into the presence of God. The Spirit of Christ Himself takes us by the hand.

2. Stage two is much debated among Bible-believing Christians. This experience commences at the time of Jesus Christ's physical return to the earth when His bride (the 'Church') is 'raptured' to join

Christ in the air. At that moment, our experience once again becomes physical despite being 'in the clouds.' Somehow, if we have experienced death, we will be transported from 'paradise' back to the upper atmosphere of the earth. Our physical body is resurrected and rejoins our spirit and soul. Our physical body is changed. But what happens next is contested. Either we will continue on from our presence in the clouds to return to the surface of the earth (which is the so-called post-tribulation rapture view), or we will once again return to where we were previously, the 'other dimensional reality' (as the 'pre-tribulation rapture' doctrine asserts). We will have physical bodies once more, but our surroundings will continue to be in 'paradise.' According to most evangelicals (within the *Dispensational* school of thought), we will likely remain in this state for at least seven more years (according to how time is kept upon the earth), until Jesus returns at the Battle of Armageddon to defeat Antichrist and his armies. We will be physical creatures but reside in a realm distinct from what we now call 'space-time.' Paul tells us, *"Then we which are alive [and] remain shall be caught up together with them in the clouds, to meet the Lord in the air: and so shall we ever be with the Lord."* (I Thessalonians 4:17) Some may object that this is illogical; the two realms cannot be traversed in this way. To that objection, I point out Jesus Christ was resurrected and possessed a physical body that could be touched. He could eat and drink. He urged his followers to see *He was not a ghost.* (See John's gospel, chapters 20, 21) He was a physical being. And yet, when he ascended into heaven, He disappeared into a cloud with His physical body intact. Here is our precedent for 'stage two' *life after death* that the Bible promises.

3. Then comes stage three. As in a novel, this constitutes the 'climax.' For those who believe the Bible and profess that the Second Coming of Christ happens in 'space-time,' we return with Jesus at the Battle of Armageddon. We are His Saints. We comprise the 'clouds of heaven.' There are so many of us, dressed all in white (thanks to His redeeming death cleansing us from all our sin), to the mortals on earth we will appear like clouds rolling in at the seashore. We will be a portentous sight. From this moment forward (for at least the next 1,000 years) our experience returns to

'space-time' and we live physically upon the earth. The Bible is quite explicit in both the Old and New Testaments: We will reside on this earth.[2] The Kingdom of the Messiah is the Kingdom of Jesus Christ. John tells us that His Kingdom will last for 1,000 years. However, that is not the end of things.

4. Finally, a New Heaven and a New Jerusalem will follow this 1,000-year period. This comprises the *dénouement*. Like a novel, it constitutes the final stage when all questions are answered and everything becomes exceedingly clear. With the race won, we are awarded the ultimate prize. John describes this as "a new world coming." Peter reveals God purges the entire universe of a persistent flaw which even throughout the Millennium is not fully corrected. John describes the New Jerusalem with breathtaking language suggesting the "streets are paved with gold" and all structures composed of a precious metal or some manner of jewel. Paul exclaims the entire creation yearns for this moment. *"But as it is written, 'Eye hath not seen, nor ear heard, neither have entered into the heart of man, the things which God hath prepared for them that love him.'"* (I Corinthians 2:9, quoting Isaiah 64:4) In this moment, suddenly time and space are reconfigured in an unimaginable way. Heaven and earth unite. Time and eternity conjoin. The sun and moon are no longer needed for light. The Glory of God persists and provides unending illumination. We cannot fully fathom this experience. What we can gather: our enjoyment of this reality will exceed our most sublime dreams.

A SHORTSIGHTED VIEW

In thinking about my father's ideas about heaven, one fault I do find: it seems somewhat 'short-sighted'—it does not look far enough into the future recognizing that God has more in store for us than we can ever realize with our finite comprehension.

---

[2] G.H. Pember poses a slightly nuanced view of this 'endgame.' He speculates that the purpose of the Saints is to replace the 'spirits' under the direction of Satan, "The Prince and Power of the Air." Our authority will extend from earth to 'the second heaven'—managing the world from a 'birds-eye view.'

Despite how wonderful the world will be when there is no longer political strife, natural disasters, or personal tragedies—when sickness is forgotten and when death is done away—we should appreciate that the best still is yet to be. An earth made like heaven constitutes a great story. But much more exists concerning the afterlife to contemplate. As stated in an earlier chapter, experiencing the afterlife might be likened to celebrating 12 days of Christmas rather than only one. Each stage of 'what comes next' builds upon the previous. Indeed, we will soon learn that there is no such thing as 'this is as good as it gets.' An infinite God has the ability to enhance the spectacular *continuously*. My concept of heaven and earth may be more complex than my father's, but I venture it holds much more promise for the both of us.

So in the years ahead, if you hear me talk or write about my ideas about heaven and earth, please allow me to repeat myself. For the prospects are too awesome to be the subject of only one or two conversations, sermons, or books.

11: DOOM AND GLOOM

And there shall be signs in the sun, and in the moon, and in the stars; and upon the earth distress of nations, with perplexity; the sea and the waves roaring; **Men's hearts failing them for fear, and for looking after those things which are coming on the earth**: *for the powers of heaven shall be shaken. And then shall they see the Son of man coming in a cloud with power and great glory. And when these things begin to come to pass, then look up, and lift up your heads; for your redemption draweth nigh.*
(Luke 21:25-28)

THE GOOD AND THE BAD GO TOGETHER

There is a common saying, "You have to take the bad with the good." Apparently, it is standard operating procedure for us common folk: When good things happen, bad things come right alongside too. We naturally believe it is impossible for everything to go perfect. The wisdom of life seems to predict bad and good are coupled. You can't have one without the other.

Like Frank Sinatra's classic song preaches, *"Love and marriage, go together like a horse and carriage... Dad was told by my mother, you can't have one without the other, love and marriage go together."* I am not saying *love* is good and *marriage* is bad... although perhaps that was the not-so-hidden message in the song! Mamma had to remind Daddy, "Hey, there is no free lunch! You want my love? Get on your knees and propose to me!"

If we think about it more deeply, I suppose we could get philosophical and assert that we can only experience the good if we know what it is like to experience the bad. Our knowledge of either depends upon comparing the two. We need contrast to distinguish one from the other. A cold glass of water tastes a lot better when we are 'dying of thirst' than it does when we are in 'fluid balance' as my wife the nurse says.   When it comes to 'getting in shape,' the adage exhorts us to recall that 'without pain there is no gain.' Perhaps we might recall that famous recipe-cum-adage for a summer beverage: "Take the lemons life gives you and make lemonade." Likewise, we could recall that other conventional wisdom, "You can't make an omelet without breaking some eggs."

KNOCKING ON WOOD

I have sometimes experienced periods during my life when if I had have a good day, it would be automatic that the next day would be bad—or at least *not as good*. Consequently, after I had concluded, "Wow, today was a great day" then I had to remind myself, "Beware: the next day may not be so happy." Time after time, this experience played itself out. Perhaps it was the failure on my part to be positive and optimistic. Indeed, maybe the bad that followed the good was something of a self-fulfilling prophecy. Those who promote *the power of positive thinking* would certainly fault me for expecting the worst. It is hard to argue against that point—you often get exactly what you expect.

In my defense, my *peculiar* outlook actually seems pretty typical. It comes from a universal, deep-seated superstition built upon this same recognition: "Do not be too enthusiastic about your success today—do not say anything out loud about it. The 'spirits will hear you and spoil your fun.'" We golfers joke about 'the golf gods' that *get even with us* when we brag too much about how great a shot we just made. Sure enough, a great shot is more often than not followed by a *laugher* (not that we find it easy to laugh when this happens!) Even the old superstition about 'knocking on wood' (after any positive affirmation) links to this idea: rapping on the nearest wooden object awakens the spirits living inside the wood. These spirits promise protection from fates who seek retaliation for such boisterous confidence (i.e., 'smacking us down' as my kids might say).

One of the most common reactions amongst those of us who are excited about biblical prophecy is for someone around us, typically someone we love, to chide us for being full of *doom and gloom*. We might even be asked, "How can you sleep at night believing what you do about the end of the world?" Perhaps in self-defense I have come to call myself jokingly, "Doomsday Doug" since I am a published author on the topic of Bible prophecy. Perhaps I expect a frontal assault in reaction to my public stance. By calling myself a self-deprecating name and going 'not okay' (as they teach in Transactional Analysis, or 'TA'), I defuse the anticipated missile soon to be launched my way.

GOING TO HELL IN A HANDBAG

Still, it remains hard to escape the reality of what the Bible teaches. The redemption we pursue arrives at the height of worldwide calamity. 'Going to heaven' comes at the time when the world is literally 'going to hell.' Our joy arises simultaneous with the terror of those around us who do not share the same hope. Jesus predicted that in our times (paraphrasing), "Men's hearts shall fail them for fear of what they see coming to pass in the world." (Luke 21:26, paraphrased) If we willingly admit to those around us we believe in Bible prophecy and expect to witness terrible signs in our lifetime, we know we are destined to 'hear about it.' It seems getting 'raked over the coals' by those who do not share our enthusiasm—being a proponent for *doom and gloom*—just goes with the territory.

To be sure, most of the experts in Bible prophecy agree: Fearful signs in the heavens, massive earthquakes, terrible storms, plagues, and catastrophes one right after another accompany the time of Jesus' return. If a particular cataclysm appears especially heinous, we often hear the descriptive phrase, "it is of biblical proportions." The populace may know little about Bible prophecy. However, everyone seems to know that if a cataclysmic transpires, many conclude Bible prophecies about the end times are coming true. Even the biblically illiterate recall the freakish judgments of the Bible: water turning to blood, locus attacks, the sun growing dark, and stars falling from the heavens. Yes, even the unbelievers remember the 'bad' in the Bible. We can certainly thank lots of apocalyptic movies and TV shows for this little bit of Bible education among the masses.

THE AFLOCKALYPSE OF 2011

In January of 2011, just after New Year's Day, we heard portentous reports worldwide regarding thousands of birds falling down dead from the sky. News anchors could hardly contain themselves. They quickly labeled it, the "A-*flock*-alypse." They intimated we could laugh about it, even if it was no laughing matter. This not-so-funny quip suggested this strange event might be an omen of the world's end. Of course, immediately after spouting their well-turned phrase, our news people reassured us the situation is under control. They reported several noteworthy naturalists had clarified these 'die offs' happen all the time—no need to worry.

Well, perhaps that stands to reason. Then again, perhaps there *really was* something apocalyptic concerning these puzzling deaths. Could this have been the start of a pole reversal where the North and South Pole flip? We know that animals navigate by sensing the 'lines' in the planet's magnetic field. We could logically assume that if our magnetic field becomes so radically altered, nature will not teach animals all that rapidly how to adjust to this change. Predictably (and sadly), millions of animals could die.

We know Science believes our poles could flip at any time and that we are 'past due' for this to happen.[1] When this pole reversal occurs, our magnetic field virtually dissolves until the polarity completely reverses, whereupon Nature reinstates it. Many of the 2012 doomsayers believed this event would occur at the same moment when the Sun's sunspot activity peaked. The Sun will spew higher levels of radioactivity our way at just the same time our planet's *shields are down* (to borrow a phrase from *Star Trek*). The result: we could experience power blackouts, radiation burns, and massive die offs of animals of all sorts, including *Homo sapiens*. Does the Bible confirm this will happen? No, but science reasons it constitutes a plausible scenario.

If you study the Bible from cover to cover, the plain meaning of Scripture remains steady: 'the day of reckoning comes.' *The Day of the Lord* is so labeled by most Old Testament prophets, while the New Testament renames this timeframe *The Day of Jesus Christ*. (Some try to differentiate the two, but that approach seems contrived). This period will be an unmitigated season of colossal judgment. The Scripture confirms this scenario again and again. If we believe the Bible, even if we do not like to think about such horrible possibilities, we must affirm *it constitutes a frequent subject*.

---

[1] This flipping remains recorded in the composition of rocky material at the bottom of the ocean. Fault lines where the 'spreading' originates on the ocean's floor, serves as a magnetic recorder of the direction of the polarity of the earth at certain times in the past. We know these 'flips' occur every 100,000 to 200,000 years.

The Sun also reverses its polarity in 11 year cycles, coinciding with sunspot activity. When these two cycles coincided as they were predicted by some to do in 2012, we might have seen a cataclysm 'of biblical proportions.' But it did not happen in 2012 or in 2013. Major Ed Dames, the head of the military's Remote Viewing team predicted in his book *Killshot* that the misbehaving sun would launch a solar flare to end all solar flares. He said he saw the future in 2013 and it was going to happen. Of course, it did not.

Several near misses have been discussed during 2014, but someone seems to be looking out for us. As the song says, "He has the whole world in His hands."

Without question, the cataclysms described in the prophecies of both the Old and New Testaments frighten us. We are told the experience of these 'last days' results from God's wrath directed at an unbelieving world.

The Book of Revelation delves into grave details using remarkable symbols of judgment. There are S*even Seals, Seven Trumpets,* and *Seven Bowls of Wrath.* Each broken seal discloses a new horror; each trumpet portends a new calamity greater than the previous; each vial of wrath pours forth judgments whose description grows increasingly more horrible.

If we dwell on these images of doom, no doubt we too would become gloomy. Nevertheless, the Bible consistently offers a starkly contrasted message: *the greatest day for those who believe in Christ, comes on the worst day for those that don't.*

Furthermore, the Bible instructs Christians not to focus on this message of doom and gloom. We must "*lift up our heads for our redemption is at hand.*" Therefore, we must choose to accentuate the positive! We should not dwell on the horrors soon to happen. We should set our minds on the good things just ahead.

WHAT REALLY HAPPENED IN SODOM AND GOMORRAH?

The story of Lot and his family fleeing the judgment of Sodom and Gomorrah holds a lesson for us today. Most everyone (once again, even the biblically illiterate) knows of Sodom and Gomorrah. This city was so evil God determined to destroy it in a manner unlike any other judgment mentioned in the Bible. Archeologists studying this area in the Holy Land consider the possibility Sodom and Gomorrah was destroyed by an atomic explosion: 'Fire and brimstone' literally rained down from the heavens. Could God have 'nuked' the city?

Ancient alien astronaut theorists are certain this happened. While I may not agree with their depiction of God (who they believe to be an extraterrestrial intelligence), intriguingly the non-orthodox corroborate an exceptional source destroyed this area of the Middle East 4,000 years ago through some heretofore matchless method.

In the biblical account, we learn a problem existed in God's plan to judge these two cities on the plains of Israel. God had 'His people' in the city of Sodom: *Lot, the brother of Abraham* lived there. Furthermore, Lot had two daughters and a wife. The book of 2 Peter (2:7) tells us Lot was a righteous man tormented by the sin of this contemptuous city surrounding him.

Consequently, like a special team of commandos, God prepared an extraction of the righteous before the unrighteous of Sodom and Gomorrah would be destroyed.

Genesis 18 and 19 tells us God sent three special agents (His angels) to carry out this plan of judgment. However, first the three angels traveled to see Abraham and Sarah (his wife) in order to give

FIGURE 24 – LOT AND HIS FAMILY FLEE SODOM AND GOMORRAH

Abraham a 'heads up' that they were on their way to destroy these cities; whereupon Abraham began negotiating with the angel-in-charge (who many scholars believe was the pre-existent Christ and whom the Bible identifies as "the LORD"). Abraham questioned the first angel about how many righteous persons had to be in the city before God would forsake His plan.

This negotiation took place because Abraham misunderstood God's plan and more importantly, because he misunderstood *the nature of God.* Quite clearly, God did not intend to destroy the city with the 'good guys' still living there. First, God would rescue the righteous, extract them, and then judge Sodom and Gomorrah. In this discourse, therefore, God sought to express to Abraham that while judgment was coming He would protect Abraham's brother and his family. If Abraham had thought about it further, perhaps he would have realized, "Why else would God come see me first?" However, God was teaching Abraham a lesson: *God rescues His people before He sends judgment.* Unlike the gods of Sumeria that Abraham grew up learning about as a child, Abraham's God was a *just* God—free of any taint of capriciousness. God did not need Abraham or anyone else to tell Him 'how to do the right thing.'

Nevertheless, having not yet learned this lesson, Abraham negotiated with the LORD. He bargained with God and made the LORD agree He would drop His plan of judgment on behalf of no more than a mere *ten* righteous persons who might live in Sodom and Gomorrah (a number no doubt that Abraham calculated would include Lot's family, son-in-laws, and possible children Abraham supposed might be present).

In the account, two of the angels press ahead to Sodom while Abraham and the LORD finish their negotiation. When these two angels arrived at Sodom, Lot greeted them, bowed down before them (recognizing their other-worldly nature), and then brought the angels into his house where they would spend the night—but not without incident. The Sodomites (all men, both young and old) bang on Lot's door and demand these guests be given to them to exploit sexually. Lot goes out to bargain with them and even offers his two virgin daughters to the crowd instead (apparently his daughters were betrothed to his son-in-laws but not married).

However, the angels refused to stand by and let Lot go through with his offer. They came to the door, pulled Lot back into the house, and smote (one of my favorite biblical verbs) the crowd with blindness. Early the next morning (before the town was awake), the two angels gathered Lot, his wife, and his two daughters together in order to flee the city (without the son-in-laws who mocked Lot when he asked them to join the escape party). The angels warned their little group of 'rescuees' to look forward and not backwards as they fled. The Scripture hints the party traveled from the plains into the mountains, an appreciable distance. Later we learn Lot's wife apparently hears the thunder of judgment and senses the city's destruction. She turns to look from far away and instantly, turns into a pillar of salt having disregarded the angel's warning.[2] This was probably more than 'the curiosity that killed the cat.' Evidently, Lot's wife could not fix her eyes on the good to come—she was still stuck in the mire of what lay behind.

The Bible says this event could be seen from many miles distant: *"And Abraham gat up early in the morning to the place where he stood before the LORD [negotiating]: And he looked toward Sodom and Gomorrah, and toward all the land of the plain, and beheld, and, lo, the smoke of the country went up as the smoke of a furnace."* (Genesis 19:27-28) Did it resemble the ominous mushroom cloud of an atomic explosion? Abraham surely wondered whether Lot and his family were 'free and clear'

---

[2] Many have speculated why Lot's wife received this peculiar judgment. The speculation suggests that she was unwilling to depart from the city. She did not want to leave her life 'in the city' behind, perhaps proving her unworthiness to be saved. Her turning around was a willful decision and not an accidental glance. It probably was not the first 'about turn' she had done that day.

of this destruction. If God had not warned Abraham, we can imagine Abraham would have headed right toward Sodom to learn of his brother's fate. Hence, we can see why God made sure Abraham knew what was about to happen.

We are told the next action of Abraham was to 'head south'—no doubt to put more distance between his family and the awesome destruction he had just witnessed. Were radiation involved, the story makes even more sense. God would not have wanted the father of many nations walking amidst a ground covered in such poisoning. This would have put a real kink in God's greater plan—generating mutations in the progenitor's DNA would not be wise.

SALVATION AND JUDGMENT MAY HAPPEN CONCURRENTLY

The Bible provides many lessons on how God moves to protect His people before His brings judgment on the unrighteous. We see this with Noah and his family, protected in the Ark while the world is judged with a massive flood. The lesson is consistent: *rejoice in God's upcoming salvation, even though His judgment comes too.* Praise Him for protecting and yes, *rescuing us from the terrors of the wrath to come.* We do have to take the bad with the good. It is sad the world is heading toward a horrible climax as the 'signs of the times' continue to mount. We are, however, to *"lift up our heads for our redemption draweth nigh."* Despite the impending doom, we are to rejoice that the good comes right alongside. The two must happen together.

So how should we respond to those who label we who fastidiously study Bible prophecy as 'doom-and-gloomers'? Perhaps we should remind them the Bible teaches we all have a choice. We rejoice in His provision to pull us out before doom strikes. We express sorrow that so many will choose not to embrace the opportunity to be *extracted.* Like Lot's son-in-laws who ignored the warnings of angels, unbelievers mock believers who hope to see even these 'mockers' rescued. At day's end, however, those who mock us remain responsible for the choices they make. If they castigate us (however seriously or not-so-seriously) for bringing up the subject of the end times with the implicit allusion to the doom and gloom which lies ahead, we should be quick to point out it is not that we focus on doom and gloom, *it is just our redemption, that which we seek, happens at the same time.*

CHOOSE LIFE THAT YE MAY LIVE

Perhaps the Apostle Peter said it best when he reminded us that the apocalypse remains a future event because God's 'extraction program' comprises an ongoing activity (the 'snatch and grab' mission as they say in the military). He intends to pull to safety as many as He can. *"The Lord is not slack concerning his promise, as some men count slackness; but is longsuffering to us-ward, not willing that **any should perish**, but that all should come to repentance."* (2 Peter 3:9)

Mama said, "We have to take the bad with the good." But God's offer looks beyond the destruction to the redemption and opportunity that lies on the other side. He reminds us our decisions have consequences. And yet, His offer *beckons us to choose life.*

After 40 years wondering in the wilderness, Moses exhorted the Children of Israel at the moment when they reached the cusp of their new life, as they stood ready to cross the Jordan, and enter into the Promised Land: *"I call heaven and earth to record this day against you, [that] I have set before you life and death, blessing and cursing: therefore choose life, that both thou and thy seed may live"* (Deuteronomy 30:19).

The choices are clear: blessing or cursing, life or death. Which will you chose?

12: FINDING MEANING IN DOOMSDAY[1]

And as it was in the days of Noe (Noah), so shall it be also in the days of the Son of man. They did eat, they drank, they married wives, they were given in marriage, until the day that Noah entered into the ark, and the flood came, and destroyed them all. Likewise also as it was in the days of Lot; they did eat, they drank, they bought, they sold, they planted, they builded [built]; but the same day that Lot went out of Sodom it rained fire and brimstone from heaven, and destroyed them all. Even thus shall it be in the day when the Son of man is revealed.
(Luke 17:26-30)

EMBRACING DEATH RATHER THAN DENYING IT

IT IS NOT THAT UNCOMMON TO HEAR SOMEONE SAY, "THAT WHICH DOES NOT KILL US, ONLY MAKES US STRONGER." THE PHRASE IS ACTUALLY A POPULAR, ALBEIT SOMEWHAT CORRUPTED ADAPTATION of a statement of Friedrich Nietzsche: "That which does not destroy us, defines us." There is considerable truth in this notion. I might personalize the wording even further: *Any challenge we overcome provides a compelling disclosure of who we really are.*

But in an unexpected way, those limits we cannot overcome—especially the ultimate ones—also define who we are. Limitations, once accepted and embraced, can reveal *character* and what course our lives should take. This is what the philosopher Martin

---

[1] This chapter is adapted and expanded from a portion of the concluding chapter of my book, *Decoding Doomsday*.

Heidegger taught. For him, death was the ultimate issue. Once we understand it characterizes *the* inescapable reality, *paradoxically*, we may experience real meaning. By denying death, we delay discovering the limited capacity we have to plot our course in this life and consequently, what our life stands to mean.

In 1973, an important book was published that crossed the lines of philosophy, anthropology, and psychology. Written by Ernst Becker, it was entitled, *The Denial of Death*. It won the Pulitzer Prize for non-fiction in 1974.

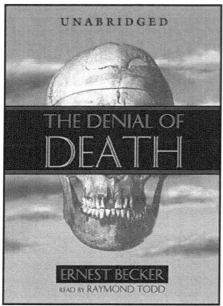 

FIGURE 25 - ANTHROPOLOGIST ERNST BECKER, AUTHOR, THE DENIAL OF DEATH

Becker asserted that, when it comes to the subject of our mortality, *human beings are double-minded*. On the one hand, we know we will die. On the other, we seem called to do something with our lives that is heroic, which proves our meaning. We seek a positive legacy. In short, *we strive to amount to something*.

Becker says, "The hope and belief is that the things that man creates in society are of lasting worth and meaning, that they outlive or outshine death and decay, that man and his products count."[2]

The nightmare scenario: *Death* remains both certain and permanent while *significance* is not only fleeting, it is ultimately fictional. Our lives are full of attempts to deny death. We build our character and identity upon our 'claim to fame.' We try to attach our worth to something we do or 'someone' we believe we are. This endeavor typically consumes us.

Becker believed that this effort was a necessary exercise for human beings to live in the world. However, this 'immortality project' (as he called it) prevents self-knowledge. We live in denial, hiding in dark shadows throughout our days, avoiding any light of awareness that might uncover the truth we are nothing more than finite beings with an unpredictable destiny. As Shakespeare laments in Macbeth's soliloquy:

> *Tomorrow and tomorrow and tomorrow,*
> *Creeps in this petty pace from day to day*
> *To the last syllable of recorded time,*
> *And all our yesterdays have lighted fools*
> *The way to dusty death. Out, out, brief candle!*
> *Life's but a walking shadow, a poor player*
> *That struts and frets his hour upon the stage*
> *And then is heard no more: it is a tale*
> *Told by an idiot, full of sound and fury,*
> *Signifying nothing.*

In short, whether it is conscious or not, we persist in our self-deception. We ignore the Socratic admonition, "The unexamined life is not worth living." We disregard the hard truth about what makes us tick. We may fool others—but we surely fool ourselves.

---

[2] For additional information on Ernst Becker, please see *www.ernest-becker.com/thedenialofdeath*. Quote taken from the following page: *www.ernest-becker.com/ernest-becker-quotes*.

DESTROYING THREATS TO MEANING BEGETS EVIL

Becker presses the point that *evil* comes from what happens when we *deny our mortality and seek to destroy all threats to what we deem our source for meaning.* Religious wars would certainly fall into this category, but so would the efforts to overturn religion in the name of science.

While Becker may be guilty of dramatizing *the evil that men do* being so heavily influenced as he was by the holocaust, it remains inadequate to offer a summary characterization of his views with no more than a clichéd phrase like *human behavior is selfish and self-seeking.* Indeed, his insight into our underlying motivation begets a genuine breakthrough: we do evil primarily to protect our *immortality project*, our claim to fame. If someone dares to upset what we perceive substantiates our self-worth, we are quick to strike out against any and all such perpetrators. We feel compelled to eliminate such threats because we preserve the basis for life's meaning—it is sacred—nothing stands more important to us whether we are conscious of it or not.

While Becker did not use these exact words, nonetheless they concisely state his position: Our *quest to protect life's meaning becomes the root of our evil.* Perhaps we best administer a self-test:

- What is your most 'cherished' belief giving meaning to your life?
- *What happens when someone challenges this belief?* Are you angry or threatened? Are you quick to strike back?
- *What is the reason for your belief?* Is the foundation of your faith immune to any sort of *proof to the contrary*?

If we are being honest, any contradiction posed to our most treasured belief, if unexamined, constitutes a *flash point*. We will not let the matter go and walk away. We will strike back—no holds barred—to reassure ourselves we *still have it right*. My point being: it is dangerous to ask ourselves why we believe what we do;

but it is even more dangerous *not* to face the possibility our beliefs could be dead wrong.

WOULD GOD REALLY ALLOW US TO DESTROY OURSELVES?

In light of these insights which mirror so much wisdom from many other religions and philosophers through the ages, what should we to make of the phenomenon we call *doomsday*?

If we are like most people, we avoid thinking about it. At some point, however, we may conclude, it is a topic we cannot evade. After all, there is now so much discussion about the threats of war, disease, planetary catastrophe, and wild weather—the apprehension grows daily. *Doomsday remains impossible to ignore.*

Confronted as we are with the realistic possibility of *doomsday,* how should we react? Certainly, we must feel endangered. However, do we easily dismiss this fear? Does doomsday mirror *the denial of death,* since it includes the 'whole-species'? After all, could anything be more shattering to our notion of meaning, if something—no matter how simple or sinister—was to wipe our entire species off the face of the planet?

It quickly becomes apparent our notion of God (is He real or not?) has a lot to do with how we handle our predicament. For those who believe in an infinite creator God, a personal being who broods over his creation, that (as evangelical Christians preach) desires a 'personal relationship with us,' how could we possibly believe God would allow such a thing? Certainly, we base our *shared sense of meaning* upon an overt notion our existence on this planet comprises no accident. Something or someone greater created us— no way would God allow all of life to expire! Surely, He would even overturn our free will if we were hell-bent on destroying the planet (and ourselves). For those of us who believe in the reality of a divine presence in the universe (however we understand *the divine being*), there is little doubt about our conclusion: *Evil will not prevail.* The good guys come out on top.

On the other hand, if we believe God does not exist, perhaps we might sooner come to grips with at least the theoretical possibility that a future cataclysm will end civilization and the entire human species. With the absence of *God as a protector,* there no longer remains any insurance against annihilation—there stands no guardian upon which we can rely—no higher-power exists to watch over us. We are *left to our own devices.*

Some would state stoically, "The sooner we accept this bleak truth, the better off we are." Indeed, many would counsel this constitutes a much more honest way to approach the matter of doomsday. After all, is counting on God's intervention on our behalf that He would prevent us from destroying ourselves—a dishonest, negligent, and even reprehensible position to take? Does not atheism, in this context, demand we take responsibility for our actions far more than relying upon God?

WHEN BAD THINGS HAPPEN TO GOOD PEOPLE

For the moment, suppose we say this is so. The question then arises, "When it comes to whether we should dismiss all meaning to our existence, is the atheist capable of being consistent with his or her own presuppositions?" Can he or she actually get comfortable with the starkness of a universe without God? We ask this question because we know that, despite what we say we believe, at the end of the day we are all very much alike. The quest for meaning comprises part of our makeup just as much as our denial of death; in fact, it remains one and the same.

Just consider how the *unbeliever* acts when tragedy occurs. He might cry out, "Why me?" just like anyone else—when he should remember such questions imply faith in life's purpose—which his stated belief system expressly denies. How can there be *misfortune* if we begin with no guarantees and no destiny? If there is no God to offer explanations, how can we obtain answers? If there are no fates to cause the occurrence, how can we expect a reason to explain it?

When bad things happen to good people, the last person that should be shocked is the atheist. The atheist truly cannot label any catastrophe *a tragedy*. It is what it is. The cry goes out to the stars and the sky, but the universe answers with silence.

That is why atheism stands so inconsistent with humanity's wiring. When calamity strikes, *even the most pessimistic atheist is stunned.* The unbeliever, just like the believer, expects better. The atheist too feels the same initial *sense that there must still be hope*. Accordingly, we should not wonder why the atheist, just like a person of faith, gets upset if something bad happens. The reality is *even the atheist loses his or her equanimity* when an outcome seems brutal or unjust. In our better moments, we all anticipate social justice and positive outcomes. It may only be instinctual in the human 'animal.' Nevertheless, we believe somewhere there *is a guarantor for the good*.

That is why, even for the atheistic materialist, an indisputable aspect of human expectation insists *there is something beyond ourselves*. The reality of this underlying conviction defies even the hard-core atheist to mutter 'so what' at our demise. Our optimism, our *assurance* (which often needs to be *re-assured* by our loved ones, a good book, or an uplifting sermon) remains a part of humanity's essence. Therefore, we build our love and aspirations upon a rock called *meaning*. What happens *does matter*, not just to us, but to *the grand scheme of things*. We want to believe every person deserves a happy ending. We all share this confidence in life's meaning because God planted this impulse within us. It remains *an innate testimony to God's existence* because it inspires our best moments and causes us to seek justice, love, and ultimately the knowledge of Him. I would not go so far as to say this recognition provides 'proof' of God's existence. This 'theorem' does not measure up to Thomas Aquinas' 'unmoved mover' or other cosmological arguments, but it seems a standard human attribute implying God left His thumbprint on our 'inner person.'

WHAT WOULD THE UNIVERSE BE LIKE WITHOUT GOD?

Perhaps paradoxically, and very much on the other hand, we must meditate on the possibility *of a universe without God*. Even the faithful should thoughtfully consider this perspective despite giving appearance to a moment of infidelity.

From this vantage point, the search for *meaning* could indeed be nothing more than a primal delusion to which we all succumb—a survival mechanism we must outgrow. We may all share in a happy but false fantasy about what life means. Perhaps it stands as nothing more than *a diabolical curse* because every day we uncritically quest after fairness and significance. If it consists of nothing more than a diabolical trick, then our best and most noble ambitions are destined to fail.

While our optimism may be nothing more than a deception making life bearable, Becker (and others who consider themselves existentialists), nevertheless insist we squarely face this possibility, however theoretical. The *absurd* could be our lot. Before we seek a way out of this metaphorical dungeon, we should recognize we might not find a doorway.[3] We must consider the distinct possibility we cannot rid ourselves of the malaise of meaninglessness.

As a teenager, I remember a popular expression cast about by many to help keep things in perspective: *Today is the first day of the rest of your life.* This notion was a refreshing way of recognizing we can put our past behind us and start anew. Yet, the abrupt converse of this statement may be better medicine awakening us to our 'existential situation:' *Today could be the last day of our life.*

For believers and unbelievers alike, we do not awaken in the mornings with this thought firmly in mind as we live out each day. If we did, we probably would not get out of bed! However, it does not make the possibility any less stark. The fact remains: a bus

---

[3] Jean Paul Sartre's *No Exit* comes to mind here.

might run over us today or tonight an asteroid could decimate our planet. Either way, our mortal life ends. Our consciousness comes to a halt. Perhaps we can avoid the former by staying at home. However, the latter possibility remains one we can literally do nothing to circumvent.

So how should we deal with such fear? How do we *put doomsday into perspective?*

WHY FAIRY TALES ARE NOT JUST FOR CHILDREN

When they are young, we read fairy tales to our children. But the tales we read today are highly sanitized versions of the old *Grimm's Fairy Tales* (first published in 1810). What we may not realize is just how grim these fairy tales were. The monsters and witches were much darker then, heroes were much more vulnerable, and the deaths of the villains much more gruesome.

Why did our forebears tell such frightful stories to their children? It was not because these parents loved to frighten their kids. We know now it was how parents prepared their children for the reality of the dark world in which they lived. Evil was commonplace. Better to scare them to death early exposing them to the horrors of life, for such things were to be their firsthand experience sooner rather than later. It was in the parent's best judgment this sort of *tough love* was necessary conditioning as part of growing up.

This perspective contrasts so much with our protective methods of child rearing today, perhaps we should ask ourselves a series of questions: "Which generation was right? Should we teach our children evil exists but requires little effort to defeat, that death is easy to cheat? On the other hand, do we help our children understand that death constitutes a part of life? Should they learn evil sometimes wins and disasters occur? What type of reassurance comprises the proper balance between hoping for the best and not being surprised if bad things happen?"

The prayer I used to say at bedtime (like many other baby boomers) included the line, "If I should die before I wake, I pray the Lord my soul to take." As a child, I did not fear death. Nor did this prayer scare me to death either. Somehow knowing God was watching over me, even as I slept, was a comforting thought. We sometimes employ the phrase *whistling in the dark* when we are afraid to face the dire circumstances in our way. What do we mean by this adage? What is the underlying motive for whistling a happy tune while we 'walk about' fearing what might come next?

In essence, our whistling *normalizes* the situation; it makes our circumstances less imposing. Sometimes psychiatrists will describe this phenomenon as *minimizing* whatever threat disrupts our normal course of life. You know the familiar phrase, "The bigger they are the harder they fall." We may not believe it. Nonetheless, by invoking this phrase sincerely, we muster the courage to face our enemies.

My family did this so very well it took me many years to learn how to deal with death and suffering. Our approach was to laugh it off or get things back to normal as quickly as we could. We might typically say something like "Oh, it's no big deal." We would avoid the possibility the worse could happen and that we might be unable to cope. Instead of learning to square up to bad times and face the music, it was our habit to escape the pain. This failure to come to terms with tragedy and suffering almost ended my marriage 30 years ago when my father-in-law died from Lou Gehrig's disease (ALS) and I could not relate to my wife's feelings as she watched her father's health disintegrate before her eyes.

HOW TO COPE WITH THE INEVITABILITY OF DOOMSDAY

My supposition is this: we have two essential methods of dealing with death from doomsday—one healthy, the other, *not so much*. These are deep-seated human techniques to cope with drastic situations.

Method One: *Recognize that the cataclysm not only* **can** *happen, it stands inevitable.* Furthermore, our encounter may be immediately ahead. We may embrace it and calculate how we should live our lives in its light. We may make our meaning no longer contingent upon the denial of mortality and our particular and cherished plan for self-worth. We may recognize we are finite beings who trusts our value secured *only after* it is linked to something much bigger than us. In the case of those in the Judeo-Christian tradition, we may connect who we are and what our life means *to God*, whose infinite status assures our value. He is our point of reference. In other words, *we have meaning because God tells us we mean something to Him.* Moreover, the proof is in His promise—our lives are so valuable He will transform them—making them fit for eternity. As the evangelical intellectual Francis Schaeffer asserted: *Finite beings have meaning only if they have an infinite point of reference.*

Method Two: *Find ways to reduce the potential for doomsday.* Our culture, now more than ever, obsesses over *the end of days*. Doomsday captivates us. Our popular culture provides examples galore. So then, as a culture, do we *really* deny doomsday? It seems—at least on the surface—that nothing could be further from the truth. Sometimes though things are not what they seem.

In our defense, we insist we are taking action. We seek to dispel the worry and the gloom of doom. We read books. We go to movies. However, our captivation appears much more akin to *whistling in the dark* than assimilating frightening images medicinally *through the fairy tale*. We encounter the darkness to reassure ourselves it is not a menacing presence after all. We vaccinate ourselves with just enough of what could happen to comfort ourselves that it will not. It simply remains too fantastic after all—so out of the question—why would we lose any sleep over it? We venture out to a movie and watch the world end in the best special effects ever. After all, it is *only a movie*. The sun will rise again tomorrow. Life will go on.

If the reader accepts my contention as true, what does the doctor prescribe? Simply this: It is best to acknowledge the end can happen *at any moment*. We may realize our worst fears. We should not deny it. We should embrace it. This does not mean we have to rejoice in it. But we best acknowledge its reality. Even if we cling, I believe rightly, to faith as our means to overcome anxiety and to resolve what may otherwise appear absurd, it remains wise to recognize the dilemma in which we find ourselves. Once we appreciate our *existential* condition, we live a far more authentic life. Even from the perspective of the most pious and stalwart Christian, before any of us can fully appreciate *the salvation message*, we should fully understand *our predicament if we did not have God's gift of salvation*.

Who has not experienced a *narrow escape*, when someone you loved nearly 'bought the farm?' Perhaps it was a spouse. Perhaps it was a child. When we finally realize our loved one is okay, this resolution quiets our worst fears. Yet, we still never quite forget the feeling of *dread* we just experienced. Being grateful, we may be forever changed. Living in light of that experience reminds us to keep our eyes wide open, be a bit more cautious, and take extra pains to protect those we love. After this happens, if we fail to appreciate this impact, we have wasted what the calamity sought to teach us. A wise person once said: "Pagans waste their pains"—which comprises a statement of concise conviction that something or someone greater than ourselves was teaching us a lesson we must learn. Nietzsche scolded his readers for not recognizing *all progress comes through pain*. Seeking only pleasure as a cherished goal in life is a death knell for personal growth and meaning.

LIKE NOAH, WE MUST PREPARE FOR THE RAINY DAY

The 'conventionally wise' wonder why people like 'prophecy buffs' believe doomsday constitutes a historical inevitability and is more than a myth. We can imagine those folk casting aspersions along the lines of: "Why are you so consumed with such bleak prognostications? Why don't you look on the bright side?"

Our response could be simply, "Because we have to face facts. And the fact is sooner or later, whether you listen to science or to the Bible, one manner of doomsday or another is inevitable." Like Becker and other existentialists who proposed that death is the inescapable destiny which awakens us to reality—teaching us how to live—doomsday exists as an unavoidable reality causing humanity to come to grips with our limits and what actions we must take *now*. Some disasters we can avoid altogether while others we can do little more than reduce their effects. But who disagrees with the admonition that it is better to be prepared than to live blithely as if nothing like doomsday could ever happen, even if it is only 'regional', i.e., in our neck of the woods?

Noah was a unique person. He was told by God that doomsday was coming. What is more, he was told specifically what he must do in order to assure his family (and all land creatures from lambs to lions) would survive doomsday. We can imagine how believing in doomsday would cause his contemporaries to laugh him to scorn for such a crazy thought. How much more would they scoff at him for building a boat miles from an ocean? And yet, he knew doomsday was inevitable; God had told him so. While everyone else continued on, living life as usual, eating and drinking (thinking short-term), marrying and giving in marriage (thinking long-term), Noah and his sons were preparing for the end of the world. Clearly, in a very unique way, doomsday gave Noah purpose and meaning.

Today, we know there are many types of regional and even global catastrophes science can prove have precedent. There are also warnings about future wars we read plainly in the Bible. Will we be like Noah who took extraordinary measures to be prepared or like his neighbors who gathered just to jeer him? God may not be asking us to build an ark; nonetheless He implores us to prepare ourselves and those we love for the inevitable. Perhaps we should adapt the prayer of theologian Reinhold Niebuhr, made famous by Alcoholics Anonymous:

God grant us the serenity to preempt those catastrophes we can, prepare ourselves for the calamities we are helpless to deflect, and the wisdom to know the difference.

13: LINKING OUR ORIGIN TO OUR DESTINY

Knowing this first, that there shall come in the last days scoffers, walking after their own lusts, and saying, "Where is the promise of his coming? For since the fathers fell asleep, all things continue as they were from the beginning of the creation." For this they willingly are ignorant of, that by the word of God the heavens were of old, and the earth standing out of the water and in the water: Whereby the world that then was, being overflowed with water, perished.
(2 Peter 3:3-6)

STEP BY STEP, OUR LIVES SHOWCASE A GRAND DESIGN

WHEREVER WE ARE ON THE ROAD OF OUR LIFE, WE DID NOT JUST APPEAR WHERE WE FIND OURSELVES WITHOUT TAKING A SERIES OF OTHER HIGHWAYS TO GET US HERE. FIRST WE take one road. Then we take another. We make choices. Sometimes we are puzzled and ask ourselves, "How did I wind up here?" But memories serve as breadcrumbs lying in the paths taken, marking the trail we chose along the way. Another way to express this observation: Our lives are like steps on a vast stairway. Each day comprises one step. Where we are now results from the many steps taken to arrive at our destination.

How we explain 'who we are' begins with where we started out. Who I am today results of a collection of people I have known, events I have experienced, lessons I have learned, and decisions I have made. It is a combination of what is happened to me and how I have reacted to those myriad events each and every day.

Surely whoever we are at this moment results from many such matters. Like stones placed on the exterior wall of a giant house, each stone is placed precisely one at a time. Unlike bricks, each stone is unique and has to fit exactly with all the others in a very specific way. Fitting the stones together takes creativity. To build a good looking house takes a master mason to perform the stonework, someone who knows exactly what he or she is doing.

The nutritionist says, "You are what you eat." The existentialist says, "You are what you do." A Christian should say, "I am what God enables me to become."

For those who believe in the providence of God, without denying our personal responsibility, we believe somehow God constitutes that expert mason, placing the stones we call 'life events' in exactly the right spot, considering carefully the shape of every stone, so that once the house stands complete, it looks *smart*; it evinces a grand design. Undoubtedly, we want our lives to appear like that when the 'mason' puts the last stone of our life in its place.

A LIFE WELL-LIVED LIVES ON IN THE LIVES OF OTHERS

When I spoke at my mother's funeral a few years ago, I quoted a particular saying that she loved. It was a simple verse. I once employed my gift of calligraphy to 'engross' it upon parchment. The verse was, "What I am is God's gift to me; what I become is my gift to God." Being artistic and eager to make a few dollars for my work, I became quite adept at practicing the art of the medieval monks. When I was a teenager, folks knew me as an artist.

At the funeral, I talked about the influence of my mom, how she contributed to the person I then was. Despite my mom's idiosyncrasies (some of them not so charming), she loved her kids and cared for us as only a loving mother could (indeed, sometimes maybe too much!) At the service my main point was that how we influence others comprises a 'gift that keeps on giving.' A life well-lived lives on, continuing its influence in the world through the lives of those so enriched by the life now past—others who continue the journey. It may seem a rather obvious tribute to the person eulogized. And yet, it remains an awesome thought: We affect the world long after we are no longer walking on this earth. The footprints we make are not easily washed away. May those footprints we have left, the impressions we made while on this earth and the minds of those who knew us, become footsteps others seek to follow for guidance and stability.

As I have reflected on that service afterwards, and what I related to the audience, I realized I had never felt prouder of anything I have ever said in a public forum. I still feel that way today. Perhaps someone will find something inspirational to say about me that profoundly affects attendees in a transformational way at my funeral. I can only hope!

Decoding prophecy involves a paradox: to learn about our future we must study our past. Whether we search ancient sources of wisdom or study megalithic monuments holding hidden meanings, both archeology and written history hold the key to *eschatology*.[1] In our personal lives, the same dynamic holds true. We can fathom our future only after we meditate on the meaning of previous life lessons. *We learn more about what our future holds, as our understanding of our past grows.*

As we have discussed, for many reasons Christians believe that prophetic studies are vital. Part of this intensity stems from the knowledge that *the world in which we live will soon be rehabilitated.* This transformation will be massive and life-changing. This appears to be especially so for those who anticipate the new world.

However, in this chapter I may astonish many readers because, on the surface, my method relies upon the past to tell us how the world will be transformed *in the future.* I venture some readers will

---

[1] From *eschaton* in the Greek, meaning the study of 'last things.'

be astounded by what I share regarding how our world *was destroyed and then recreated in the aeon past,* preparing for this *epoch of humankind.* The reason the topic proves so relevant relates to the verse from 2 Peter quoted as the epigraph for this chapter. The connection: to properly appreciate what will happen on the earth *after* Christ returns, we must comprehend what really happened to our world *before* Adam was created 'from the dust of the earth' by Elohim, the Creator.

THE CONTROVERSIAL BOOK OF SECOND PETER

Many scholars consider the New Testament book of 2 Peter the most controversial book in the Bible. Bible critics doubt its authenticity. Aspects of the book seem to draw upon sources that are unique to its message. That is, a few of its passages appear to have no canonical precedent elsewhere. My personal position: it contains some of the most intriguing and 'hidden' insights into the nature of the world, the cosmos, and what will happen in the millennium ahead. To gain such insights, the author must have experienced direct and special revelation from God. Following Christian convention, such revelation was uniquely given to Christ's Apostles. Besides, since the book possesses a claim to be written by Peter and its author testifies it is his second epistle, I readily side with tradition and ascribe it to Peter.

At the base of what many assume to be my gullibility comprises a principle I hold to be trustworthy: It remains difficult to give credence to a work written under a 'pen name' (i.e., a pseudonym).[2] Ultimate matters are made more sure when the author

---

[2] Of course, higher criticism suggests all the books of the Bible, except about half of Paul's letters, were not written by the authors as claimed by tradition. In liberal theology, it's fashionable to allow fraudulent claims, just because some ancient writers did this in order to impress and influence their audiences to 'heed what the authors wrote.' Since the liberal perspective believes spiritual truth constitutes 'views' and not 'news,' for liberal theologians it does not really matter who spoke them.

does not mislead his audience about who is responsible for the ideas contained within.

The passage cited above from 2 Peter makes little sense until we understand that Peter disputes the notion *that the world today remains the same as the world has always been.* Peter implies that what we see—the form of the world as we observe it—is *not* because of the current and 'standard' processes we normally perceive all about us. Dramatic, indeed radical events outside of the norm fashioned the world in which we now live. Peter provides a startling analogy. Once we understand his intended meaning, it becomes a powerful argument for rethinking why our world 'takes the shape that it does.' In short, it dramatically alters what many typically believe the first chapter of Genesis teaches. Additionally, it opens the door to a completely different *cosmology*—including a proof that future changes are all the more likely than what we would have guessed *if* we did not have this spectacular insight.

SEEING THE WORLD IN A FAR DIFFERENT LIGHT

While it remains quite common to doubt our world is subject to radical change in the future, Peter wants us to realize this 'time-bound' outlook is wrong. We may assume that 'nothing new ever happens around here'—but in actuality, something categorically different did happen at select times in the past. In short: the truth regarding the nature of our earth, our solar system, and our universe constitutes a far different world than what we suppose.

Peter's argument, reduced to its most basic form, seems rather simple: "Because the world has been dramatically transformed once before, it can and will be radically altered again in the future." Peter indicates that scoffers base their doubt regarding Christ's return because of their common everyday observations. They are strict empiricists—they believe we acquire all knowledge through sense perception only.³ The guiding rule could be stated with the following sentiment: "If I have never seen it happen before, it certainly will not happen that way today." This dubious but standard day-to-day perspective lies behind the denial regarding the Bible's teaching concerning the world to come. That is, repudiating Christ's Second Coming begins with the wrongheaded opinion that the principles we see in operation today are exactly the same as they have been for millions of years gone by—and the way they will be for millions of years to come.

In geology, we call this the principle of 'uniformity.' This principle assumes the processes we witness today (slow and incremental), are the same processes that go back to 'time immemorial.' Peter argues how holding this view begets a fabricated understanding of the way the world came to be. He teaches the world in which we live has gone through at least one dramatic *re-creation* and will go through another re-creation after Christ returns. This geologic principle we know as 'catastrophism.' It stands in stark contrast to the empirical heuristic. While often mocked throughout the twentieth century as a result of science's embrace of Darwinism (from the standpoint as a *theory of origins*), by referencing recent scientific discoveries⁴ we now know there have been many enormous global cataclysms. From caldera eruptions to comet collisions, our world has experienced far more catastrophes than we once thought. Disasters have shaped our world and will continue to shape it in the future. Succinctly put: *what we witness as first-hand observers today does not tell us how we got to where we are now or where we are going next*. That comprises the essence of Peter's perspective. So what does Peter actually mean regarding the nature of how the present world came about?

---

³ In philosophy, this perspective is called *positivism*. As the world progresses toward spiritualism (an occult view), positivism is becoming passé. This is discussed in the classic, *The Morning of the Magicians* by Pauwels and Bergier.

⁴ Most of these discoveries have occurred in the past two decades.

IN THE BEGINNING, GOD CREATED. BUT THEN...

The stunning truth many classic Bible scholars teach us[5] is that the Bible does not begin with 'today's creation'—the world as we know it—that is as it originated in Genesis 1:1. True, in the beginning God made the heavens and the earth. However, the next verse assumes something happened after verse one and before verse two. Thus, the creation of the world as-we-know-it today begins *in Genesis 1:2*.

What was this 'in-between' event? The whole of creation (or at least our solar system so some scholars suspect) became *chaos*. Unlike the gnostic and Greek notion, it did not start out that way. But something happened causing things to go haywire. Therefore, God's creating in Genesis 1:2 constitutes a rectification of this chaos. It was literally, a '*re*-creation.'

The Bible through Moses (with God as the real author), wants us to recognize that God created the heavens and the earth (Genesis 1:1). But between Genesis 1:1 and Genesis 1:2 there was a gap of time in which violent things happened. Once we respect the entirety of Scripture's teaching, we discover this startling fact.

A straightforward summary of this biblical cosmological theory, known as 'Gap Theory' (or alternatively the '*Ruin and Restoration Theory*') can be found on Wikipedia.[6]

I paraphrase it here:

- The earth existed before the six days that began in Genesis 1:3. Its form and its inhabitants are not fully understood, but the fossil record and artifacts that date hundreds of thousands or millions of years tell us the earth is ancient.

---

[5] Such scholars would include Clarence Larkin, J.N. Darby, and G.H. Pember and most 'dispensational' theologians of the twentieth century.

[6] See http://en.wikipedia.org/ wiki/Gap_Theory.

- God is perfect and everything He does is perfect, so a newly created earth from the hand of God should *not* have been 'without form and void'—and shrouded in darkness. (See Deuteronomy 32:4, Isaiah 45:18 1 John 1:5) To be precise, it was not created first as chaos and then subsequently put into its present order.

- The Holy Spirit was "renewing" the face of the earth as He hovered over the face of the waters. (See Psalms 104:30)

- Angels already existed in a state of grace when God "laid the foundations of the Earth", so there had been at least one creative act of God before the six days of Genesis. (See Job 38:4-7)

- Satan had fallen from grace sometime after the initial creation but before the chaos mentioned in Genesis 1:2, which, since the serpent tempted Adam and Eve, had to have occurred before the 'fall' of humankind. (See Isaiah 14:12-15, Ezekiel 28:11-19, John 8:44)

Consequently, Genesis 1:2 was mistranslated and thereafter, has been generally misunderstood. In the King James Version (and essentially most other versions echo the King James), we "The earth was without form and void." But by taking it one-word-at-a-time and looking carefully at the Hebrew, the correct translation appears much more likely to be as follows: "But the earth *became* chaotic and a wasteland."[7] The Hebrew transliterated reads *tohu va bohu*. Another article in Wikipedia addressing this specific language deepens the important implications with these words:

---

[7] I have studied several books, pro and con, on this theory before committing to my position. Perhaps the best treatment is by Arthur C. Custance, *Without Form and Void*. It is, however, a highly technical study in Hebrew grammar pertaining to the Genesis account. A much simpler study was written by Finis Dake: *Another Time, Another Place, Another Man*. Dake's book was written almost 50 years ago but is still relevant and useful. A much more recent study takes up the subject in light of what may be discovered in the way of *artifacts beyond the earth* (demonstrating that intelligent life has existed elsewhere, and the age of the solar system proves to be quite ancient). See Allan Cornford, *Genesis and the Rahab Conspiracy* for a well-written and carefully crafted 'Bible study' should such disclosure of 'alien' artifacts on other spheres in our solar system come to light.

There is evidence that the sentence "And the earth was without form and void" (tohu v'bohu) indicates destruction, not simply primitive creation. This phrase is rendered more strongly elsewhere (i.e., in other ancient versions). For example, the Chaldee Version has "But the earth had become desert and empty," the Septuagint has "But the earth had become unfurnished and empty," and the Aramaic has "And the earth had become ruined and uninhabited."[8]

FIGURE 26 - THE BAALBEK MEGALITHS

Now that language conveys a meaning quite different from the standard perspective. Apparently, something happened which caused the world to be corrupted and turned into a chaotic mess. We do not know exactly what ensued. Most scholars who subscribe to this interpretation of Genesis believe that it was the rebellion of Lucifer which caused the world to become a wasteland.

---

[8] See http://en.wikipedia.org/wiki/Tohu_wa-bohu.

There are many unanswered questions arising from this explanation of Genesis 1:2. This viewpoint, however, also offers some satisfying solutions to challenges often posed to Bible believers.

HOMO SAPIENS PRIOR TO ADAM AND EVE?

G.H. Pember in his classic work, *Earth's Earliest Ages*, digs deep into the Bible's language to draw out these amazing truths buried in the original wording of the Scripture. Pember argues, I think correctly, that the fossil record and many artifacts of intelligent life dating perhaps ten thousand or more years in the past are not necessarily from the current 'epoch' of humankind. They date

FIGURE 27 - THE RUINS OF PUMA PUNKU

from before the time of Adam's creation and the 'six days' of Genesis chapter 1. We learn that there is also a Hebrew tradition from the Targum (an Aramaic version of the Bible and related 'commentaries' written during the Second Temple period (beginning roughly 400 BC and lasting until the Middle Ages), that a 'pre-Adamite' race of humanoids existed. And their view was not alone among the ancients. Other distant cultures possessed myths supporting the same interpretation.

For instance, artifacts such as the ruins of Baalbek in Lebanon or Puma Punku in Bolivia, which may date from 10,000 to 15,000 BC, have been adduced by ancient astronaut theorists to prove 'extraterrestrials' have been here and were misunderstood by early humanoids to be deities.9 Pember would agree such relics and monuments attest to the presence of another form of intelligent life pre-dating the re-creation of the world and Adam's origination. One possible interpretation of the data suggests another form of Homo sapiens existed with many of the same intelligent properties that *'Homo sapiens sapiens'* possess but without the *'imago dei' (God's image)* placed within Adam.

Such predecessors to Adam would be reflected in the fossil record we attempt to decipher today. Likewise, cave art that dates from perhaps 35,000 BC forward, as well as other 'Stone Age' artifacts indicate a 'naked ape' with expansive capabilities but not the full equivalent of today's human being. This seems implicit in the twentieth century scholar Finis Dake's work entitled *Another Place, Another Time, Another Man* (emphasis added) Indeed, one of the great puzzles of anthropology remains, "Why have we witnessed civilization only in the past 6,000 years when scientists assume that the intrinsic capabilities of humankind (brain capacity primarily) have not changed appreciably in the past 200,000 years?" Civilization came into being with a sudden explosion precisely at the time the Bible indicates the Lord God created Adam and his progeny, roughly six millennia ago.

---

9 The working theory among many who write today on these subjects suppose that an angelic incursion in which 'the Sons of God' came into the daughters of men, and created a hybrid race, drawing upon he premise of Genesis 6:4. This Pre-Adamic race would be understood to be like the Nephilim which came about after Adam was created but before the Flood of Noah.

The 'Gap Theory' as described here may present a plausible explanation (this is speculation on my part). When God created Adam, an additional capacity was added. This quality caused humankind to behave differently, eventually giving rise to civilization. It also made God directly knowable to human beings. The Bible does not tell us this—it is speculation, but educated speculation building upon numerous biblical facts.

Therefore, it appears possible that a different form of life lived on the earth contemporary to 'pre-Adamite' humanoids. We do not know if these other life forms were angelic or some form of hybrid race; but what we do know is that God began with the current 'human family' in Genesis 1:2 and the verses that follow, moving forward from there.

It is in this act of 'recreating the world' (after a massive calamity left the earth 'without form and void—literally chaotic') where the Spirit of God hovered over the waters that covered the world, and set about to bring life back to the earth. In this process, Elohim assigned new roles for the sun, moon, and stars (for days, months, years, and for signs) where the first Adam (as Paul refers to him in Romans 5) came into being and where 'our story,' the tale of humanity actually began. [10]

INTELLIGENT DESIGN AND OTHER CREATION THEORIES

The Gap Theory of Creation does not necessarily conflict with *intelligent design,* today's most popular and biblical response to Darwinism. Principles exist within the universe, which testify that creation was designed with 'life on earth (and maybe *elsewhere!*) in mind.' Proponents call it *the anthropic principle.*

---

[10] See my most recent book *Lying Wonders of the Red Planet,* for a detailed discussion of the theory that intelligent beings once existed on Mars (and possibly on the Moon!) In that book I recap the groundbreaking work of the late David Flynn whose research provides a strong argument that the Bible supports a now defunct angelic civilization in our solar system (and probably upon the earth) *prior* to Adam.

Young Earth Creationism as well as the so-called Gap Theory both assume this principle to be true. Even the hybrid theory labeled *theistic evolution* would see much in the anthropic principle to applaud. Also known as *directed evolution* some evangelicals and most liberal Jewish and Christian theologians espouse this perspective.[11] Implicit within the anthropic principle are scores of purely scientific data arguing God created the universe to sustain life. Without His creating the world based upon these principles, life as we know it could never have happened.

However, we must recognize that *so-called Young Earth Creationism (YEC)* conflicts with 'Gap Creationism.' This former creationism held by William Jennings Bryan in the Scopes Monkey Trial (who faced Clarence Darrow) asserts that the world and the universe are no older than Adam. Creationists assert that the earth was created with an appearance of age; and it is only 6,000 years old (or perhaps as old as 10,000 years, assuming that the chronologies of the Old Testament are not meant to be fully inclusive of every generation). Creationists contend scientific dating methods like 'Carbon-14' (and about 40 others) are not reliable. Consequently, YEC cannot accept the earth's actual age to be billions of years as science postulates. If Creationism is your view, I do not wish to fuss about whether you are right or wrong. However, I side with the 'Gap theorists' because I believe it better fits 'the facts' of what we find buried within the earth and yet, still allows upholding the infallibility and authority of the Bible. The issue remains succinctly, *what does the Bible teach?* In my opinion Genesis 1:2 is better translated in accordance with Gap Theory.

Some protest that Gap Theory comprises an accommodation to modernity and science (although we find it in many writings of

---

[11] This view suggests that God worked through evolution; there is continuity from ancient times to the present. Most evangelicals would object for a variety of reasons, believing science as well as biblical teaching are at odds with this notion.

Christian scholars throughout the last 2,000 year period—not just since the time of Darwin). Those who promote a rigid or strict Creationism maintain adhering to a 'young earth' amounts to a test of orthodoxy. I disagree: the Bible can be interpreted either way; it most certainly does not constitute a test of orthodoxy. There simply is insufficient detail in what the Bible tells us about the timing of our origins to be dogmatic.[12]

NOT ONE FLOOD IN THE BIBLE, BUT TWO

Another interpretative mistake that is generally made about the passage in 2 Peter: misunderstanding Peter's meaning regarding the "waters." We assume the overflowing of water discussed in 2 Peter relates to the flood of Noah. But this does not follow from the context of his argument. Instead, what Peter reveals is that God created the heavens and earth, but then (without explanation) the world was overflowed with water and life subsequently perished. The world became a chaotic wasteland. Like the title of the famous but failed Kevin Costner movie, it became a 'water world.' God had to *recreate* (restore) the world to make it capable of sustaining life once again. This suggests that there have been *two* global floods. That is, thousands of years before the Flood of Noah, another flood encompassed the earth. The flood of Noah constitutes a much more recent catastrophe.

Recall that evangelical scholars (who rely upon Bishop Ussher's calculations from the genealogy of Genesis), establish the date of Noah's flood at 2348 BC. The prior flood was at least 2,000 years

---

[12] Even if we treat the account of Genesis as a 'mythical' story which affirms only that humankind is a special creation of God, I could still base my faith on that position. But the emphasis must be on (1) 'special creation of God' and that (2) humankind possesses the image of God in a unique way unlike any other creature that the LORD God made. The story tells us that humankind held a unique place in the world and communicates with God unlike any other creature in the Garden. There is a very special 'connection' between Adam and God. Of course, I do not treat it mythically.

before that time, and logically would have been even further back in the 'annals of time.'

What caused the first flood? Authors like Pember and Dake concluded it was the rebellion of Lucifer aka Satan. Dake discusses a passage from Isaiah and the part that 'the son of the morning' played in the destruction of the prior 'aeon' (properly translated as *age* and not *world*):

> Turning the pages of Isaiah, we find a prophecy concerning the king of Babylon in the fourteenth chapter. At first, the text is referred to as a "proverb against the king of Babylon" (Isa. 14:4). As we study this passage, however, we find several statements which cannot possibly be made of an earthly king. These verses are generally accepted as referring to the fall of Lucifer:
>
>> *How art thou fallen from heaven, O Lucifer, son of the morning! How art thou cut down to the ground, which didst weaken the nations! For thou hast said in thine heart, I will ascend into heaven, I will exalt my throne above the stars of God: I will sit also upon the mount of the congregation, in the sides of the north: I will ascend above the heights of the clouds; I will be like the most High.* (Isa. 14:12-14)[13]

Dake provides this commentary:

> Through Isaiah's eyes we can peer down the corridor of time and see fragments of history that took place before Adam was formed. Angels walked the earth in the purity of holiness as each did the will of his Creator. Lucifer, an angel created by God, was given widespread authority and power. His position and influence were such that the archangels themselves were hesitant to confront Lucifer under their own authority.[14]

---

[13] Dake, Finis (2011-01-06). *Another Time...Another Place...Another Man* (Kindle Locations 420-426). Dake Publishing, Inc.. Kindle Edition.

[14] Ibid., Kindle Locations 435-438.

Dake continues to make his perspective perfectly plain:

> It seems clear that Lucifer must have held a position of rulership second only to God Himself. In this passage Isaiah portrays Lucifer's exalted status prior to his fall through rebellion. Writing under the inspiration of the Holy Spirit, Isaiah records that Lucifer had a throne, obviously signifying rulership or kingship. Likewise, rulership implies subjects to rule. Furthermore, since Lucifer was charged with weakening the nations, *there must have been nations in existence for him to weaken.* In the sense of a visible, personal rule on earth, Lucifer had no kingdom at the time of Adam's creation and hasn't had one since; he has only ruled through others since Adam's day. *Therefore, Isaiah's prophecy must refer to a time before Adam.* Isaiah declares that *Lucifer's kingdom was on earth.* "I will ascend above the heights of the clouds," Lucifer boasts in verse fourteen. How could he have attempted to ascend above the clouds and stars and into heaven itself if he already lived in heaven? Why would this kind of language be used, if not to *emphasize Lucifer's earthly position* prior to his rebellion against God? [Emphasis added][15]

SCOFFERS UNDERSTAND NOTHING ABOUT EITHER AGE

Peter's commentary (in my interpretation and those of the authors I have cited) reinforces the 'Gap' concept and, as stated above, employs this understanding as an analogy to *undercut the arguments of scoffers who claim the promise of the Second Coming is preposterous.*

> *Knowing this first, that there shall come in the last days scoffers, walking after their own lusts, and saying, "Where is the promise of his coming? For since the fathers fell asleep, all things continue as they were from* **the beginning of the creation**." *For this they willingly are ignorant of, that by the word of God the heavens were of old, and the earth standing out of the water and in the water:*

---

[15] Ibid., Kindle Locations 441-449.

Whereby the world that then was, being overflowed with water, perished. (2 Peter 3:3-6, emphasis added)

Note the context of Peter's argument. Scoffers say all things are the same as they have been since *the beginning of the creation*—not since the deluge that destroyed life (aka Noah's flood). We can make this point because it is highly likely that the memory of the global flood was ubiquitous—everyone assumed that this had occurred. But a flood that took place prior? A 'water world' from which God had to restore the earth to make it habitable? That was something that many schooled in the Scripture would believe, while the unlearned would not necessarily acknowledge.

In essence, Peter says to his readers, "Why pay attention to scoffers who base their point of view on a fallacious understanding of the creation. Because they do not understand how we got here, why should we care if they scoff about our where we are going? They base their understanding upon what they see. As such, they are without insight from God's revelation. Since they do not understand the past. How can they predict the future?" Peter's argument emphasizes God *intervenes* in space-time. Unlike the Gnostic notion that matter is too evil for God to handle directly, God 'touches' the material world. He directly alters the world we see.[16]

The issue we must consider, and in my opinion what the Bible teaches, is that the *aeon (epoch or age) of humankind* may be only a small, yet paramount parenthetical time period in an otherwise vast period of earth history.

Might the earth be 4.5 billion years old? Yes it might, just as secular science says. But the context of the creation account in Genesis may only be referring to the past 10,000 to 15,000 years (or

---

[16] Of course, this is also why Gnostics could never accept a true incarnation (God becoming flesh), because flesh, being matter, is evil.

less, perhaps only 6,000 years) of that immense timespan. If we accept that the Bible's interest consists of only *this final epoch* (from the moment of the 're-creation' of our world to the time Christ returns and restores the earth to a redeemed state), Peter asserts it makes the promise of His coming *even more certain*. God has intervened supernaturally twice before in a global and dramatic way to change the course of life on this planet. He can and will do so again.

Therefore, to comprehend the end of this age, we must correctly 'reckon' its beginning. Understanding the surprising if not astounding origin of life on this earth makes our incredible destiny of a new heaven and new earth all the more plausible.

14: SEEKING THE IDENTITY OF ANTICHRIST

Let no man deceive you by any means: for that day [the Day of the LORD] shall not come, except there come a falling away first, and that man of sin be revealed, the son of perdition; Who opposeth and exalteth himself above all that is called God, or that is worshipped; so that he as God sitteth in the temple of God, shewing himself that he is God. Remember ye not, that, when I was yet with you, I told you these things? And now ye know what withholdeth that he might be revealed in his time.

For the mystery of iniquity doth already work: only he who now letteth will let, until he be taken out of the way. And then shall that Wicked be revealed, whom the Lord shall consume with the spirit of his mouth, and shall destroy with the brightness of his coming: Even him, whose coming is after the working of Satan with all power and signs and lying wonders...
(2 Thessalonians 2:3-9)

LOOKING OUT FOR THE ANTICHRIST

NO PROPHETIC TOPIC COMPRISES THE SUBJECT OF MORE BOOKS, BOTH SCHOLARLY AND SENSATIONAL, THAN THE ISSUE OF "WHO IS THE ANTICHRIST?" LIKEWISE, THERE IS NO MATTER MORE inclined to generate debate and speculation than the issue of, "How we can identify the 'Man of Sin?'" Movies have had a field day with the issue. We think of the 1960's cultural phenomenon *Rosemary's Baby* or the popular horror picture *The Omen* and its various sequels.

Virtually every author who writes on the subject of the Antichrist offers extensive analysis on the matter—many even going so far as to name names. It stands as a matter of fact that the Bible nowhere instructs us to keep on the lookout for the Antichrist. However, for many who study biblical prophecy, we dive into this search with both feet.

Why do we do it? After all, is keeping an eye peeled for the 'Devil's Man of the Hour' really a good idea? Why do we appear to have no *misgivings* in doing so? Are we who call ourselves Christians *to watch for the Antichrist instead of Jesus Christ?*

Although the Bible explicitly directs us otherwise, nonetheless, many are swayed by curiosity and 'calculating the number of his name.' Indeed, logic drives the quest. We reason that once we detect the signs of the Antichrist—drawing a bead on his identity— the return of Jesus Christ *must then be even more proximate.* "Spotting the Antichrist" promises an early warning of Christ's return—that is, if you believe the rapture of the Church happens *before the Antichrist appears*. Since a slight majority of evangelicals believe this to be the case (the rapture comes first), it seems to be why many are obsessed with this hunt for the man of sin.

HOW THE TIMING OF ANTICHRIST AFFECTS OUR WATCH

To flesh out the argument more precisely:

1. In the passage of 2 Thessalonians, Paul leverages the connection between the appearance of Antichrist and timing of the Day of the LORD, drawing a crucial conclusion regarding the order of these events. Paul describes the initial act of Antichrist to be "exalting himself above all that is called God, or that is worshipped." This action is 'officially' known as the 'Abomination of Desolation' as depicted by Jesus and before Him, as predicted by Daniel the Prophet (Matthew 25:15; Daniel 9:27). Antichrist declares his divinity inside God's Temple (most likely in the holiest place, known as the 'Holy of Holies,' where the Ark of the Covenant—and on its top, the Mercy Seat—was placed in Solomon's ancient Temple). Antichrist's declaration constitutes 'an abomination.' Thus, his declaration desecrates the Holy of Holies.

2. Going to the 'top of Paul's argument' (verses 3 and 4), Paul indicates that 'the Day of the LORD' cannot precede the Abomination of Desolation. The Abomination of Desolation comes before the Day of the Lord. Because the Day of the LORD is specifically a time of judgment when God directs His wrath toward the unrepentant world, Paul wants to make it clear that the Antichrist reveals himself *before* God releases His judgments. Subsequent to Antichrist's revealing (remember the 'apokalyptō discussion' from earlier in this book), the judgments of the 'Trumpets' and the 'Vials' commence. We know this revealing of Antichrist happens exactly half-way through the Seventieth Week of Daniel (see Daniel 9:24-27), kicking off the Great Tribulation. Therefore, the world

FIGURE 28 - DRS. STRANGELOVE AND KISSINGER

does not experience God's wrath until sometime in the latter portion of the final seven-year period leading up to Christ's return.

3. Because Christians are to be saved from God's wrath and the inference is that the judgments of the Great Tribulation qualifies as the *wrath from which we are saved* (we take this up in detail in a

subsequent chapter), then logically, the rapture of the Church must happen *before* Antichrist reveals himself.[1]

4. Given it comprises a logical syllogism, the thinking flows this way: (1) If we see signs the Antichrist will soon be revealed; and (2) we believe the Coming of Christ for His Church must happen sometime before Antichrist appears; then (3) Christ's advent must be VERY SOON indeed.

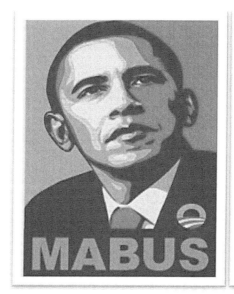 

FIGURE 29 – BARAK OBAMA AS MABUS; RAY MABUS, SECRETARY OF THE NAVY

Being a student of prophetic subjects for over 40 years, I have studied strong arguments for many Antichrist candidates. At one time, Henry Kissinger appeared to be the odds-on favorite. The movie, *Dr. Strangelove* strengthened His standing since the good

---

[1] Pre-wrath advocates argue, 'No, the Rapture can happen after Antichrist is revealed, but it absolutely must happen before God's wrath commences.' Since the *Trumpets* and *Vials* may not take place until later in the final portion of the *Great Tribulation*, i.e., later in the final 3.5 years, the rapture may finally occur with only a few months remaining in the Seventieth Week—according to Pre-Wrath advocates. My stance, of course, remains that the rapture occurs before the Tribulation begins.

doctor had a not-so-hidden resemblance to Henry Kissinger. Supposedly, the author of the screenplay had met Kissinger, an 'intelligence advisor' for the military, before HK was well-known. He foresaw how Kissinger would influence world politics in the years to come. At a minimum, this guess was astute. Kissinger's aggressive anti-communist stance and thick German accent dramatically enhanced his persona making him attractive not only as the role model for the eccentric Strangelove (the centerpiece of this outstanding cold-war political satire envisaging the nuclear apocalypse), but a probable if not clever choice for Mr. AC as well.

The three Antichrists of the French seer Nostradamus—Napoleon, Hitler, and a third persona (possibly tied to the mysterious *Mabus* of Nostradamus' quatrains)—*fascinate many in our day.* As discussed in my previous book, *Mabus* as the jumbled name of the Antichrist appears to be a stretch, especially since many followers of Dr. No decode the name into familiar and current appellations like Bush, Hussein, and Obama. Therefore, if we select any one candidate over the others by trying to decode *Mabus*, our choice amounts to little more than a wild guess since no one truly stands out from the pack. Even if we could fathom Dr. No's meaning regarding Mabus, his other descriptions of the third Antichrist seem to imply Nostradamus did not intend *Mabus* to represent the third Antichrist.[2]

RESPONSIBLE STUDIES ON THE IDENTITY OF ANTICHRIST

However, two important books written and published during the past five years provide substantial and compelling new information about the identity of the Antichrist. Written by popular author Tom Horn, one of those books was entitled, *Apollyon Rising: 2012.* The other book, written by the late J.R. Church possesses the lengthy title, *Daniel Reveals the Bloodline of the Antichrist.*

---

[2] See my chapter on Nostradamus in *Decoding Doomsday* for the details

Both books yield rich historical analysis as well as fresh insights into the biblical material concerning Antichrist. For those interested, both books are 'must reads.' Here I provide but a short summary and commentary.

Church's book studies the chapters of Daniel in sequence, interpreting Daniel's visions consistent with most other evangelical authors over the past 150 years. But J.R. adds remarkable insights from the church fathers of the third-century, including Irenaeus and Hippolytus. As one studies the quotations from these two third-century authors (direct 'descendants' of the teaching of John the Apostle and Polycarp, John's personal disciple), the consistency of their teaching with the writings of many pre-millennial evangelical authors today surely captivates (especially since these authors wrote almost 1800 years ago).

In Irenaeus' book, *Against Heresies*, Book 5, Chapter 28, he employs several common titles for Antichrist including the *Man of Sin*, a *'man with fierce countenance'* (attributed to the angel Gabriel in his explanation of the *little-horn* of Daniel 8), and the *abomination of desolation* (so-called by Jesus in Matthew 24). Irenaeus also indicates the Antichrist likely springs from the *tribe of Dan*[3], quoting passages from the Old Testament books Jeremiah, Genesis, and given the fact there is no mention of the tribe of Dan in the book of Revelation. Could the Tribe of Dan be the Jewish forebear of the Antichrist? Many scholars think so. J.R. certainly did as does his colleague, Gary Stearman.

OUTRAGEOUS ROOTS OF THE MAN OF SIN

From studying the Old Testament and several apocryphal books, we learn that supposedly around 1400 BC when the Israelites conquered the land of Canaan, the Tribe of Dan settled near Mount Hermon (today's Golan Heights in Syria). This mountain

---

[3] One of the 12 sons of Jacob/Israel and original tribes of Israel.

marks the precise location where Canaan, a son of Ham, established his abode after the Flood of Noah. According to the non-canonical books of Enoch and Jasper, the peak of Mount Hermon identifies the location upon which angels "leaving their first estate" (see Genesis 6:4) descended to earth.

A quick reminder: supposedly, 200 angels, also known as 'the Watchers,' begat offspring with the daughters of men, which gave rise to the *Nephilim*. Moses, whom tradition holds as the author of Genesis, indicated the Nephilim were in fact the historical characters from which ancient mythology originated.

As I have discussed elsewhere, since scholars generally designate these beings as demigods—part-human and part-god—we can describe them correctly as *chimeras*.[4]

So it is that Dan located his people at 'ground zero.' But for some undisclosed reason (perhaps because he realized his tribe lived at 'Spook Central' to quote a line from *Ghostbusters*), the **Dan**ite's did not reside in this location for long.[5] Given the tribe of Dan was known for its sailing skills, Dan's descendants determined to leave their land in northern Israel and travel to the isles of Greece, where (according to Church) they became the **Dan**aans (circa 1200 BC). From Homer, we learn it was in their ships the

---

[4] We come to appreciate from Genesis and other apocryphal books that these Nephilim dominated the antediluvian world. Additionally, they may have been the primary reason that the Flood was brought upon the world, to destroy the 'mixed' blood of 'gods' and men. Only Noah was found "perfect in all his generations" such that he and his three sons (and apparently their 'sister' wives!) would restart the human race after the flood, to reassert the purity of human DNA.

[5] Some scholars indicate that the Danites were unwilling to fight the Philistines or the giant Canaanites to preserve their land. A lack of courage might have been the reason. If this is true, it becomes all the more remarkable that the Danites are destined to become the Spartans as we discuss later. As you may recall, the Spartans were known as the fiercest fighters of ancient times. It just goes to show that if you try to escape the lesson God wishes to teach, you best buckle down and learn it sooner rather than later. You can't escape the Almighty's lessons forever. He follows you, even to the Greek Isles!

Greeks set sail to retrieve Helen from her lover Paris, the Trojan prince (circa 1000 BC).[6] While these details are fantastic to say the least, the story bestows other fascinating facts.

Church cites strong historical records from sources such as Josephus and apocryphal books like *2 Maccabees*. He indicates that following the Trojan War, a (now mythically famous) survivor named *Aeneas* fled to the Italian peninsula after seven years of travel.[7] His progeny, the twins Romulus and Remus, founded Rome several generations later (approximately 758 BC). While generally regarded as purely mythical, the historian Plutarch assumed their historicity, remarking that Romulus was 53 at his death. Hence, we discern how through this progression of ancestry, the Romans may be in fact the offspring of the Trojan *Aeneas*; through his great grandparents the Greek Spartans; and from these forebears, the Jewish tribe of Dan. From Daniel's visions, Church identifies the 'little horn' and the 'people of the prince to come' as being both Greek and Roman. Therefore, the conclusion offered by Irenaeus and Hippolytus: *Antichrist comprises a descendant of all three peoples*. The evidence appears to be backed up by details coming from classical, historical and biblical sources.

In summary, Church's analysis of the bloodline of the Antichrist substantiates the traditional, historic viewpoint that 'the Beast' will come from European ancestry and yet be Jewish (though one might conjecture this will not necessarily be obvious.)

AN APOLLO CREED: ANTICHRIST FROM THE PYTHON PIT

The other work that explores compelling new insights concerning his *Infernal Highness* is Tom Horn's *Apollyon Rising: 2012*. Horn also refers to various classical sources to demonstrate

---

[6] Helen was the 'face that launched a thousand ships,' ships built by the **Dan**ites!

[7] Aeneas is the subject of Homer's *Aeneid*. Aeneas was a descendant of Dar**dan**us, the founder of Troy. The Dar**dan**elles also refer to this lineage as it is adjacent to the ancient city of Troy.

that the persona behind the Spirit of Antichrist is none other than the god, *Apollo*. The Bible certainly indicates the Beast is known as *Abaddon* in Hebrew and *Apollyon* in Greek. Revelation 9:11 says: *"And they had a king over them, [which is] the angel of the bottomless pit, whose name in the Hebrew tongue [is]* **Abaddon***, but in the Greek tongue hath [his] name* **Apollyon***."* Horn quotes several historians to demonstrate the connection between the names *Apollo* and *Apollyon*. The evidence, however, hardly stops there.

The case is made stronger still when one considers the various antichrist figures in history connected to Apollo. Indeed, the old-

FIGURE 30 - THE DESECRATION OF THE TEMPLE BY ANTIOCHUS EPIPHANES IV

est *figure or fore type* for Antichrist is *Antiochus Epiphanes IV*, the Greco-Syrian king who reigned over Syria and most of what is today Iraq and Iran from around 200 BC to 166 BC. Antiochus and his descendants were the obvious subjects of many of Daniel's very specific prophecies; plus, AEIV associated himself with the god Apollo. It was this king, Antiochus, who halted the ritual sacrifice of the Jews in Jerusalem in 170 BC, establishing an altar for Apollo in the Temple, and thereby desecrating the Temple by this abomination.[8] For three years, Antiochus' troops fought (and finally lost to) Matthias and Judas Maccabeus, ultimately leading to the liberation of the Jews—and the Jewish holiday *Hanukkah*. The Feast of Dedication draws its name from this story—the re-dedication of the Temple once ritually cleansed following the abomination of desolation—Antiochus Epiphanes IV 'style.'

Moving forward in time, we learn how *Domitian*, the Caesar most likely contemporary to John the Apostle (when John wrote his apocalypse), expressed a wish to be regarded as Apollo incarnate.[9] But the Apollo connection does not stop there. Tom Horn indicates the name 'Napoleon'—one of Nostradamus' three Antichrists—actually means, 'the new Apollo.' (I would add another familiar name to the list: Adolf Hitler who identified with the sun god Apollo through his ubiquitous use of the *swastika*, a Hindu symbol of the sun.)

Horn references several authorities in classic Greek studies who confirm that *apoleia*, the Greek word for 'perdition' (which Paul appropriates in 2 Thessalonians 2:3), is rooted in the name *Apollo* just as its spelling suggests. Therefore, the Apostle Paul equates the *Man of Sin* to the *Son of Perdition*, implicitly conveying the *Antichrist constitutes the reincarnated Apollo*.

I will mention other linkages later; but first, the 'minority report.'

---

[8] In *Decoding Doomsday*, I provided an illustration of a coin minted by this king bearing his profile on one side, while portraying Apollo—also known as the god of music, seen playing his harp—on the other.

[9] Recall that Apollo is so named in both Roman and Greek mythology whereas *Zeus*, the highest Greek God and father of Apollo is renamed *Jupiter* in Roman accounts.

THE MINORITY REPORT—THE MUSLIM ANTICHRIST

Considerable debate rages today surrounding several verses in the Old Testament which name the Antichrist 'the Assyrian,' proposing that the Antichrist will not originate from Europe (or America, Europe's former colonies in the New World). Instead, Antichrist will hail from the Muslim world.

Isaiah refers to the Assyrian in several different passages. The first, Isaiah 10:24 says, *"Therefore thus saith the Lord GOD of hosts, O my people that dwellest in Zion, be not afraid of the Assyrian: he shall smite thee with a rod, and shall lift up his staff against thee, after the manner of Egypt."* Hosea also mentions the Assyrian (Hosea 5:13 and 11:5). Micah refers to the Messiah who will defeat the Assyrian when he says: *"And they shall waste the land of Assyria with the sword, and the land of Nimrod in the entrances thereof: thus shall he deliver [us] from the Assyrian, when he cometh into our land, and when he treadeth within our borders."* (Micah 5:6). Some suggest the label 'the Assyrian' connects the Antichrist to Nimrod. Genesis 10:8, 9 comments concerning Nimrod's lineage:

FIGURE 31 - NIMROD, THE MIGHTY HUNTER

> "And Cush begat Nimrod: he **began to be a mighty one** in the earth. He was a mighty hunter before the LORD: wherefore it is said, 'Even as Nimrod the mighty hunter before the LORD.' "[10]

Nimrod founded the city of Babel (later, Babylon) leading the people to make bricks and create its famous tower 'reaching unto heaven.' His goal: form a single government keeping everyone together in one place so that humankind might grow stronger.

> "And they said, Go to, let us build us a city and a tower, whose top [may reach] unto heaven; and let us make us a name, lest we be scattered abroad upon the face of the whole earth (Genesis 11:4).

But the implication of his comment 'that we might make a name for ourselves' conveys something beyond strength alone. My sense: it suggests striving to achieve equivalence in power to God or at least to the Nephilim who continue to reappear *after* the Flood of Noah. Aggregating everyone to maximize the power of humanity would support this goal. At minimum, it signifies how a united humanity forming a single 'state' can more forcibly work its will. We see this from God's statement that He must confound them lest they prove that they can accomplish anything that they 'set their minds to' (Genesis 11:5-9).

Consequently, we may regard Nimrod as a foreshadowing of Antichrist. As he was an 'Assyrian,' it is certainly conceivable that the mention of *the Assyrian* symbolically (as an archetype) refers to Nimrod and implies an Antichrist figure.

Chuck Missler, one of today's most popular and highly regarded writer/teachers concerning Bible prophecy (from the evangelical perspective) proposes Antichrist could be called,

---

[10] Evidently, this was a popular saying in the time of Moses. Today, being a Nimrod means being stupid as Nimrod who thought He could build a tower that would reach all the way to heaven. In ancient times, however, being a Nimrod likely meant being overpowering or visionary. Nimrod was literally the King of the ancient world. As I will argue, being a Nimrod, biblically, means being an archetype of Antichrist!

'Nimrod II.' Missler does not fully commit to this Islamic Antichrist, but proffers it as a distinct possibility.

My view is this: rather than a literal Assyrian (coming from today's Iraq), the Antichrist as an Assyrian (the 'Nimrod' of the latter times and the Bible's depiction of him as an enemy of the Jews) *is only symbolic.* If this be so, it explains how the Antichrist could descend from Greek, Roman, and Jewish blood, yet *remains* pre-figured as *Nimrod*, the Assyrian. Therefore, all four races are accommodated from a biblical perspective.

ORION, GIZA, AND THE CULT OF THE ALL-SEEING EYE

Going further still, other scholars connect the fact that Nimrod was the great hunter and in fact, it is he who is foreshadowed in the 'gospel of God in the stars.' It is certainly undeniable that the Egyptians connected the constellation *Orion the Hunter* with their god Osiris (believing Osiris and Orion were one and the same). Furthermore, the mythology of the stars suggests the Hunter *Orion* (Nimrod, aka Antichrist), is the enemy of Virgo (Mary) and her offspring (Jesus).[11] Thus, from the 'originating source'—Egypt—we can see how Nimrod, Osiris, Orion,

FIGURE 32 - THE ALL-SEEING EYE OF OSIRIS

---

[11] According to some scholars, even Freemasonry ascribes to the preeminence of Nimrod. Rather than identifying the origin of 'The Craft' with Solomon and his first temple, the most hidden of secrets known only amongst the 'inner circle' specifies that Nimrod is the real King of interest, and the Temple where the Craft began was actually the Tower of Babel.

and Apollo all relate to the personage we know today as Antichrist. But is this conclusion supported by the science of archeology?

Robert Bauval and Adrian Gilbert in their 1994 ground breaking book, *The Orion Mystery*, set forth a thesis that Osiris is the God celebrated in the famous Pyramids of Giza. The very layout of the Giza complex—notably the location of the three great pyramids—reflects the belt of Orion. Osiris is the sun God and comprises the same god that the Greeks and Romans named *Apollo*.

As I have documented in my previous books, this mythology which centered on Apollo occupies the cornerstone of pagan religions worldwide; it also lies at the center of that contemporary 'non-religion' religion known as Freemasonry. Many of the most sacred Mason symbols are clearly Egyptian (the *pyramid*, the *all-seeing eye* of Horus (aka Orion or Apollo), and the *eagle*—a contemporary replacement for the mystical Phoenix). Therefore, current scholars insist that Antichrist has been the subject of religious worship for over 5,000 years. He continues to be worshipped today in sophisticated, yet secretive halls many of which we are not aware. [12] Because this remains the case, does it not suggest the spiritual war between God and Lucifer is reflected throughout this universal religion and the countless megalithic monuments we find across the world? The story, however, goes deeper still.

MIGHT ANTICHRIST BE 'MORE THAN HUMAN'?

Genesis says that Nimrod 'became a mighty one'—a *gibborim*—the Hebrew word for 'a mighty one.' In Genesis 6:4, this word is

---

[12] Hoagland and Bara in *Dark Mission*, disclose how NASA is thoroughly captivated by Egyptian mythology, primarily because its principals are Freemasons. The mission to the moon was named *Apollo*. The new mission to the moon sponsored by George W. Bush in 2004 was named *Orion*. The 'Mission Patches' worn by astronauts featured the constellation Orion and highlighted the three stars in Orion's belt. But this only scratches the surface on NASA's fascination with Osiris/Orion/Apollo.

used as well as *nephilim*, suggesting that the two words are connected in some way.

> "There were giants (**nephilim**) in the earth in those days (before the Flood of Noah); and also after that (after the Flood), when the sons of God came in unto the daughters of men, and they bare [children] to them, <u>the same [became] mighty men</u> (**gibborim**) which [were] of old, men of renown."

This association leads Tom Horn to speculate that Nimrod was not only 'mighty' but may in fact have become a *demigod*, equivalent to the Nephilim. Perhaps in a Faustian manner, Nimrod became 'more than mere man.' His new found power, supplied by

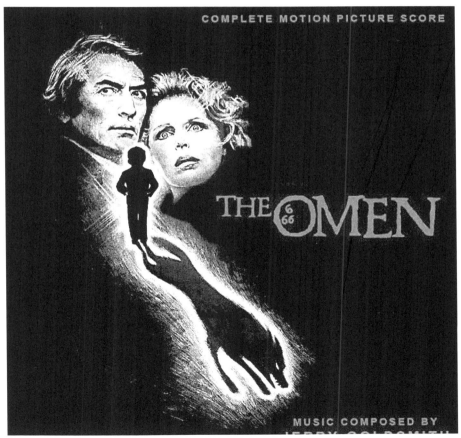

FIGURE 33 - THE ALL-TIME GREATEST MOVIE ABOUT THE ANTICHRIST: *THE OMEN*

the fallen angels described in the *Book of Enoch*, enabled him to emerge as the dominant leader of humankind after the flood. We are thus left wondering, "Was this 'becoming' a result of genetic engineering? Was he 'made into a mighty man' as a result of what the fallen angels accomplished on his behalf?" Was he a mighty hunter because of superhuman strength or stature?

This association between Nephilim, *gibborim*, and Nimrod has many authors contemplating whether the Antichrist *may be more than a human entity.* Is it possible that the Antichrist will have 'god-like' capacities through an alteration of his DNA? Perhaps, the premise of *Rosemary's Baby* and *The Omen,* that the Antichrist is the 'seed' of Satan possessing genuine satanic DNA, is not so far-fetched after all.

The Book of Revelation indicates it is this destroyer spirit, *Apollyon*, who reigns over the 'bottomless pit' and who is resurrected possessing the 'Man of Sin.' From the spiritual perspective, there seems to be little doubt that the Devil controls the Antichrist. But could the human possessed by this most evil of evil spirits also have demonic DNA as well? Horn takes the possibility even further, considering whether a genetic 'splice,' perhaps first applied to Antichrist, becomes the *Mark of the Beast.* In my book *Decoding Doomsday*, I examined whether Nietzsche's Übermensch might be a modern description for Antichrist. In some ways, the Antichrist appears to be the literal fulfillment of Nietzsche's visionary 'superman.' [13] At the very least, in our day, Nietzsche's Übermensch expresses this 'spirit of Antichrist'. He comprises a man who chooses his own values relying only on himself since he proclaims that *God is dead.*

---

[13] Certainly Hitler believed he was the fulfillment of the Messiah that many occult writers discussed late in the nineteenth century. Dietrich Eckhart, the spiritual father of Nazism according to Hitler, believed this literally. Hitler was quite committed to genetic engineering. He drew upon the poetic myths of the Nordic *Edda*, in which the purified Aryans would be supermen, no longer contaminated by Jewish blood.

ANTICHRIST AS THE WOLFMAN—THE LYCOS FROM LYCIA

There are even more visual cues which must be considered. Horn mentions the connection between *Apollo and the wolf*.[14] He indicates that Herodotus, the 'Father of History,' writing in the fifth century BC, discussed a great people to the north of Greece known as the Hyperboreans,[15] who worshipped Apollo and made an annual pilgrimage to the land of Delos where they participated in the famous Apollo festivals there.

Lycia, a small country in southwest Turkey, also boasted a connection with Apollo, known there as *Lykeios, which ties* to the

FIGURE 34 - ZEUS TURNING LYCAON INTO A WOLF, ENGRAVING BY HENDRIK GOLTZIUS.

---

[14] Horn, op. cit., pg.163.
[15] Early on in his book, *The Antichrist*, Nietzsche has his Antichrist proclaim, "We are Hyperboreans." Nietzsche also called his followers 'fellow Hyperboreans.'

Greek word *Lycos* and means 'wolf.'[16] 'Wolfmen' are called *Lycans or lycanthropes* for this reason.[17] Since *Apollo and the wolf* are connected, perhaps the wolf is an image we could associate with the coming Antichrist! In this context, we must recall Jesus' teaching, *"The wolf comes to destroy. But the Son of Man comes to give men life abundantly."* (John 10:10, paraphrased).

OTHER MANMADE BEASTS MAY BE COMING TO HAUNT US

With the science of *transhumanism* now appearing on the front page of our newspapers—coming as it were to the foreground—we witness a frightening development. In laboratories today, scientists create chimeras just as depicted by H.G. Wells in his classic, *The Island of Doctor Moreau*.

Likewise, the fear of Mary Shelly inherent in her novel *Frankenstein* reaches beyond a mere tale of horror. Should we create a new kind of human by altering our DNA, what manner of beast do we unleash upon the world? The distinct possibility now exists

---

[16] A strong case can be made that Britain is the island of Hyperborea. While Plutarch (writing in the first century AD) identified Hyperboreans as the Gauls, an ancient historian, writing 300 years earlier, Hecataeus of Abdera, identified this race as living on a northern island bigger than Sicily with a temperate climate capable of growing all manner of crops. The North Sea was called the Hyperborean Sea. According to Hecataeus, the island also possessed a circular temple (which many scholars identify as *Stonehenge)*. Interestingly, Stonehenge has been known as Apollo's Temple since classical antiquity (See Squire, Charles, *Myths & Legends of the Celts*, p. 42). It is a remarkable fact that supports the premise of the breath-taking book by Knight and Butler, *Before the Pyramids*, which provides compelling evidence that Stonehenge (built circa 3,000 BC) was based on Thornborough Henge (built circa 3,800 BC, in northern England), and that the Egyptian pyramids built 1,000 years after Thornborough Henge (in 2,800 BC) were in fact based on these giant stone circles. Thus, the Egyptian monuments were more sensational versions of what had already been created in England. (See Knight, Christopher, and Butler, Alan, *Before the Pyramids: Cracking Archeology's Greatest Mystery*, Watkins Publishing, London, 2009). Apparently, all three monuments connect to Apollo. A discussion of Hyperborea can be found in Wikipedia (see *en.wikipedia.org /wiki /Hyperborea)*.

[17] The original search engines included not only Yahoo! but also **Lycos,** whose symbol was a dog—specifically a black Labrador.

that humans may soon face decisions regarding our openness to the scientific manipulation of our DNA (presumably) for beneficent reasons. It appears entirely conceivable that in a few short years governments could demand the population receive some manner of genetic alteration as a vaccination against a horrendous plague, as the movie *I Am Legend* portends.

Alternatively, individuals in a marketplace where human attributes can be bought and sold—may opt to 'enhance' their genes in order to obtain super human capabilities. For the past decade, ethicists and scientists have debated this possibility. Some are now calling for setting ground rules for this oh-so-serious game. How should Christians respond?

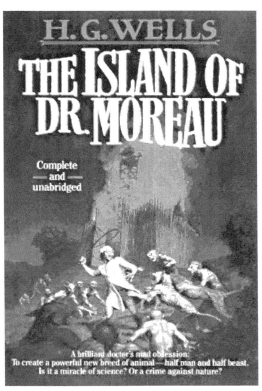

FIGURE 35 - THE PRESCIENT SCIENCE FICTION OF H.G. WELLS

LOOKING FOR THE ANTICHRIST: MORE THAN A CURIOSITY

At a minimum, we should recognize that the matter of seeking Antichrist's identity takes on a completely new meaning. It stands no longer solely as a curiosity. It becomes a discreet means to detect the evil he represents and that inevitably looms just ahead.

Does this also suggest, however, we should be trying to play a game of 'pin the tail on the donkey' by striving to name who the Antichrist is in today's world? While staying alert to the means by which Antichrist may make the ultimate power play to capture humanity and its very genome, I strongly advise against naming names when it comes to identifying the Antichrist.

The actual human identity of Antichrist is unlikely to become apparent before Mr. AC reveals himself. Biblically, we may be able to discern his bloodline and build a case from what portion of the world he will arise (as my colleague authors and I have done in our book *The Final Babylon*), in which we unswervingly identify the United States as the likely power base of the Antichrist. We can certainly determine the Spirit of the Antichrist, but not Antichrist himself, before he reveals who he is. We must remember that Paul indicates Antichrist's revealing is an *apokalyptō*, something that stuns and surprises us. *Knowing the man's name before he 'confirms the covenant' with Israel and then desecrates its Temple, may be a fool's errand.* And yet, deciphering the nature of the Antichrist spirit possessing him has surely been accomplished and made evident in these last days by such great works as offered by Church and Horn. Whether we call him Nimrod, Osiris, Orion, Apollo, Abaddon, Apollyon, Lycos, or the Übermensch, we know who that spirit resembles and what his agenda most likely entails. For now, that knowledge is enough.

Sir Isaac Newton, a great student of eschatology writing in the seventeenth century, admonished his readers to be alert and determine who this Antichrist might be. He wrote this directive in his 300 year-old English dialect (including all manner of strange spelling), "And therefore it is as much our duty to indeavour to be able to know him that we may avoyd him, as it was theirs to know Christ that they might follow him." [18]

---

[18] And Newton continues, "Thou seest therefore that this is no idle speculation, no matters of indifferency but a duty of the greatest moment. Wherefore it concerns thee to look about thee narrowly least thou shouldest in so degenerate an age be dangerously seduced & not know it. Antichrist was to seduce the whole Christian world and therefore he may easily seduce thee if thou beest *not well prepared to discern him.* But if he should not be yet come into the world yet amidst so many

Watching out for the 'Man of Sin' entails much more than engaging in obsessive study as prophecy enthusiasts. It encompasses *an obligation for those who take the Bible seriously*, believing our mission in this world demands we stand firmly against all manner of evil. *"For there shall arise false Christs, and false prophets, and shall shew great signs and wonders; insomuch that, if [it were] possible, they shall deceive the very elect"* (Matthew 24:24).

Keeping watch for the return of Jesus Christ also entails being on the lookout for the Antichrist. While many of us believe we will not see the Antichrist reveal himself (because the rapture may come before his apocalyptō), we will likely see the conditions that immediately precede his revelation. Warning those who are not capable of discerning the signs of the time (and the biblical signs of the coming apocalypse), may the last and best hope they have to bring them to repentance before it is too late.

---

religions of which there can be but one true & perhaps none of those that thou art acquainted with it is great odds but thou mayst be deceived & therefore it concerns thee to be very circumspect." (Sir Isaac Newton, *Untitled Treatise on Revelation*, Section 1.1, *emphasis mine*).

15: ESCAPING THE WRATH TO COME

*"And take heed to yourselves, lest at any time your hearts be overcharged with **surfeiting**, and drunkenness, and cares of this life, and so that day come upon you unawares. For as a snare shall it come on all them that dwell on the face of the whole earth. Watch ye therefore, and pray always, that ye may be accounted worthy to escape all these things that shall come to pass, and to stand before the Son of man."*
(Luke 21:34-36)

A REVERSAL OF FORTUNE, FOR ALMOST EVERYONE

WHEN TIMES ARE GOOD, IT IS EASY TO FORGET THE MASTER'S DIRECTIVE TO 'KEEP WATCH.' ON THE OTHER HAND, WHEN WE LIVE AMIDST THE 'WORST OF TIMES,' THERE IS A GREATER likelihood we turn our thoughts to heaven and consider the proximity of Jesus Christ's predicted return to this earth. In fact, when we find ourselves despondent about life's prospects, it is all too easy to wish that Jesus would "just come back right away and get us out of this mess" (a mess which we ourselves likely made without much help from anyone else!)

Most of us are not caught up in overindulgence at the moment. That is what the old word *surfeiting* means. We struggle just to get by. Such is especially true for me and many of my friends who worked in the biggest and highest up, high-flying 'high tech' business in the U.S. (that one in Redmond, Washington). Ten years ago we had plenty of money, we drove fancy cars, and we lived in big houses. Some in their late 30s and early 40s had already retired.

Today, however, houses in my old Woodinville neighborhood have fallen in value by 50%. Virtually everyone remains 'under water' (that is, holding an asset worth less than what you owe). A lot of the youthful retired have had to go back to work. If you do not have any sympathy for 45-year-olds that have to go back to work, I can relate as I myself have experienced a severe change in lifestyle and struggle every month just to get by and pay the bills. Retirement? Not in this lifetime. Even Social Security may go broke in the decade ahead. That 'safety net' now has gaping holes. With ObamaCare striving to bring more people into a status of 'insured' an equal or greater number of the formerly insured are now without health insurance altogether. More people have fallen into poverty. The gap between rich and poor has widened. CEO salaries reach 300 times the pay for the average worker (comparing the U.S. to Japan—Japan's CEOs enjoy only a 12 multiple over the pay of their average worker). *American greed* (the business TV network, CNBC has a popular program by that name) has reached new heights.

Looking at the bigger picture, financial prospects are not so good. In Europe, we see governments failing. In America, state and city governments, and even the Federal Government struggle to balance the budget.[1] Protests are becoming frequent. We weathered the 'Occupy Wall Street' movement (which meant to stymie the operation of Wall Street), a protest that should have featured the 'average Joe' (members of the middle class), instead of today's version of hippies and anarchists. But at least someone took to the streets and lodged a vociferous complaint.

---

[1] The Federal Government has less of a problem since its partner in crime, the Federal Reserve Bank, literally invents money and loans it to the government at interest in its self-devised form of legal larceny known as the Fractional Banking System. We the taxpayers pay the interest. The principal is never at risk. The banks invented the principal at the beginning of the 'loan process.' The bankers collect the interest.

Many predict that widespread rioting stands ready to break out. Martial Law may not far behind. Perhaps the predicted financial collapse of the world (which contributes to the coming of Antichrist) will begin soon. Regardless, most everyone would agree that we are not living in the good ol' days any more. Almost everyone yearns for better times.

Times are indeed tough. I must confess I have had desperate thoughts many times in the past couple of years. But one of the good things about these challenging stretches: we are much more inclined to contemplate the 'real meaning of life' than when times are good. We do not cling to material things. Should we pray, however "Come Lord Jesus" to escape the circumstances?

GOD DESIRES TO HELP US MAKE ENDS MEET EVERYDAY

It is not that uncommon for believers in the Second Advent to have such thoughts and comment accordingly (and in their weak moments complain just a bit). All too often, we hope to escape the bad times in which we find ourselves. In our better moments, we recognize this niggling escapism does not constitute the right reason to hope for Christ's coming. Although our personal circumstances may at times be most dire, wishing for Jesus to come back to save us, trivializes what is in essence the culmination of history. Moreover, it consists of a convenient means to a selfish end.[2]

Why do I say this? Because when we leap to this 'way out' way out, we demonstrate *a lack of faith.* Jesus said He came that we might *"have life... more abundantly"* (John 10:10). That does not mean we will always have a *surfeit* of material goods. Neither does it mean we will only know peace and quiet. But it does promise that despite hard times, we can maintain our equanimity. Our outlook on life should remain positive because Jesus taught us to ask our Father in Heaven to provide our *"daily bread."* Likewise, God

---

[2] It is interesting how this expression is uttered more often by men than women!

shall provide *"all your need"* as Paul tells the church at Philippi (Philippians 4:19). *We serve a God who wants to provide for us and does not mind the daily 'grind' of helping us make ends meet.*

Yet, this assurance remains a far cry from promising a Porsche for every garage. Indeed, perhaps the biggest heresy in Christendom during the past 50 years concerns the so-called 'Gospel of Wealth' which suggests all believers should prosper materially. Prosperity preachers teach we are doing something wrong if God does not bless us with wealth and health. Perhaps we have 'unconfessed sin' in our lives? Perhaps we 'lack faith?' I shudder when I hear such counsel. Indeed, I find this 'gospel' repugnant as well as unbiblical. Just consider the examples in the New Testament. While on earth, Jesus (and His disciples) had no more money than what Judas could carry in the common purse. The early Church shared possessions and conducted their 'church services' secretly in Roman catacombs and individual homes. Paul had to make tents lest he be a burden on his churches. Such outward signs do not convey great wealth amongst the brethren.

Nevertheless, these believers were living life 'abundantly' Being filled with the Spirit to the point of 'bursting' and witnessing miracles 'left and right,' they would not have traded their new found faith and the joy they gained for all the riches in Rome.

Consequently, it comprises neither a practical nor righteous motive *hoping for the Lord's return that we might escape our personal bad times.* This should not be a part of 'keeping watch.'

THE MEANING OF THE MILLENNIUM

Most of my readers are *Pre-Millennialists*. Therefore, they know what this awkward label means: It refers to the *Millennium Kingdom* in which Jesus Christ reigns physically on this earth for 1,000 years—just as *John the Revelator* predicts in the last book of the Christian Bible (if we take his words to be *literally true regarding their fulfillment in space-time*).

John's discussion of this magnificent epoch stands as the only passage in the Scripture specifying the length of the Christ's earthly Kingdom which will last literally for 1,000 years. It also seems somewhat ironic that although the term *millennium* is never used in the Bible, it remains the *key term used to distinguish the various ways in which Protestant Christians interpret the meaning of the coming Kingdom.* Eschatology, the study of last things, is distinguished by how one interprets *the meaning of the millennium.*

As a refresher (and for my readers that do not know), there are three protestant prophecy 'schools of thought:' The 'Pre,' 'Post,' and 'A' (pronounced 'Ah') Millennialists—reflecting a 'before,' 'after,' or 'not so relevant' perspective of when Christ comes (and what happens next) vis-à-vis the Millennium.

Today, most evangelical Christians are *Pre-millennial* while *Amillennial* best denotes 'reformation' Christian doctrine regarding when Jesus Christ (physically) returns to earth.[3] Interesting, Catholics are in the same camp as today's 'reformed theologians'— both groups do not believe in a literal millennium.

Perhaps only in the last 40 years or so have the 'Pre's' have outnumbered the 'Post's' and the 'A's.' [4] We can thank Hal Lindsey's *Late Great Planet Earth* and Tim LaHaye/ Jerry Jenkins' 'Left Behind' series of fiction books which fomented this modern-day 'sea change.' It is the Dispensational school that has made this happen.

---

[3] Neither Martin Luther nor John Calvin, the preeminent reformers of the sixteenth century had much use for the Book of Revelation. They believed *Antichrist* was the Pope and the Catholic Church *was Mystery Babylon*. That they didn't believe in a literal millennium should not be surprising. Covenantal Theology as it is known today (J.I. Packer and R.C. Sproul, wonderful Christian authors are prime examples), remains strongly tied to strict Reformation views and consequently, Covenantal theologians often criticize those who hold to a literal Millennium.

[4] I examine these various views, what underlies them, and ultimately, how our method of interpretation eventually leads us to the most biblical perspective. See my book, *Are We Living in the Last Days?* for a thorough treatment of these topics.

Still, despite the fact this 'popular' perspective boasts a majority view, no consensus exists on this topic and the resulting reality regarding this issue could be characterized as mostly 'rough seas'. Lots of acrimony remains between these different schools of thought.

FACING THE POSSIBILITY OF GREAT TRIBULATION

Hand-in-hand with the notion of the Millennium stands the notion of the *Great Tribulation*. All *Millennialists* (and some Christians that are not so 'into' the Millennium), believe there will be a final period of time in which the earth will suffer the greatest distress it has ever known. If you think times are tough now, just wait.

So does this mean that when the *Last Days* are 'full on' (and the judgments of God are about to be unleashed upon the world), we just need to 'buck up' and deal with the horrible pressures and catastrophes the Bible predicts will happen? Or is there something fundamentally different about these final days? As we approach the period known as 'The Great Tribulation,' no doubt our destiny in this scenario stands as one of the most momentous issues we could ever face. Therefore, we should study this matter in earnest.

Of course, some might argue it would be better not think about it—the less we know the better. Instead, we should assume the 'ostrich position' (i.e., have one's head buried deep in the sand). Saner heads, however, would keep their heads up and their eyes peeled.[5]

---

[5] A great expression, keeping one's eyes peeled. The web site World Wide Words explains from whence it comes to us. "It derives from an old verb *pill*, "to plunder", which is the root of our modern word *pillage*. It came to us from the Latin root *pilare*, meaning "to take the hair off, pluck" (closely connected with our [word] *depilate*), but which also had the figurative meaning of "plunder, cheat", almost exactly the same as the figurative meaning of our modern verbs *fleece* or *pluck*. From about the seventeenth century on, *pill* was commonly spelt *peel* and took on the sense of "to remove or strip" in the weakened sense of removing an outer covering, such as a fruit. The figurative sense of keeping alert, by removing any covering of the eye that

Many would reply that the only responsible thing to do is consider whether we do have to go through the 'worst of bad times.' We must square up to the issue and ask the tough question: will believers who trust in Jesus Christ live through the 'Tribulation' that final seven years when literally 'all hell breaks loose'?

Most believe this time period is equivalent to the Prophet Daniel's final (70th out of 70) 'weeks of years' (totaling 490 years of prophecy related to the God's plan for salvation of His people, the Jews). Daniel specifies that this last seven years of 'normal' history (in which humans apart of Jesus Christ 'run the show') consists of 2,520 days—that is, seven, 360-day years.

Also, it appears the second half of this period, the final 1,260 days (aka 3.5, 360-day years) will be particularly difficult. In this vein, some scholars regard this period to be equivalent to the so-called **time of Jacob's trouble**: *"Alas! For that day is great, so that none is like it: it is even the time of Jacob's trouble, but he shall be saved out of it."* (Jeremiah 30:7).

THE *DAY OF THE LORD*—TO WHAT DOES THIS REFER?

Likewise, some scholars align the *time of Jacob's trouble* with the *Day of the Lord*,[6] a period which begins (as discussed previously), with the appearance of Daniel's prophesied *Abomination of Desolation*. Indeed, Jesus seems to be very, very specific about when the times of greatest tribulation begin. He connects it to the

---

might impede vision, seems to have appeared in the US about 1850." See http://www.worldwidewords.org/qa/qa-kee1.htm.

[6] This phrase might refer to an even more specific period of time, perhaps days, weeks, or months, in which the final judgments of God are experienced by the inhabitants of the earth sometime within the Great Tribulation rather than being totally equivalent to the final 3.5 years. Dispensational teaching, however, typically associates the *Day of the Lord* specifically to the final seven years (Daniel's 70th week), and the Age that immediately follows the conclusion of the Church Age at the rapture of the Church. It also includes the Millennium and even the time just after the 1,000 years are concluded (when the New Heavens and New Earth are created by God).

specific action, the 'abomination of desolation'. In context, Jesus has supplied His disciples a listing of events that must come to pass, but advises them that those signs he has mentioned, by themselves do not constitute the end of the age. However, after the gospel has been preached throughout the world, at that specific point in time, the kickoff event takes place. It commences with the *abomination of desolation*:

FIGURE 36 - THE ABOMINATION OF DESOLATION

*15 When ye therefore shall see the **abomination of desolation**, spoken of by Daniel the prophet, stand in the holy place, (whoso readeth, let him understand:)*

16 Then let them which be in Judaea flee into the mountains:

17 Let him which is on the housetop not come down to take any thing out of his house:

18 Neither let him which is in the field return back to take his clothes.

19 And woe unto them that are with child, and to them that give suck in those days!

²⁰ *But pray ye that your flight be not in the winter, neither on the sabbath day:*

²¹ *For **then shall be great tribulation**, such as was not since the beginning of the world to this time, no, nor ever shall be.*

²² *And except those days should be shortened, there should no flesh be saved: but for the elect's sake those days shall be shortened.* (Matthew 24:15-22, emphasis added)

Recall, this Abomination constitutes the claim by the Antichrist that he alone is God—and he alone deserves worship from everyone worldwide. He speaks blasphemies beyond imagining. According to traditional conservative scholarship, not until the Antichrist *proclaims himself to be God* and his self-declared worthiness of worship (perhaps within the 'Holy of Holies' in a newly rebuilt Jewish House of Worship[7]) will we know with certitude[8] (1) who the Antichrist is and (2) we know the Great Tribulation has 'officially' begun. Once this occurs, scholars suggest this moment commences the countdown to Christ's physical and visible return. Also, after this amazing event transpires, *we can calculate the exact day Jesus returns.*[9]

---

[7] This Jewish house of worship may be a rebuilt Temple or it might be a rediscovered ancient *Tabernacle* that is placed in the courtyard on the Temple Mount. Some scholars believe it will be either the Tabernacle of Moses, or more likely, the Tabernacle of David that served as the shelter for the Ark of the Covenant until Solomon completed his temple (circa 1004 BC) and the Ark was transferred for what was intended to be its permanent resting place. Others disagree and assert that the Third Temple will not be built after until the Messiah returns. An interesting discussion on the subject of whether or not the Temple need be fully rebuilt may be found at this location: http://heavenawaits.wordpress.com/where-does-the-abomination-of-desolation-really-stand/.

[8] Daniel indicates there will be a covenant with the many for seven years. It appears from the language used that the Antichrist confirms the covenant but breaks it halfway through its term. It is at the time when this personage breaks the covenant that we can draw a bead precisely on who he is. Whether the Antichrist is responsible for inking the origination agreement does not appear to be as clear as is his revealing (his *apocalyptō*).

[9] Either 1,260, or 1,290 days depending upon one's interpretation of Daniel.

Paul makes the sequence particularly clear. He specifies that this abomination must come first, and then the *Day of the Lord* (aka the Day of Christ, the Day of the Wrath of the Lamb) will occur.

*² That ye be not soon shaken in mind, or be troubled, neither by spirit, nor by word, nor by letter as from us, as that **the day of Christ is at hand.***

*³ Let no man deceive you by any means**: for that day shall not come**, except there come a falling away first, and that man of sin be revealed, the son of perdition;*

*⁴ Who opposeth and exalteth himself above all that is called God, or that is worshipped; **so that he as God sitteth in the temple of God, shewing himself that he is God**.* (2 Thessalonians 2:2-4, emphasis added)

That day (the Day of the Lord) cannot happen until first there comes *a falling away* (an apostasy) or a *departure* (another scriptural way to translate the Greek word used here, *apostasia*. (See Appendix 2 for a detailed analysis of this discussion.) Then the 'man of sin' will be revealed.

From Daniel and from Revelation, we know this crucial event does not occur until half-way through the final seven years. Daniel 9:27 states, *"And he shall confirm the covenant with many for one week: and in the midst of the week he shall cause the sacrifice and the oblation to cease, and for the overspreading of abominations he shall make it desolate, even until the consummation, and that determined shall be poured upon the desolate."*

Therefore, the Day of the Lord, according to Paul, refers to the time AFTER the abomination of desolation—after Antichrist declares himself the only god worthy of worship and speaks great blasphemies: *"And there was given unto him a mouth speaking great things and blasphemies; and power was given unto him to continue forty and two months. And he opened his mouth in blasphemy against God, to blaspheme his name, and his tabernacle, and them that dwell in heaven."* (Revelation 12:5-6).

Suppose we assume that the Abomination of Desolation (the forthcoming debut of the Antichrist) takes place sometime within the next decade or two. At that moment in time, a whole series of events commence including the issuance and enforcement of the *Mark of the Beast*, the appearance of *God's 'Two Witnesses'*[10] to preach against the Antichrist, and the miraculous ability of the False Prophet to make the image of the Antichrist appear anywhere in the world. (Note: these events constitute the most overt biblical signs of the coming apocalypse).

Then God unleashes judgments against the Antichrist and those who accepted his Mark (remember our discussion on *owth*, a sign aka mark of a covenant). These judgments consist of the 'Trumpet and Vial judgments' as expressed in the language of Revelation. These judgments are so destructive that they annihilate most of the world's population. Enormous geological processes take place that drastically reshape the topography of the world (mountains will be flattened, islands will disappear). Animals on land and fish in the sea will be virtually wiped out almost to the point of complete extinction. So the obvious question is, "Will Christians be here during this tumultuous time?"

---

[10] Most likely these two witnesses appear 'in the spirit of Moses and Elijah.' As John the Baptist was Elijah who came before Jesus to fulfill the Messianic prophecy (so said Jesus), these two personages will likely be distinct human beings but preaching and working miracles in the same power and authority as these two heroic figures of the Old Testament. The two witnesses will preach against Antichrist possibly for the entire 3.5 years of the Great Tribulation until they are murdered by Antichrist. Others, like my colleagues Dene McGriff and Douglas W. Krieger (my co-authors of *The Final Babylon)*, propose the two witnesses are (1) the Church which remains on earth during all but the last 30 days of the Tribulation period, and (2) the Jewish people who have become believers in Jesus Christ as predicted in Zechariah 12:10, *"And I will pour upon the house of David, and upon the inhabitants of Jerusalem, the spirit of grace and of supplications: and they shall look upon me whom they have pierced, and they shall mourn for him, as one mourneth for his only son, and shall be in bitterness for him, as one that is in bitterness for his firstborn.."* I do not agree with my colleagues, but I find it an interesting, if not worthy theory to investigate.

THE TIMING OF THE RAPTURE

'Pre-Millennialists' have *three* different answers to that most pertinent and urgent question. Here we encounter the next three 'sub-groups' with traditional but equally awkward labels applied by those engaged in the debate. There are the 'Pre-Tribbers,' 'Post-Tribbers,' and the 'Pre-Wrath' folk, aka 'somewhere-in-the-middle Tribbers.' This terminology relates to *when* the *rapture of the Church* occurs and if so, precisely when it happens in relation to the seven year 'tribulation period.'

Up front, we should remember that the term *rapture* in Latin means to 'seize' or 'snatch up.' This word *rapturae* is the Latin word Jerome selected to translate the Greek word *harpazo* when he created the Vulgate in the fourth century.[11] 1 Thessalonians 4:17 employs it, *"Then we which are alive and remain shall be* **caught up** *(harpazō) together with them in the clouds, to meet the Lord in the air: and so shall we ever be with the Lord." Harpazō* means *"to forcibly snatch out of the way."* Paul says in I Corinthians 15:52, *"In a moment, in the* **twinkling of an eye**, *at the last trump: for the trumpet shall sound, and the dead shall be raised incorruptible, and we shall be changed."* [Emphasis added]

In other words, this event will happen faster than you can say "Hallelujah! I am going home." Those that believe in the 'Pre-tribulation Rapture Theory' advocate for Christ to return secretly before the Tribulation begins and 'snatch' away His Church. Most Pre-Tribbers consider the rapture to be a 'signless event' that could happen at any time. It is therefore always imminent.

The 'somewhere-in-the-middle Tribbers' believe this happens after the Tribulation begins but before the actual judgments of God are *loosed*. That is why its adherents call it the 'Pre-Wrath Theory' of the rapture. Advocates of the Pre-Wrath theory believe the 'Day

---

[11] The Vulgate is the Latin Bible of the Catholic Church.

of the Lord'—associated exclusively with the time of God's wrath—comprises a particular period transpiring at the very end of the Great Tribulation (perhaps lasting two to six months).

The final group, the 'Post-Tribbers,' believe Christians will face martyrdom and most will be killed by the forces of the Antichrist (although some will pass through the entire Tribulation period unscathed—until the exact moment of Jesus' return). At that moment when Jesus appears 'in the clouds of Heaven' believers are 'translated' and immediately return with Christ to judge the Antichrist and his armies in the Battle of Armageddon.

So which view is right?

We have recounted the story of how Lot and his family were saved from Sodom and Gomorrah's destruction by God's angels entering into the city, collecting the family, and sneaking out before the break of dawn. Those that advocate for the *Pre-Trib* view believe this represents a universal biblical principle: *before God sends judgment, He delivers His people.* In other words, His children do not experience His judgments.[12] At the very least, we could say He puts His people in protective custody. Better yet, we should use an even more relevant analogy: believers go into a witness protection program and are transported safely out of town altogether.

The Post-Tribbers argue Christians have always been subject to martyrdom; we who are alive at the time of the Great Tribulation should not expect special treatment. Furthermore, Post-Tribbers implicitly accuse the Pre-Tribbers of *a lack of faith*. We often hear them proclaim, "You are looking for an easy way out." The implication: Pre-Tribbers are cowardly and unwilling to face the inevitable persecution in the days ahead. To Post-Tribbers, the *Pre-Trib rapture* constitutes the 'great escape.' As a Pre-Tribber myself, you might expect I would be a bit upset by these accusations. Well, perhaps a little. After overcoming those ill-advised

---

[12] 'Discipline' yes—but 'judgment' no.

emotions as Jesus' disciple, the question becomes, "How should Pre-Tribbers respond to what is something of a reprimand?"

RESPONDING TO THE 'ESCAPIST' REBUKE

To clarify things, it is essential to distinguish between 'human-inflicted' malicious acts such as torture and murder (aka *martyrdom*) versus 'God-inflicted' acts of punishment as depicted in the many judgments described in Revelation. As believers, we are told to expect persecutions. Certainly, it is considered a badge of righteousness to be seen 'worthy to be persecuted' for the sake of Jesus Christ.

In the Book of Acts, we see this language spoken by those who are beaten and tortured for their commitment to the gospel of Christ (See Acts 5:41). The accounts are clear, however, that such persecutions and even martyrdoms were not the acts of God, but of humankind. Christ's disciples did not blame God when they are stoned or thrown in prison by spiteful pagans. Instead, they praised God that they were found worthy to suffer for the sake of the Gospel of Jesus Christ.

Of course when it comes to determining who is right, the squabble between the Pre-Tribbers and the Post-Tribbers ought not to be settled solely based upon 'logic' but upon what the Bible teaches. Furthermore, accusations of one group targeting the other—questioning the quality of the other groups' commitment—should have no relevance to who is right and wrong. In logic class, we learn this is an *ad hominem* argument. This occurs when the *value of a premise is linked to a characteristic of a person.* It is like saying, "You are wrong, because you have red hair!" Nevertheless, we see this type of sniping in books arguing for the Post-Tribulation point of view. Unfortunately, it continues today even among otherwise sincere Christians. The argument that Pre-Tribbers are cowardly and unwilling to face the music of the Great Tribulation and martyrdom consists in this kind of chastisement. The argument against the Pre-Trib position gets connected to the personal attribute presumed within or about that person who professes this particular point of view: *(1) The Pre-Trib position (the argument) must be false because (2) the person who affirms it is unwilling to experience persecution (the pejorative attribute).* But is persecution the same as the wrath of God? Of course not.

Throwing the ad hominem argument into the fray adds to the heightened vitriol. Indeed, the level of acrimony can grow quite intense, with one group speculating that the view of the other group constitutes heresy, an unforgivable foible sure to cripple the proclamation of the gospel, today and in the Great Tribulation to come. Some go so far to assert that an incorrect profession of faith on the rapture topic now will cost the believer their place in heaven for eternity! (To that I politely reply, "Balderdash!")

Alas, we forget that Jesus said, *"By this shall all [men] know that ye are my disciples,* **if your doctrine remains perfect on every topic."** Well, actually, he did not say that. Instead, the condition for disclosing to others that we are his disciples would be *"if ye have love one to another."* (John 13:35) We forget we should never directly attack a person (or persons); *just the idea* with which we disagree. It remains well within bounds to *battle over ideas*; but not so commendable to attack against others *personally* (especially our brothers and sisters in Christ) with opposing views. Elevating this issue to the point of a curse ("You will go to Hell!") places the accuser only small step away from burning the accused at the stake! Such behavior may have been acceptable in Geneva during the sixteenth century. And unless we wish to emulate radical Islam and cut off the heads of infidels, it would seem advisable to steer clear of this approach.

SO WILL CHRISTIANS GO THROUGH THE TRIBULATION?

What does the Bible teach? There are numerous powerful verses which appear to state plainly that true believers *will be rescued from the coming judgments.* One such verse is from Paul's first letter to the Thessalonians: "[We are] ... *to wait for his Son from heaven, whom he raised from the dead, [even] Jesus, which* **delivered** *us from the wrath to come."* (I Thessalonians 1:10) Yet, this sounds like something that happened in the past and is not relevant to the future. Does this reinforce the view that we must pass through the Tribulation?

The key problem with the translation of the King James Version is that it incorrectly translates the Greek verb '*rhyomai'* in the *past tense*. 'Delivered' should be 'delivers' (implying present or future tense). Plus, according to the *Blue Letter Bible* the verb means "to draw to one's self, to rescue, to deliver." *Young's Literal Translation* of 1 Thessalonians 1:10, brings the meaning alive: *"and to wait for His Son from the heavens, whom He did raise out of the dead—Jesus, who is rescuing us from the anger that is coming."* The New American Standard Version provides a similar translation: *"and to wait for His Son from heaven, whom He raised from the dead, that is Jesus, who rescues us from the wrath to come."*

The *Vines Dictionary of New Testament Words* provides this explanation:

> Here the AV [King James Authorized Version—AV] wrongly has "which delivered" (the tense is not past); RV, "which delivereth;" the translation might well be (as in Rom 11:26), "our Deliverer," that is, from the retributive calamities with which God will visit men at the end of the present age. **From that wrath believers are to be "delivered."** (Emphasis added)

The passage employed as our epigraph for this chapter has something important to say here as well: *"Watch ye therefore, and pray always, that ye may be accounted worthy to* **escape** *all these things that shall come to pass, and to stand before the Son of man."* (Luke 21:36) The key word used in this passage is the Greek Word '*ekpheugō.*' This term conveys "to flee out of a place" (such as prisoners escaping from prison). It does not mean "preserved through" the calamity, but *being entirely removed from it*. One is not removed from prison by being safeguarded within it. The context of Luke's account strongly suggests the same thing: We are saved 'out of' the earth in order to "stand before the Son of Man." We must be taken out of one place to appear in another. God does not clone and only He has the ability to be in multiple places at the same time.

Perhaps one of my favorite verses in this regard is 1 Thessalonians 5:9. I memorized it in college (as translated in the New American Standard Version) and it has stayed with me for 38 years: *"For God has not destined us for wrath but to the (full) attainment of salvation for our Lord Jesus Christ."* The King James Version says: *"For God hath not appointed us to wrath, but to obtain salvation by our Lord Jesus Christ."*

Vines Dictionary explains what the word *'peripoiēsis' (obtainment)* means in this context: "the act of obtaining" anything, as of salvation in its "completeness"—referencing this verse and 2 Thessalonians 2:14: *"Whereunto he called you by our gospel, to the obtaining of the glory of our Lord Jesus Christ."* The connotation of the term comes across in a particularly strong way: *If you have it, you have all of it.* You will not be partially saved or 'saved' metaphorically. You will be *completely* saved. God intends that you receive all *the possible salvation you can get.* You will not be *left in the lurch*[13] when God pours out His judgment upon the world.

Once again, the context of 1 Thessalonians Chapter 5:1-11, clearly reinforces this same interpretation. Paul's admonition to his audience relates to *"knowing the times and the season;"* they

---

[13] A great phrase, whose origin is from the French board game of *lourche* or *lurch*, which was similar to backgammon and was last played in the seventeenth century. Players suffered a lurch if they were left in a hopeless position from which they could not win the game. Another possible origin: The lurch held casketed bodies awaiting a funeral. It was a small 'out building' lying next to the Church. To be 'left in the lurch' would be a bad place to spend time, to be sure. An outlier one might say!

are not in the *Day of the Lord* as they may have been assuming before he wrote. When we consider the context, it seems clear this was the reason Paul penned this particular epistle. Paul teaches:

> ¹*But of the times and the seasons, brethren, ye have no need that I write unto you.*
>
> ²*For yourselves know perfectly that the day of the Lord so cometh as a thief in the night.*
>
> ³*For when they shall say, Peace and safety; then sudden destruction cometh upon them, as travail upon a woman with child; and they shall not escape.*
>
> ⁴*But ye, brethren, are not in darkness, that that day should overtake you as a thief.*
>
> ⁵*Ye are all the children of light, and the children of the day: we are not of the night, nor of darkness.*
>
> ⁶*Therefore let us not sleep, as do others; but let us watch and be sober.*
>
> ⁷*For they that sleep sleep in the night; and they that be drunken are drunken in the night.*
>
> ⁸*But let us, who are of the day, be sober, putting on the breastplate of faith and love; and for an helmet, the hope of salvation.*
>
> ⁹**For God hath not appointed us to wrath, but to obtain salvation by our Lord Jesus Christ,**
>
> ¹⁰*Who died for us, that, whether we wake or sleep, we should live together with him.*
>
> ¹¹*Wherefore* **comfort yourselves together**, *and edify one another, even as also ye do.* (1 Thessalonians Chapter 5:1-11, emphasis added)

Paul conveys an explicit instruction (paraphrasing): "Everyone calm down! We cannot be in *The Day of the Lord*. We would know if we were. Why? We would already be with the Lord!"[14] As

---

[14] Whether we are "wake" or "sleep" at this time, we shall *"live together with Him."* This is analogous to the language of the Apostle's Creed: "We believe in the resurrection of the quick and the dead"—that when Christ returns He resurrects both

Paul says elsewhere, *"to be absent from the body is to be present with the Lord."* (2 Corinthians 5:8) We are to speak these words to *"comfort yourselves together and edify one another."* In fact, Paul must remind them once again of this very same truth in his *next* letter, 2 Thessalonians (as we mentioned earlier). Clearly, the Thessalonians were obsessed with the prophecies of the Lord's Second Coming. Apparently, matters were made worse because those who forged a letter (from Paul) made the frightening claim *that all Christians were going to go through the Tribulation:*

> *¹Now we beseech you, brethren, by the coming of our Lord Jesus Christ, and by our gathering together unto him,*
>
> *²That ye be not soon shaken in mind, or be troubled, neither by spirit, nor by word, nor by letter as from us, as that the day of Christ is at hand.*
>
> *³Let no man deceive you by any means: for that day shall not come, except there come **a falling away** first, and that **man of sin be revealed**, the son of perdition;*
>
> *⁴Who opposeth and exalteth himself above all that is called God, or that is worshipped; so that he as God sitteth in the temple of God, shewing himself that he is God.*
>
> *⁵Remember ye not, that, when I was yet with you, I told you these things? (2 Thessalonians 2:1-5)*

Paul supplies his followers with two distinct clues as to how they can know whether they had missed the rapture. First: there must come a 'falling away' (which either means an apostasy leading up to the revelation of the Antichrist—the apocalyptō; or means a 'departure' of the force that is restraining his appearance at the present time—to be expanded upon later). Then, secondly, *you will see the Antichrist reveal himself in the Temple of God,*

---

those living at that time and those that have already died, i.e., are *asleep.* We are removed from the earth to "live with Him."

declaring himself to be God. If you witness these two things, the Tribulation has begun! The Day of the Lord has come. However, if you were found worthy to be rescued from the wrath to come and to stand before the Son of Man, you will not be here to watch this event (no doubt televised worldwide) when it happens sometime in the future. Where will you be instead? Preoccupied—talking with loved ones in Heaven. The *Parousia* will have taken place. We will all be together and with the LORD from thenceforth and forever.[15]

BEING KEPT FROM THE HOUR OF TRIAL

Finally, Revelation 3:10 reinforces the very same concept yet again: *"Because thou hast kept the word of my patience, I also will keep thee from the hour of temptation, which shall come upon all the world, to try them that dwell upon the earth."* The King James Version uses the word temptation to translate the Greek word *peirasmos*. Vines indicates that a better English word for *peirasmos* would be 'trial.' The intention would be to 'prove something true or false,' as the remainder of the passage describes. The point is that God does not tempt humankind; but He sometimes tries us or tests us to prove (to us, not to Himself) what He has said about humankind in His Word stands true.[16] Since this statement is made in the context of the book of Revelation, the testing that comes upon the earth will be distinct. This tribulation involves *great vials of wrath.* Jesus' promise excludes His own from such 'testing.'

To dig deeper: The promise of Revelation 3:10 was given to the church at *Philadelphia* (in ancient Turkey). Many scholars for

---

[15] Additionally, those of us that have had physical infirmities (I have an artificial left leg) will likely be checking out our new bodies. Remember that line in Isaiah, "The lame shall leap?" I plan to be doing some serious leaping! Amen and amen.

[16] In this case, the lesson is likely that despite the severe 'testing' humans will curse God rather than repent. See Revelation 9:20, 21.

the past two centuries have taught that each of the seven churches in Revelation 2-3 provide a prophecy related to seven historical periods for Christ's church; in other words, each church represents one of seven consecutive stages in church history. The Philadelphia church is thought to represent the church which lives immediately before the Lord returns. This church was characterized by fervent evangelism and generally, orthodox teaching. The following verse, Revelation 3:11 begins: *"Behold I come quickly."* Thus, the context strongly implies that *the Lord comes quickly to keep this church from the hour of trail* that is just around the corner (and directed to the unrepentant world at large).

EMPLOYING A BIT OF LOGIC IN THE RAPTURE'S TIMING

While I mentioned earlier the Bible *and not logic* should teach us the answer to the question of whether the rapture of the Church is before, during, or at the end of the Great Tribulation, it would seem appropriate nonetheless to point out two logical arguments *derived from Scripture* suggesting the Pre-Trib position constitutes the correct perspective.

First, there is the admonition of Jesus t*o watch for His coming*. Many of His parables convey this sobering message. We are to be watchful and alert. However, if the coming of the Antichrist precedes the coming of the Lord—that is to say, if the rapture does not happen until the moment of the actual Second Coming (the visible return of Christ to earth at the Battle of Armageddon)—logically we *should be watching for the Antichrist instead*. Once the man of sin appears, we can do the math and recognize that we still have 3.5 years remaining before Jesus returns. The Antichrist's announcement would be the 'tripwire.' [17] Keeping watch

---

[17] In my opinion, this is where the 'Pre-wrath' theory collapses. Since God's wrath comes later in the Great Tribulation and Antichrist has already appeared at the midpoint, Pre-wrath theorists argue we will witness the Antichrist. Our blessed hope may still be three or more years away. Until he shows up, logically we would be able to allow our lamps to remain empty.

is shifted from watching for the coming of the Bridegroom to watching for the coming of the Antichrist! This may seem repugnant to my friends who affirm the Pre-wrath or Post-Trib viewpoint, but the logic remains difficult to defeat.

So is this viewpoint biblical? I hardly think so. Not only is it out of character with the Lord's direct admonition, it is inconsistent with His statement that we "*know neither the day nor the hour*" of His coming. Once Antichrist appears, we *will know the exact day* of Christ's return. That constitutes another logical reason implying that the rapture must precede the *apocalyptō* of the Antichrist.

Secondly, we are to comfort one another with the promise of His coming *to deliver us from the wrath to come.* If we know we must face the likelihood of martyrdom, the 'comfort factor' is dramatically diminished. Not only that, we would then face the fearful judgments and catastrophes that shall cause "*men's hearts to fail them for fear of what is coming upon the earth.*" (Luke 21:26) This seems glaringly inconsistent with the Scripture and the nature of God's care for His children. We should be looking forward to the return of Jesus—not dreading the coming of the Apocalypse.[18] Otherwise, our reward for studying 'what should soon come to pass upon the earth' would be a more thorough knowledge of how we may suffer. We might wish we were not so thoroughly informed!

IS THE RAPTURE A FEAT TOO DIFFICULT FOR GOD?

Is accomplishing the rapture such an incredible task for God? True: it transcends what we, limited by our finite minds, can comprehend. But is that a reason we should dismiss it as outside God's ability to accomplish? I presume many believe it to be 'non-sense' for this reason. They wonder how could God suddenly 'translate'

---

[18] See Appendix One and Two for additional arguments for the Pre-Tribulation Rapture; the first providing a series of additional 'logical' arguments and the second providing a discourse on the explicit meaning of the key word, *apostasia*, a word according to some scholars meaning "departure," used by Paul to imply the rapture.

perhaps one billion bodies of the living and perhaps another two billion bodies of the dead—at the very same moment—from a corrupted (dead) or corruptible (mortal) state to an incorruptible (immortal) state. How could He do all that *"in the twinkling of an eye?"* Just directing the traffic alone would overload the circuits of the biggest computer we can imagine.

But then, God does not use computers to accomplish His will.

So if that challenge causes us to doubt, we should realize our problem is: "W*e underestimate God's power to save."* God asks Abraham (and us) if we consider *"anything too hard for the Lord?"* (Genesis 18:14) I, for one, do not wish to suggest our God is incapable of anything. He remains *Elohim*, the Creator, as well as *Jehovah*, the covenant keeper. After all, what is the rapture, but another stupendous act of creation, converting a form of matter subject to decay to another which can never die or degenerate? Doing such things is what our God, as made known to us through the earthly life of Jesus Christ, does best. Doing the impossible is His trademark!

Finally, if we believe that God attends to every detail of our lives (each and every day of our life—which is what the scripture teaches) and He remains capable of keeping everything straight (and not becoming mixed up with what happens at all times with 7 billion people simultaneously, all the while keeping track of what is transpiring with billions more animals who He created and loves (of whose lives he remains fully aware), why would we puzzle over how God could accomplish the rapture, all in the twinkling of an eye?

Just because we cannot understand something does not make it fail when we put it to use. I do not understand the principles of aerodynamics, but I still board an airplane and it still flies through the air getting me to my destination. My understanding of the technology being employed to serve my needs has nothing to do with whether it can or cannot work. Someone smarter than me figured out exactly how it could work. I rely upon their competence.

And God is fully capable of performing ANY feat. Peter makes this very point: *"The Lord **knoweth how to deliver the godly out of temptations [testing or trial]**, and to reserve the unjust unto the Day of Judgment to be punished."* (2 Peter 2:9, emphasis added) The LORD knows how to deliver the godly.

Perhaps the Psalmist said it best when he exclaimed: *"[Such] knowledge [is] too wonderful for me; it is high, I cannot [attain] unto it."* (Psalm 139:6)

Happily, God does not rely upon our ability to comprehend His ways in order to accomplish His plan. He expressly tells us we cannot fully understand His ways. They are beyond knowing.

The Book of Job states this far more poetically that I can ever hope to express: *"God thundereth marvellously with his voice; great things doeth he, which we cannot comprehend."* (Job 37:5)

16: WALKING WORTHY OF OUR VOCATION

*I therefore, the prisoner of the Lord, beseech you that ye **walk worthy** of the vocation wherewith ye are called*
(Ephesians 4:1)

*That ye might **walk worthy** of the Lord unto all pleasing, being fruitful in every good work, and increasing in the knowledge of God*
(Colossians 1:10)

*That ye would **walk worthy** of God, who hath called you unto his kingdom and glory.*
(I Thessalonians 2:12)

THE PRACTICAL IMPORTANCE OF THE APOCALYPSE

I HAVE PUT FORTH MY CASE WHY CHRISTIANITY COMPRISES A DISTINCTLY APOCALYPTIC FAITH, STANDING APART FROM OTHER RELIGIONS IN THE STUDY OF THE FUTURE. AS SUCH, CHRISTIANITY satisfies one of our most cherished quests.

By the same token, orthodox Christianity opens itself to be proven true or false based upon *its prophetic accuracy*. Additionally, because it is a 'space-time' faith, Christianity intends to be a highly relevant faith. Even the 'signs of the times' speak to how Christ proclaimed God's incursion in our space-time realm.

To further emphasize God's connection to history, Jesus related the stories of Noah and Jonah, the most notorious 'mythical' characters of the Bible, insisting that their historical reality confers certain details of coming events. While many highly regarded religious thinkers in our day espouse the distinction between the hard-core fabric of history and the ethereal nature of spirituality, the God of the Bible as disclosed through Jesus Christ, makes no such epistemological distinction. No dichotomy exists between *truth* in spiritual matters and what we see printed in the news.

Given that Christian truth demands it be characterized as "down to earth" in a philosophical sense, we should inquire *"what is the practical value for believing in these things?"* If we believe that Jesus will soon return in our space-time realm, how does this affect us? The point being: since the apocalypse of Jesus Christ hovers close to the intellectual center of Christianity, *this notion should have a vital impact upon how we live our daily lives.*

There is the old joke about two priests talking. One says to the other, "Father John, I have just discovered and it is confirmed: *The Lord is returning tomorrow*! Whatever shall we do?" Father John—somewhat perplexed—replies without thinking, "I do not know. But one thing is for sure. We better look busy."

Certainly one practical conclusion we can draw is simply this: W*e are accountable.* We are to be good stewards. We must remember when 'the Master returns' we are required to give account of ourselves and what we have accomplished. Did we invest our time wisely? Did our stewardship yield a return to the Master? Did we do unto others as if we were doing what we did, unto the Lord? As I write these words, I am sure the many relevant parables of Jesus come quickly to the reader's mind reinforcing how frequently Jesus taught such things to His disciples.

The Master never indicated that being His true disciple was an easy task requiring little commitment and no modification to the way we live. He cautioned we must 'count the cost of discipleship.' We must make tough choices.

Consequently, following Christ was more than practicing meditative spiritual disciplines. It meant altering our priorities. It meant putting the interests of others ahead of our own.

COUNTING THE COST OF DISCIPLESHIP

In Luke, Chapter 14:27-33, we read the stark conditions of following Christ:

> *"And whosoever doth not bear his cross, and come after me, cannot be my disciple. For which of you, intending to build a tower, sitteth not down first, and counteth the cost, whether he have sufficient to finish it? Lest haply, after he hath laid the foundation, and is not able to finish it, all that behold it begin to mock him, saying, 'This man began to build, and was not able to finish.' Or what king, going to make war against another king, sitteth not down first, and consulteth whether he be able with ten thousand to meet him that cometh against him with twenty thousand? Or else, while the other is yet a great way off, he sendeth an ambassage, and desireth conditions of peace. So likewise, whosoever he be of you that forsaketh not all that he hath, he cannot be my disciple."*

Becoming a disciple of Jesus Christ requires extensive self-examination. Too often, we are *not* challenged to count the cost by messengers of the gospel. After all, did not Jesus say, *"My yoke is easy and my burden is light" (Matthew 11:30)*? Many preachers sell solace to 'parishioners' for mending broken hearts; some promise prosperity to perk up their hopes and dreams as if "godliness is a means of great gain" (I Titus 6:6). But God's Grace, as Dietrich Bonhoeffer diagnosed, is cheapened by such promises. Suffering a martyr's death for his association in several assassination attempts on the life of Hitler, Bonhoeffer knew firsthand what the cost of discipleship meant. He died hanging naked from a piano wire wrapped around his neck. And yet, he went to the gallows with such serenity his imprisoned colleagues were astonished.

I could continue to beat this drum, since I believe it worthwhile to underscore our obligation to follow Christ authentically. True, we should admit we have squandered many opportunities—we have failed to follow Christ perfectly. Indeed, we have sinned as the Bible asserts. It is not surprising that the return of Christ causes us to 'clean up our act.' The Bible states that reflecting on the soon coming of Jesus Christ sanitizes our incentive. *"And every man that hath this hope in him purifieth himself"* (I John 3:3).

But dwelling on the 'stick' rather than the 'carrot' is not really my style. My motivation always is to accentuate the positive. I realize *benefits* from conviction about the Second Coming. There seems to be little need to focus on our failures to heed the Master's call. Christ's coming should not provoke fear we will be found wanting. Consequently, my focus remains *on the 'upside.'*

FIGURE 37 - BONHOEFFER - THE COST OF DISCIPESHIP

In part, I confess this positive approach owes to my suspicion that many who read this book present a pretty clean act to begin with—not to mention are also well grounded in the knowledge that our salvation depends not upon what we do, but because of *what God has done for us through the death of Jesus Christ on the cross* (Romans 5:8). So then, was there any reason readers who strive to live a consecrated life should have bothered to read this book? Obviously, I would not have put pen to paper, (metaphorically speaking that is, since I make good use of my word processor), if I did not believe there was a need worthy of my effort.

WHY WE MUST LIVE IN LIGHT OF THE APOCALYPSE

Let me cite several important reasons for living 'informed' by the nearness of the apocalypse. We must adopt the right motives, consider what others see as the message of the gospel as illustrated by the way we live today, refresh our message according to a more thorough and scholarly interpretation of the Bible, and consecrate the time we have left in order to maximize our impact upon the unbelieving world. These hopeful goals summarize my intent in writing and also serve as a proposal for a sound, albeit abbreviated agenda to follow, as we examine ourselves daily.

Why do we need to 'have our wheels continuously realigned?' All too often, those inclined to study prophecy appear compelled for the wrong reasons. Consequently, I propose several questions for our self-examination:

- Are we fascinated by the end of the world because it is a scintillating topic?
- Are we 'code breakers' hoping to finally discover a hidden secret about the nature of the Second Coming of Jesus Christ?
- Do we believe that the Bible holds a hidden date that tells us exactly when Jesus will return to this earth?
- Are we depressed about our personal predicament and hoping for an 'out-of-this-world' quick escape?"

Because it affects the way in which we live, it is appropriate—even necessary—to examine why we focus on the subject of prophecy. Moreover, we should question if we have 'gone out of balance' regarding the entirety of the gospel message. Much more remains to be learned from the Bible than just predictions about the future. While experts point out the Bible devotes 25% of its content to the subject (typically an argument for why we should study prophecy), there is another 75% addressing other topics, such as: establishing biblically sound theology, learning the lessons of ancient history, how to worship God properly, and how we should treat one another. Consequently, the challenge to consider is, "Are we so concerned about prophecy that we pay little attention to other matters important in the present day?" No doubt, we all need to balance learning and living.

There is an oft quoted cliché how some Christians are "so heavenly minded that they are no earthly good." Are we 'guilty as charged?' Or do we engage in activities underscoring the Love of God and His plan for humankind? Do we understand who our neighbor is? Do we come to his/her aid? Do we defend the doctrine—God created the world and expects us to be its caretakers? Or do our actions present a point of view evincing an unbiblical understanding of our responsibilities (i.e., our stewardship) of this planet?

When it comes to matters of 'social justice'—a term often associated with the 'leftish agenda' (and the wrong-headed notion that 'social justice' is a non-issue for evangelicals)—do we seek support for those society puts down or represses? Whether it is a simple case of kids being bullied in school, gang violence in the 'hood,' or the corner grocer run out of business by a national supermarket chain, do we sit on our laurels offering little to no help? Do we even care when we learn of the misery of others?

As Christians, doing 'the right thing' remains our responsibility even if we believe we only have a few months or years left before Christ returns. How we behave morally, ethically, and socially reflects upon who we are and, lest we forget, *who God is*. If we take seriously the message of Genesis that we are image bearers of God, how can we fail to realize our actions communicate louder than words? A tree is known by its fruit.

LIVING SALTY LIVES THROUGH DOING GOOD WORKS

It is not that these public or civil actions take precedence over our commitment to personal piety, virtue, and evangelism; nonetheless God commands us to "do good works"—it is for this purpose we are called. *"And let us consider one another to provoke unto love and to good works"* (Hebrews 10:24, see also 1 Timothy 6:18; Titus 3:8, 14). As mentioned, Jesus taught: "We are the salt of the earth"—therefore, we must maintain our 'saltiness.' *"Ye are the salt of the earth: But if the salt have lost his savour, wherewith shall it be salted? It is thenceforth good for nothing, but to be cast out, and to be trodden under foot of men"* (Matthew 5:13).

Consider the story of William Wilberforce (1759—1833), a fervent evangelical and the essential catalyst bringing an end to the slave trade in England.[1] The exploitation of slaves was hardly something he could accept in good conscience and sit idly by, doing nothing. His intent glowed pure and consistent with the gospel of Christ. But he was ignored, threatened, and mocked for his witness that slavery must end in England.

Whether it was Parliament, the leaders of the Church of England, or successful businessmen (mind you, all 'members in good standing in the Christian Kingdom of England!'), Wilberforce risked his life and health to make a difference. Ultimately, his actions brought enormous change to the world and relieved the suffering of millions upon millions of persons.

Sometimes the 'full gospel' of Jesus Christ is associated with being 'baptized in the Holy Spirit.' There is no question that Christians should showcase they live not just on their own power, but through the power of the Holy Spirit—the Spirit of Jesus Christ—living within and through us. *"For as many as are led by the Spirit of God, they are the sons of God"* (Romans 8:14). Nevertheless,

---

[1] The movie, *Amazing Grace (2007)*, tells this inspirational story

while we are commanded to be filled with the Spirit (Ephesians 5:18), the *fullness of the gospel* means far more than expressing a *supernatural* means enabling a genuinely spiritual life. Each of us is required to "walk a walk" worthy of His calling:

- *I therefore, the prisoner of the Lord, beseech you that ye **walk worthy** of the vocation wherewith ye are called (Ephesians 4:1)*

- *That ye might **walk worthy** of the Lord unto all pleasing, being fruitful in every good work, and increasing in the knowledge of God; (Colossians 1:10)*

- *That ye would **walk worthy** of God, who hath called you unto His kingdom and glory. (I Thessalonians 2:12)*

How we conduct ourselves constitutes proof of God's calling. If we do not walk worthy of His calling, logic leads us to question the legitimacy of our commitment, and therefore, our salvation. *"Brethren, give diligence to make your calling and election sure: for if ye do these things, ye shall never fall" (2 Peter 1:10).*

When it comes to 'getting the message of biblical prophecy right'—we must consider how our traditional language and concepts actually stand up to a thoughtful, fresh, and scholarly review of the Bible. Have we chosen the right words to communicate our convictions? Is our 'witness' for the veracity of biblical prophecy compelling today? Are the 'old words and usual concepts'—what we would consider tried and true—faithful to the biblical text, so that we convincingly communicate our views? Are our words *relevant* to the world in which we live?

This does not imply we must change the Bible's message. To the contrary, the Bible's message must be upheld with care taken to treat it with reverence and preach it with authority. However, if the standard terminology, the 'same old words' compromises the clarity and truthfulness of the Bible in our world today, such phrases must be retired.

I am not a friend of the language of 'soul winning.' Perhaps that phrase meant something 80 years ago. But now it smacks of doing evangelism solely for achieving an institutionally-imposed (or self-imposed) quota (how many 'souls' walked down the aisles to be saved; how many have I witnessed to this week) rather than saving the whole person—seeing the value of the individual, seeing them as their family sees them, seeing them as God sees them—individuals that can impact the society in which we live today.

Another way to express this idea: students of prophetic themes over the years have developed their own language (i.e., jargon) like any other group. Students of prophecy may be guilty of using labels and terms familiar to those of us 'on the inside' but which convey wrongs ideas to those not in the loop. Most of those 'outside our circle' know the word *rapture* but they likely entertain vivid misconceptions about what this event means. When they hear the term *millennium*, they may think 'Millenarians' and immediately assume it references current day apocalyptic advocates selling their possessions and heading to the hills.

It is a sad truth that *the craziest of the crazy are typically apocalyptic kooks*. Think Jim Jones, David Koresh, and Charley Manson. For many, believing in the Second Coming infers we are as out-of-touch as those who live in cloistered cults. After all, are not 'apocalyptics' just like the members of *Heaven's Gate* who committed suicide when the spaceship supposedly following the Hale-Bopp Comet did not come to their rescue? In the opinion of mainstream culture, those who believe in the apocalypse are not only foolish, they could be borderline criminal.

WE ARE CALLED TO BE DISTINCTIVE—BUT NOT STRANGE

If we provide a vivid and correct portrayal of the gospel of Christ by the way we live, words might seem to be less important. Nevertheless, both vital deeds and powerful words are imperative. Consequently, we must be aware of the words we use. Are we making 'best efforts' to ensure we are emphasizing the real message of

Christ? Or do we obscure His message by 'majoring on the minors?' Too many times, Christians measure spirituality by non-conformity. Indeed, Paul admonishes not to "*be contaminated by the world, but being transformed by the renewing of our minds, so we can prove that God's will is perfect*" (Romans 12:1, 2, paraphrased). We are 'not of this world.' But this phrase is often misinterpreted and an excuse for behaving oddly.

Maintaining a distinction from the world's way of doing things does not mean we have to be simpletons. There is no rule that mandates those believing in the return of Christ have to be unsophisticated and uncultured. God's creative impulse remains a major aspect of the 'divine image' within us. Few human endeavors can be more sacred than art, poetry, building, or even engineering a new bridge. Creativity, more than cleanliness, stands next to godliness.

The fact Jesus was a carpenter should be symbol enough. Furthermore, to the extent we achieve seclusion from the world for the sake of piety—we make ourselves and our message inaccessible to others. Our witness may suffer. Cloistered Christians, literally or by *liberal use of jargon in our language,* cloak the gospel making it more difficult for non-believers to comprehend. Those who have not come to a saving knowledge of Jesus Christ 'cannot relate' to the Gospel due to our failure to make the message meaningful and relevant to where they are—and we must avoid blaming them because they are 'unregenerate men or women' unable or unwilling to hear the message of the gospel.

MAKING THE MOST OF THE LITTLE TIME REMAINING

Finally, as believers who sense the end draws near, it is paramount we prayerfully consider how we live during the remaining time we have on this earth. As the Psalmist said, *"So teach us to number our days, that we may present to You [God] a heart of wisdom"* (Psalm 90:12, *New American Standard Version*).

We are all familiar with the stereotypical doomsday prophet walking the streets hoisting a sandwich board upon his shoulders. The board broadcasts a stark message painted with black paint on the white background: "THE END IS NEAR." Some might be critical of this singular demonstration; sizing him up as a laid-off roustabout, typically sporting a long beard and tattered clothes, who *does more harm than good*. But I would suggest drawing this conclusion comprises more than arrogance—it is patently false. It is more likely this unsavory character was not called to testify *to you*.

Furthermore, it begs a related and personally difficult question: while we may not don a disagreeable sandwich board, *"Is our testimony doing more harm than good"?* As believers in Bible prophecy, how we carry ourselves and convey the message that *'The End is Near!'* may be the only warning that many of our family or friends will heed. If so, the question we must ponder is, "Can those to whom God wishes for me to speak take me seriously?" While Bible prophecy and the Second Coming of Jesus Christ may be the most solemn and sobering theme of the calamitous times in which we live, do our lives and words bear witness to it?

Certainly, we profess faith and perhaps few would doubt our sincerity. But do we 'transmit' *hope for the future* despite the desperate times? Do we share the love of Christ with others in such a way those around us know we are Christian? Are we making the most of the time remaining? If we practice the evangelical imperative to share our faith with those 'who are without hope' (Ephesians 2:12), we should be encouraged. As times grow more difficult, the "open doorway" opens wider. *"Behold I have set before thee an open door."* (Revelation 3:8)

The Apostle John reminds us the time is short. *"He which testifieth these things saith, 'Surely I come quickly.' Amen. Even so, come, Lord Jesus."* (Revelation 22:20).

Keeping watch is our foremost responsibility in these last days before the return of the Savior. But note: keeping watch includes walking a walk worthy of the vocation to which we have been called. We can easily see the morning sky is red and the storm heads our direction. The blood moons may signal the end of days. So are we prepared? Remember this: much of our preparation lies in the way we live this very day. We may emit great words of encouragement and edification. But our lifestyle and our behavior towards others supplies a non-verbal demonstration with even higher decibel levels than any mode of speech. We show our maturity and readiness for the Kingdom. Or we illustrate just the opposite. It is time we take a self-assessment to determine which outcome best reflects who we are and what we wish to accomplish in the short time we have left.

17: OBTAINING THE GLORY OF GOD

For I reckon that the sufferings of this present time are not worthy to be compared with the glory which shall be revealed in us. For the earnest expectation of the creature [creation] waiteth for the manifestation of the sons of God. For the creature [creation] was made subject to vanity, not willingly, but by reason of him who hath subjected the same in hope. Because the creature [creation] itself also shall be delivered from the bondage of corruption into the glorious liberty of the children of God.

For we know that the whole creation groaneth and travaileth in pain together until now. And not only they, but ourselves also, which have the firstfruits of the Spirit, even we ourselves groan within ourselves, waiting for the adoption, to wit, the redemption of our body. For we are saved by hope: but hope that is seen is not hope: for what a man seeth, why doth he yet hope for? But if we hope for that we see not,
then do we with patience wait for it.
(Romans 8:18-25)

TRANSFIXED BY THE TRANSFIGURATION

BEFORE JESUS DEPARTED FROM THE EARTH, NOT LONG BEFORE HE WAS CRUCIFIED, HE PROVIDED HIS CLOSEST DISCIPLES, PETER, JAMES AND JOHN—A GLIMPSE INTO THE KINGDOM.

Matthew introduces the account in this way: *"'For the Son of man shall come in the glory of his Father with his angels; and then He shall reward every man according to his works. Verily I say unto you, there be some standing here, which shall not taste of death, till they see the Son of Man coming in His kingdom.'"*

(Matthew 16:27, 28) To understand Jesus' statement, we must recognize the context. Chapter 17 in Matthew's gospel begins immediately thereafter. The first event Matthew records in this new chapter fulfills what Jesus predicted at the end of the previous.

We read:

¹*And after six days Jesus taketh Peter, James, and John his brother, and bringeth them up into an high mountain apart,*

²*And [He] was transfigured before them: and His face did shine as the sun, and His raiment was white as the light.*

³*And, behold, there appeared unto them Moses and Elias [Elijah] talking with Him.*

⁴*Then answered Peter, and said unto Jesus, "Lord, it is good for us to be here: if thou wilt, let us make here three tabernacles; one for Thee, and one for Moses, and one for Elias."*

⁵*While he yet spake, behold, a bright cloud overshadowed them: and behold a voice out of the cloud, which said, "This is my beloved Son, in whom I am well pleased; hear ye Him."*

⁶*And when the disciples heard it, they fell on their face, and were sore afraid.*

⁷*And Jesus came and touched them, and said, "Arise, and be not afraid."*

⁸*And when they had lifted up their eyes, they saw no man, save Jesus only.*

⁹*And as they came down from the mountain, Jesus charged them, saying, "Tell the vision to no man, until the Son of man be risen again from the dead."*

If I am correct that the context provides the key to understanding the assertion Jesus made (that "*there be some standing here, which shall not taste of death, till they see the Son of Man coming in His kingdom*"), then Jesus' understanding of the coming of the Kingdom becomes more mystical than conservative scholarship usually allows. The coming of the Kingdom began with the event we know as the *Transfiguration*. Jesus calls it a vision in Matthew 27:9. And a vision it might well have been. And yet, the account in the gospels and in 2 Peter, locks this vision into a particular place and time. Clearly, the Kingdom intersects two dimensions. Also obvious: *Jesus' glorification lies at the heart of the Kingdom.*

FIGURE 38 - TRANSFIGURATION OF CHRIST ICON, SINAI 12TH CENTURY

THE PRINCE IN PAUPER'S CLOTHES

I have not preached many sermons in my day (I teach far more often than I preach), but one sermon I was especially proud of was entitled, "The Prince in Paupers Clothes." It harkened back to Mark Twain's *The Prince and the Pauper*, a story about two boys who look alike, one the true Prince of Wales (Edward, son of Henry the VIII), and the other, a boy from a poor family. The boys meet and switch places to see if they can get away with the hoax. And they almost do, up to the end of the story when the switch is discovered and Edward is crowned King.

My point in the sermon was this: In His earthly life, Jesus was a prince wearing pauper's clothing until the day He was transfigured before His three disciples—when it was suddenly revealed to them *Jesus was the Son of God*, the voice of God Himself testifying to this truth. Jesus' glory was so stunning it seemed He shone like the sun! Furthermore, He was accompanied by two heroic Hebrew figures: Moses and Elijah, representing the two most important sections of the Old Testament and the Hebrew religion: (1) the *Law* and (2) the *Prophets*. To see Jesus in their company was an astounding confirmation to the disciples that not only was Jesus special, *He was even superior to 'Moses and Elias.'*

This snapshot of the three together reinforced the true identity of Jesus Christ. The fact He was glorified and shone bright as the sun, while Moses and Elijah apparently were not so similarly arrayed, inferred Jesus held a superior status. He enjoyed a glory neither Moses nor Elijah then possessed (later in this chapter, we will discuss when they may receive such a glorious appearance). The experience was so dramatic Peter did not know what to say. Perhaps for their own protection (lest they be considered a bit off balance by every other follower of Jesus), the Master instructed them to keep what they'd seen to themselves until after they beheld Him, the Son of Man, risen from the dead.

The location of the event was most likely Mount Hermon. The mountain is part of today's Golan Heights, west of Damascus, rising over 9,230 feet. Scholars see this sacred landmark as the northern border of ancient Israel. The tribe of Dan resided at its base until (perhaps) they set sail for the Greek Isles.

As I explained in an earlier chapter, this mountain was the precise location where Canaan, a son of Ham, established his family after the Flood of Noah. According to the non-canonical books of Enoch and Jasper, angels "[left] their first estate" (see Genesis 6:4) and came to earth literally landing on the peak of Mount Hermon. Supposedly, soon thereafter 200 angels also known as 'the Watchers,' begat offspring with the daughters of men, giving rise to the *Nephilim*—a race of demigods.

The Bible does not explain why Jesus chose this particular place for His transfiguration. But the 'coincidence' is telling. Indeed, most evangelical scholars believe it is because this location symbolized an *apex of evil*. By His transfiguration, Jesus reclaimed the ground formerly 'owned' (from a spiritual perspective) by the fallen angels. Israel's worship of *Baal* and *Ashtoreth* (a Hebrew version of *Ishtar*, the fertility goddess) 'in the high places' (inferring Mount Hermon) reaffirmed the mountain as the acquired property of 'the Evil One.' It remains fascinating conjecture to be sure; however, a bona fide historical basis exists for such speculation. Suffice it to say, the lesson of the story centers on this 'glimpse' into the Kingdom of God showcasing Jesus' glory, and positioning Him in the context of the Hebrew religion.[1]

THE GOSPEL SPEAKS OF A COMPLETE SALVATION

More often than not, those rejecting the Christian gospel do so because they have not heard the gospel presented in a biblical way. What they reject is not necessarily 'the gospel truth' but their misconception regarding what the gospel means. In a similar way, too

---

[1] It is also interesting that Moses and Elijah (Elias) appear with Christ in this vision. It comprises the considered opinion of most prophecy scholars that these two personages (Moses and Elijah) are either literally or 'in spirit' the two witnesses of Revelation 11. These witnesses oppose the Antichrist during the Great Tribulation period. At the end of their 3.5 year ministry they are murdered by Antichrist, but then are supernaturally resurrected in front of the entire world. This amazing event appears to take place 30 days before the Battle of Armageddon.

often the sound bites we throw out concerning how to *become* a Christian as well as what it means to *be* one, fall on deaf ears. To many our oft-repeated phrases regarding 'accepting Christ' have become meaningless clichés. In effect, our pearls have been trampled in the dust. Because our easy summations are meager and hollow sayings in the minds of many people, the meaning of 'receiving Christ' is not obvious to all those outside the circle of faith. We who attempt to share their faith (and that should include all who call themselves Christian), now must work harder than ever to explain what it means to come to an authentic, saving faith in Jesus Christ.

Likewise, when it comes to, if you will, explaining the essence of salvation our notions seem rather attenuated. Salvation comprises much more than most of us realize. We understand we are forgiven of our sins. When Jesus died at Golgotha outside Jerusalem, He took our sins to the cross with Him. *"He who knew no sin became sin on our behalf that we might become the righteousness of God in Him."* (2 Corinthians 5:21, paraphrased). We also know that *"While we were yet sinners, Christ died for us"* (Romans 5:8). This is indeed wonderful news. The whole story, however, involves far more that should be communicated.

Evangelicals readily acknowledge *being saved* enables us to 'go to heaven.' We recall the famous passage that shrinks the essence of the gospel down to a single verse—John 3:16: *"For God so loved the world that He gave His only begotten Son, that whosoever believeth in Him should not perish, but have everlasting life."*

Nevertheless, the culmination of Christian salvation constitutes *one of our best kept secrets*. So much more remains to be said about the afterlife than we have typically been taught. And this lack of understanding constitutes *a big chink in our armor*. Our failure to fully appreciate what lies before us could be our undoing as we enter into these increasingly perilous times where we face persecution and all manner of difficulty. We do well to remember the epistles of the Apostles were written to their churches during times of turmoil. Being a follower of 'the Way' was not an easy task. The leaders of the early church armed the flock with a deep understanding of what was at stake. As we say today, their notion was truly a 'big idea.' For the most part, the early church stood up to the opposition even when it meant martyrdom. *We can be assured what they believed about the afterlife was a major factor energizing their amazing courage.*

That is why Paul prayed for his church at Ephesus with such intensity: he strove earnestly that they might fully realize what the salvation of God through Jesus Christ meant. He prayed that: *"The eyes of your understanding being enlightened; that ye may know what is the hope of His calling and what the riches of the glory of His inheritance in the saints"* (Ephesians 1:18). He also prayed the same for the church at Colossae: *"To whom God would make known what [is] the riches of the glory of this mystery among the Gentiles; which is Christ in you, the hope of glory"* (Colossians 1:27).

Today, more than ever, this astonishing truth is crucial to our Christian perspective: Not only are we made righteous in the eyes of God; but *the glory of God* awaits those who are adopted as His children. It comprises a wonderful and remarkable gift to have 'right standing with God'—but it stands as quite another matter altogether to possess *the glory of Christ*.

WHAT DOES IT MEAN TO SHARE IN GOD'S GLORY?

"The glory of God"—what does that mean? Are we really destined to be glorious like God? Will we really share in His glory? This seems incredible—to some perhaps even heretical. Does the Bible really say such a future awaits us?

Most everyone has at least a vague concept of eternal life. But the truth of the matter goes beyond clarifying that Christians (and orthodox Jews) believe in a bodily, physical resurrection. The historical Judeo-Christian view of heaven begins with an appreciation of our *corporeal* nature there. Jews and Christians believe 'having a body' is a good thing. This stands in contrast to (1) the classic view of the Greeks, and (2) the original Gnostics (familiar to us today through the publication of the Gnostic gospels of Thomas, Judas, and Mary Magdalene), as well as (3) today's variants to Gnosticism—occultists, theosophists, and advocates for the New Age.

All of these religions, whether ancient or current, believe the afterlife implies existence as little more than a *ghost*—a spirit being that passes between 'this side and *the other side.*' They disparage the bodily resurrection because at the core of this universal pagan religion are these beliefs (1) matter is tainted with evil; and therefore (2) requires a less-than-pure being to handle matter; consequently, (3) the creation was formed by an imperfect 'middle-man' (be it the ancient notion of a *demiurge* or today's new idol implied in 'smart matter' or 'lively matter' as depicted in modern physics—a 'fantastic reality' allegedly explaining miracles and the supernatural). This worldview (or cosmology) provides an explanation for *why evil exists* despite its assumption that 'God is good.' It also provides a defense for God's goodness—known as a *theodicy*—that is, the classic (i.e., ages old) explanation for *why evil exists in the world.*

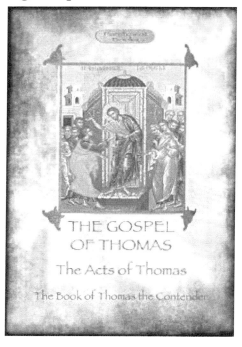

FIGURE 39 - THE GNOSTIC GOSPELS

THE CREATION WAS SUBJECTED TO EVIL FOR OUR GLORY

Nevertheless, Christians reject the notion *the creation is evil*. Instead, we believe an originally good creation was cursed because our sin (originating from humans and not God) altered what was initially made good.[2] Ultimately, both 'the sinner' and the creation are slated for full redemption by the Creator. In other words, the death of Jesus did more than pay the penalty for humankind's sin; it legally set the creation free to be made right again once Christ returns in glory. That comprises Paul's argument in Romans 8:

> *"For the creature [creation][3] was made subject to vanity, not willingly, but by reason of him who hath subjected the same in hope, because the creature [creation] itself also shall be delivered from the bondage of corruption into the glorious liberty of the children of God."*

In other words, God has a reclamation plan for our world and we are right at the very center of it! For our sakes the creation in its entirety was subjected to futility. This plan incorporates the essential gospel mystery. As Paul says, *"...we speak the wisdom of God in a mystery, [even] the hidden [wisdom], which God ordained before the world **unto our glory**"* (I Corinthians 2:7). While evil sought to wreck the creation due to our sin, God intervened in our world—in history—to redeem us and His creation. God planned from the beginning to bring good from what was corrupted. It was done this way "unto our glory"—for the purpose of *our being glorified one day*. Paul goes on to say:

---

[2] Remember after every day (save one) those statements by God in Genesis—*"And God saw what He had made and said, 'It is Good.'"* This language was an emphatic rebuttal to virtually all other religions blaming evil on the creation. God's commentary constitutes an unmistakable exclamation point for just how *good* it is! God takes all manner of creation 'dissing' personally. He reigns as the proud Creator.

[3] The word for *creation* and *creature* is one and the same: *ktisis*, (pronounced, *key-teh-sees*). Thus, it can be translated either way depending upon the context. The KJV seems to mistranslate it in the Romans 8 passage we referenced here.

> *For we know that the whole creation groaneth and travaileth in pain together until now. And not only they, but ourselves also, which have the first fruits of the Spirit, even we ourselves groan within ourselves, waiting for the adoption, to wit, the redemption of our body.*

Once fully redeemed, we will overcome *"the bondage of corruption and obtain the glorious liberty of the children of God"* as quoted earlier. We are instructed this struggle was necessary to transform us into *glorified children of God*. For from the beginning, we were predestined to become like Jesus Christ:

> *For whom He did foreknow, He also did predestinate [to be] conformed to the image of His Son, that He might be the firstborn among many brethren. Moreover whom He did predestinate, them He also called: and whom He called, them He also justified: and whom He justified, them He also glorified (Romans 8:29)*

Salvation consists of a many-step process. In God's eyes, however, all the steps have been accomplished already. There is no suspense. Everything has already been settled. Though our experience today does not include the perfection we call *glorification*, nevertheless, we are told this next step is as good as finished (or as they say in my home Oklahoma, 'it is a done deal'). According to Paul's gospel, God 'called us' for this express purpose*: "Whereunto He called you by our gospel, to* **the obtaining of the glory of our Lord Jesus Christ**.*"* (2 Thessalonians 2:14) The Lord God planned from the beginning to have many millions (at least) of sons and daughters glorified with *the same glory present in Jesus Christ.*

WHAT IT MEANS THAT JESUS CHRIST WAS MADE PERFECT

In the Letter to the Hebrews, Paul lets us in on another secret. Somehow through the incarnation, Jesus Christ was *"made perfect"* through sufferings. This occurred despite the fact that all things were made by God for Him, and He Himself (the *Logos*) made all things. Through the process of the incarnation—*the experience of becoming human and living His life in a body like ours*[4]—He was enabled to be the 'first-born' of many brethren, *"bringing many sons unto glory."* Paul refers to Jesus as *"the captain of our salvation:* "*For it became him, for whom [are] all things, and by whom [are] all things, in bringing many sons unto glory, to make the captain of their salvation* **perfect** *through sufferings."* (Hebrews 2:10)

What does Paul mean by being made *perfect*? He uses the term *teleioō (pronounced, tuh-lie-ah-oh)*—and repeats this word over *ten times* in the Book of Hebrews alone (it is used repeatedly in the New Testament as well). Note: Paul is not inferring anything regarding the nature of Jesus—no hint exists that Jesus remained less than pure or perfect in regards to sin. Rather, the issue has to do with *accomplishing what He set out to do.* That is, the term implies 'fully completed' in the sense that the goal was *achieved exactly as planned.* The word *teleioō* is translated 'fulfilled' in Luke 2:43 and 'finished' in John 4:34.[5] Think of its meaning as "mission accomplished." This word confirms God's plan is *predetermined* to be complete in every aspect.

Our tribulations contribute to the process of being made into the glorious image of Jesus Christ. *"By whom also we have access by faith into this grace wherein we stand, and rejoice in hope of the glory of God."* (Romans 5:2)

The Spirit of Christ, given to us as an 'earnest' (i.e., a down payment) commands this inner person (and ultimately outer person) 'makeover.' Visualize if you will, the following quotation from Paul: *"But we all, with open face beholding as in a glass the glory of the Lord, are changed into* **the same image from glory to**

---

[4] Jesus was "tempted in all ways just as we are yet without sin" (Hebrews 4:15)

[5] It is similar to the word *teleō* (*tuh-lay-oh*), used in regard to Jesus accomplishing our salvation on the cross, with the words, "It is *finished* (*teleō*)" (John 19:30).

glory, [even] as by the Spirit of the Lord." (2 Corinthians 3:18) We might reflect on the various 'wolf man' movies where the victim of lycanthropy watches his face change from man to beast, viewing his transformation in the mirror. Here Paul visualizes the opposite. We look in the mirror and see ourselves being transformed into the same glory as Jesus Christ! No more hairy face!

THE TRANSFORMATION HAS ALREADY COMMENCED

Furthermore, Paul indicates the process has already begun. Perhaps the transformation we witness today seems mostly minor; but it begins nonetheless while we live in our mortal bodies. *Our pains are purposeful.* And yet, Paul teaches the aches and pains we go through now are nothing compared to the enjoyment and wonder we will experience later. Why should this be so? Because God's glory will be revealed *in* us: *"For I reckon that the sufferings of this present time [are] not worthy [to be compared]* **with the glory which shall be revealed in us***."* (Romans 8:18)

Paul provides a lengthy dissertation on these matters in 2 Corinthians 4: 16-18, 5:1-8. To better analyze, we should review the entire passage before my analysis:

[16]For which cause we faint not; but though our outward man perish, yet the inward man is renewed day by day.

[17]For our light affliction, which is but for a moment, worketh for us a far more exceeding and eternal **weight** *of glory;*

[18]While we look not at the things which are seen, but at the things which are not seen: for the things which are seen are temporal; but the things which are not seen are eternal. (2 Corinthians 4:16-18)

[1]For we know that if our earthly house of this tabernacle were dissolved, we have a building of God, an house not made with hands, eternal in the heavens.

[2]For in this we groan, earnestly desiring to be clothed upon with our house which is from heaven:

[3]If so be that being clothed we shall not be found naked.

⁴For we that are in this tabernacle do groan, being burdened: not for that we would be unclothed, but clothed upon, that mortality might be swallowed up of life.

⁵Now he that hath wrought us for the selfsame thing is God, who also hath given unto us the earnest of the Spirit.

⁶Therefore we are always confident, knowing that, whilst we are at home in the body, we are absent from the Lord:

⁷(For we walk by faith, not by sight)

⁸We are confident, I say, and willing rather to be absent from the body, and to be present with the Lord.

Paul begins by acknowledging even though our fleshly body undergoes 'entropy'—it runs down and will eventually die and decay—our 'inner being' undergoes renewal day after day (verse 16). Our inner being, our spiritual life, becomes more vital.

MOVING INTO A BRAND NEW HOUSE

In verse 17, he remarks that our afflictions amount to very little and are only temporary; nonetheless, they work on our behalf to create in us that which *far exceeds in value* the 'price we are paying' now. It comprises a property which will last for all eternity—a "weight of glory" (the meaning of which we will discuss more in a moment). We are paying a small monthly rent now—but we will soon own a mansion, deed included, without any further payments due.

In verse 18, Paul reminds us that we must set our 'eyes' (to-day we would say 'our focus'), *on eternal things not seen.* For Paul, 'seeing is *disbelieving!*' We must focus on what is eternal, what we see 'with the eyes of faith.'

In Chapter 5, verse 1, Paul justifies directing our focus in this manner because our bodies on earth are growing older and running down minute-by-minute. But in heaven our eternal bodies are like houses that cannot depreciate even one penny.

In verses 2-4, Paul continues this analogy. We live in a dilapidated house now; we sigh and groan and hope for the day when we will obtain our 'new house.' Not that we want to have *no* house at all—for we do not want to be found living without one. After all, *being naked* indicates we do not possess a new house 'to come home to'—perhaps because we did not deserve one! Perish the thought!

In verse 5, Paul advises us not to worry. God's promise to us regarding owning a new house in heaven has been guaranteed by an earnest payment: He has given us *the Holy Spirit as a constant companion.* His Spirit in us confirms the house will be waiting for us to move in immediately when we arrive!

In verse 6, he switches subjects slightly, even lamenting a bit. While we live in the 'old house' we are not residing in God's neighborhood! However, just as soon as we move out of the old house, we instantly move into the new one next door to where God is! (As a quick sidebar, Paul states, *"Remember now... we live by the truth of what we know, our faith, not by what we see"* (verse 7 paraphrased). He finally concludes this discussion by saying, "You know I am so confident about this, I had rather be absent from my body right now and be in my new house, in the new neighborhood, present with the LORD." Paul is brimming with confidence.

Perhaps we should ask ourselves whether we readily concur with Paul's wish. *Do we believe our prospects to be so bright we would rather change houses right away?* Or do we just want to cling to the old real estate? Are we ready to move into the new neighborhood?

THE WEIGHT OF GLORY—WHAT DOES THAT MEAN?

At the beginning of this passage, we stumbled upon a mighty concept about what *glory* entails. Paul calls it "the *weight* of glory." What does he mean?

The word translated 'weight' in the Greek is *baros* (*bah-ross*) occurring six times in the New Testament. It is translated five times as 'burden' and only once as 'weight.' (See Matthew 20:12, Acts 15:28 for examples). The notion constitutes *assigning 'great weight' to an expert's remarks.* To be more specific, it comprises *authority*; yet possessing authority *combined with responsibility*.

In another passage but within the same letter, Paul indicates how many of his opponents complained about his personal style. They criticized him as a weakling when face-to-face, but stern when admonishing others at a distance (through his letters). 2 Corinthians 10:10 says, *"... his letters are **weighty** and powerful" (here Paul mimics his opponents).* The word employed in this verse is *barys*, an adjective form of *baros*. As an adjective, *barys* conveys not just sternness or severity *but strength and power.* His enemies were saying, "Oh, so you are a tough guy when you write, but when you are here in person you are not so big and tough after all, are you?"

If we have 'weight,' however, we are not so easily intimidated. Our strength and 'presence' convey 'weight.' In a manner of speaking, it smacks of braggadocio: "Do not mess with me! You are tugging on superman's cape!"

C.S. Lewis once wrote a book (something he was often inclined to do!), entitled, *The Weight of Glory.* While he never actually refers to the text of 2 Corinthians in the book, this Pauline text remained his touch-stone.

Christopher W. Mitchell says this, regarding what C.S. Lewis meant by "the weight of glory:"

> Lewis longed above all else for the unseen things of which this life offers only shadows, for that weight of glory which the Lord

Christ won for the human race. And knowing the extraordinary nature of every human person, Lewis longed for and labored for their glory as well.[6]

Lewis was an evangelist. He was not always eager and enthusiastic to play that part. But he believed in the eternal value of the 'soul' which, on behalf of God, he sought. Goodness knows Lewis could look upon many he who attempted to convert, surmising that in their present state, they had no 'weight' at all. But the eyes of faith saw something very different. Lewis could see the potential in all humans in the same way Christ sees them. Wright quotes Lewis from his book, *The Four Loves,*

> "But heaven forbid we should work in the spirit of prigs and Stoics," Lewis declared, writing of the ultimate purpose of love in his book *The Four Loves*. "While we hack and prune we know very well that what we are hacking and pruning is big with a splendour and vitality which our rational will could never of itself have supplied. To liberate that splendour, to let it become fully what it is trying to be, to have tall trees instead of scrubby tangles, and sweet apples instead of crabs, is part of our purpose." In his fiction, theology, apologetics and correspondence Lewis can be seen hacking and pruning with the hope that his efforts might be used to produce "everlasting splendours."

Lewis understood very well what Christ won for us at Calvary was much more than forgiveness of sins—it was an amazing future life *consisting of glory with 'great weight.'* In other words, with the glory of God becoming part of our eternal natures, we will cease being 'light weights.' Our lives will carry a presence felt by other entities we will encounter in the Kingdom to come (be they mortal humans, angelic beings, or God Himself—to His praise and glory).

Perhaps we cannot fathom what 'weight' our lives will convey then. We know we *are to rule with Christ* in the Kingdom that

---

[6] "*Bearing the Weight of Glory: The Cost of C.S. Lewis's Witness,*" Christopher W. Mitchell.

comes (*"and they lived and reigned with Christ a thousand years"*—Revelation 20:4). We are also informed specifically we will judge angels! (No doubt, to their chagrin since their might exceeds ours now—see I Corinthians 6:3.) We know after we are glorified, we are called "the Mighty Ones" (we see this in several passages cited earlier). We can surmise the "clouds of heaven" that accompany Christ are made white clouds not just because we are wearing white robes and command white horses. Somehow, our glory will shine forth too as we ride with Him. Our glory—God's ultimate gift through Jesus Christ via His death for us—will also contribute to *the brightness of the shining clouds* encompassing the heavens as the battle of Armageddon is joined.

No wonder the multitude that surrounds the throne in Revelation 4:10, casts their crowns before Jesus Christ. The Saints reflect who truly deserves 'their' crown. *The glory which they possess was won by Jesus Christ,* by His suffering on the cross. Indeed, for all but a few, our sufferings are meager compared to what He suffered on our behalf. And yet, He eagerly wants us to exchange our dilapidated 'house' for the *eternal house of glory* He has prepared for us.

THE TRANSFIGURATION MADE OUR GLORY MORE SURE

In his second epistle, Peter relates to his readers that seeing the glory of Christ made the promise of His Kingdom all the more certain. We read in 2 Peter 1:3-19:

> *Yea, I think it meet, as long as I am in this tabernacle [his body], to stir you up by putting you in remembrance;*
>
> *Knowing that shortly I must put off this my tabernacle, even as our Lord Jesus Christ hath shewed me.*
>
> *Moreover I will endeavour that ye may be able after my decease to have these things always in remembrance.*

> *For we have not followed cunningly devised fables, when we made known unto you the power and coming of our Lord Jesus Christ, but were eyewitnesses of His majesty.*
>
> *For he received from God the Father honour and glory, when there came such a voice to Him from the excellent glory, "This is my beloved Son, in whom I am well pleased."*
>
> *And this voice which came from heaven we heard, when we were with Him in the holy mount.*
>
> *We have also a more sure word of prophecy; whereunto ye do well that ye take heed, as unto a light that shineth in a dark place, until the day dawn, and the **day star** arise in your hearts.*

Peter bore witness that he saw Christ glorified "on the *holy mount*."[7] This event comprised both amazing sights and confirmation that the prophecy of the coming Christ is now made *even more sure*. Peter's goal: continue to strive, to "stir them up" (motivate them) until the day dawns when *the day star arises* in their hearts.

What is the day star? The Greek word is *phōsphoros*, the "bright and morning star." In classic mythology the day star means *the light bearer*, aka *Venus*, symbolizing in Peter's remarks the fulfillment of the glory of Christ arisen within us. Peter says (paraphrasing): *"I will continue to motivate you as long as I live and until the glory of Christ is shining in your hearts bright and clear like the morning star!"* How intriguing the 15th element, *phosphorus*, consists of an element which emits a glow on its own accord.[8] The presence of this element adds considerable *weight* to

---

[7] Signifying, by the way, that Christ *redeemed* this patch of ground in the process of His transfiguration. Peter can now call Mount Hermon *holy*. Could this be a foreshadowing of the redemption of creation that Paul discusses in Romans, Chapter 8?

[8] The philosopher's stone—an agent catalyzing non-gold metals into gold, was thought to be composed of phosphorus in the seventeenth century. "In 1669, German alchemist Hennig Brand attempted to create the philosopher's stone from his urine, and in the process he produced a white material that glowed in the dark. The phosphorus had been produced from inorganic phosphate, which is a significant

Peter's statement: it is an element contained within every human cell for all cell membranes contain its lipid form. It is the fuel used in explosives. It is also used in bleaches and laundry products to 'whiten' the load.[9] It constitutes a marvelous analogy of the glory that Christ possesses and what He eagerly awaits to impart to us.[10] This *phōsphorus* should *penetrate every aspect of our being* down to the cellular walls of our body, enlighten our natures as if we are *bleached from head to toe and set aglow*, and empower us from the 'explosiveness' of its substance. That is the manner of glory awaiting us. It comprises the glory of God.

PRESENTING SALVATION TO OTHERS IN FULL MEASURE

However, until this transformation is complete, we have a job to do. Like C.S. Lewis, we must recognize the marvelous glory awaiting those *who call upon the name of the LORD* and are saved by His death. During the time that remains, we are challenged to 'grow the family' of God by seeking others—helping them realize the wonderful gift of His love and salvation. God is Love. And as we reach out to others, our own natures grow more like His.

---

component of dissolved urine solids. White phosphorus is highly reactive and gives off a faint greenish glow upon uniting with oxygen. The glow observed by Brand was caused by the very slow burning of the phosphorus, but as he neither saw flame nor felt any heat he did not recognize it as burning." See *http://en.wiki-pedia. org/wiki /Phosphorus.*

[9] Mark's account of the transfiguration uses this analogy: *"And his raiment became shining, exceeding white as snow; so as no fuller on earth can white them"* (Mark 9:3)

[10] Some scholars believe that Adam and Eve were originally clothed in a manner of glory to some degree. Their bodies emitted light. When they sinned, in their fallen state the light ceased to shine forth and they realized they had 'lost their glow' and were naked. If true, God's clothing for them was to hide the fact that they no longer had this 'sheen.' It is also quite similar to the story Paul tells of Moses after he visits God on Mount Sinai. The account says Moses' face glowed after encountering God's glory. We learn in the story that Moses was forced to cover his face because this glow frightened the Hebrews. Deeper scholarship suggests, however, the glow eventually wore off and Moses kept the covering to hide the fact that he no longer emitted the glowing sheen he once had! (See 1 Corinthians 3:7-18)

The Apostle John shares this stunning insight: *"Herein is our love made **perfect** [fully realized], that we may have boldness in the Day of Judgment: Because as He is, so are we in this world."* (I John 4:17) As God is Love and His love transforms those who believe in Him, we too are meant to have our love *perfected* during this time. Our love is to transform others even as His love transforms us. God sets forth this duty for us now and until the day we are caught up to be with Christ. By having our love perfected (fully complete), we may be bold when we stand before Christ at the judgment for believers.[11]

Finally, we are to acquire the keen eyes God has for all those who surround us. We are to see them as prospective fellow heirs to the glory of God. We must maintain a high level of motivation. We must share the full extent of the salvation that Christ has won for us. Keeping this incredible gift in mind that is available for all who will accept it, we must express love for others and to take to heart the importance, the eternal significance, of their opportunity to share in *this weight of glory!* Are we motivated to share the gospel because of the glory that awaits those who profess faith in Jesus Christ? That is the message that the Lord God asks us to carry forth to every man, woman, and child. We should implore each and every one to believe in Jesus Christ, that they may each obtain a weight of glory that exceeds our most sublime imagining.

Keeping watch requires we be mindful of this glory that awaits.

---

[11] This judgment is not the 'White Throne' judgment of Revelation 20:11 (expressly for unbelievers) but the so-called bēma seat of Christ (bēma referenced a low platform from which civil judgments were made in the Roman Empire). "For we must all appear before the judgment seat (bēma) of Christ; that every one may receive the things [done] in [his] body, according to that he hath done, whether [it be] good or bad." (2 Corinthians 5:10) Vines comments: "At this bēma believers are to be made manifest, that each may "receive the things done in (or through) the body," according to what he has done, "whether it be good or bad." There they will receive rewards for their faithfulness to the Lord. [But] For all that has been contrary in their lives to His will they will suffer loss."

18: CONCLUSION—FACING WHAT COMES NEXT

Be watchful, and strengthen the things which remain, that are ready to die: for I have not found thy works perfect before God.
(Revelation 3:2)

But the God of all grace, who hath called us unto his eternal glory by Christ Jesus, after that ye have suffered a while, make you perfect, stablish, strengthen, settle you.
(1 Peter 5:10, NASB)

GLOBAL CRISES, CATASTROPHES, AND CATACLYSMS

WE LIVE IN TUMULTUOUS TIMES. WITH ONE CRISIS BUILDING UPON THE NEXT, THERE IS NO RESPITE FOR THE ANXIOUS. UNSOLVABLE PROBLEMS MOUNT. MATTERS ARE MADE worse as time goes forward. We cannot seem to quiet this tumult. Cable news incessantly broadcasts the latest developments, 7 by 24.

It is difficult to get past the worst calamities. Not that long ago, Japan experienced a nuclear meltdown brought on by a 9.0 earthquake while it sought to overcome the effects of a killer Tsunami most of the world watched live on television. At least 20,000 Japanese were lost—entire towns were obliterated. Millions of Japanese will be affected by radiation in one way or another from the failed Fukushima Nuclear Plant. Today in the United States, we worry about the resulting effects of its radiation on our West Coast. Will the radiation contaminate crops in California and infiltrate the American food supply?

On the other side of the world, Islamic social unrest and wars in the Middle East continue to plague millions there. Muammar Gadhafi was killed by a revolt. Egypt has waded through two revolutions. And Syria continues to be a tragedy made worse with the passing of every hour. Over 100,000 civilians have been murdered by the government there. There is no end in sight to that civil war.

Then there is the ongoing Israeli-Palestinian conflict. It continues to fester even as these other stories occupy the headlines. Despite a peace accord announced by the current Secretary of State, John Kerry, Iran likely still seeks a nuclear weapon that threatens to throw the whole region into war. Israel seems destined to take out Iran's nuclear capability. After all, they have carried out the same tactic before in both Syria and Iraq. They are not strangers to preemptive strikes.

Virtually repeating the issues leading up to World War II, Russia has recently taken control of Crimea, and the Ukraine appears up for grabs. It is not clear why the U.S. government seems resolute in its poking Vladimir Putin, the Russian President, in the eye as he seeks to stabilize an ineffective government in a neighboring country full of Russian citizens.[1] But tensions rise nonetheless.

Experts comment that the United States has been seeking to build a democratic government in the Ukraine that could create a stronger buffer between Russia and the rest of Europe. Meanwhile, Putin seems to be attempting the same thing—building a buffer—because Russia has forever been fearful of what the Germans might be up to next. Memories of two world wars that killed tens of millions of Russians—wars started by Europe (and not Russia). Therefore, those wars and their lasting effects remain hard to overlook.

---

[1] My personal theory involves the US as enforcer of the New World Order. Putin is not behaving according to plan and the US is in charge of putting him back in his place. Down with nationalism. Up with one world government.

WHAT'S THE WORLD COMING TO?

Lest we think we have only distant political problems with no effect on our daily lives in America or that our global challenges constitute only a temporary nuisance, intellectual 'think tanks' remind us that food shortages are with us to stay. The current rising cost of energy slows the chance for full economic recovery. Advances in medicine, information technology, communication, and agriculture all could back-fire as we introduce dramatic new technologies yielding unintended consequences. Future climate scenarios forecast stronger hurricanes, more extremes in temperature, and coastal flooding as ice packs in the Arctic and Antarctic relentlessly melt away. These grim prospects impact everyone.

In the U.S., the opportunity for improving our lot diminishes despite promises of recovery. Most Americans opine that the so-called *American Dream* died during the past decade. We anticipate our children will enjoy much less prosperity than what we have experienced—a gloomy expectation indeed never present before in U.S. domestic economic (and emotional) forecasts.

Over the past two decades, our popular culture grows increasingly edgy. Movies, television shows, and documentaries play on our fears, presenting catastrophes as entertainment. Disaster movies, frequently starring frightful aliens from outer space, are standard fare. Since entertainment comprises an escape from everyday difficulties, our captivation remains all the more surprising given these 'getaways' reinforce our helplessness against overwhelming forces apparently beyond our control.

We seek other kinds of relief in the strangest places with the worst substances we can manufacture. Our society has never been more addicted to hard alcohol, recreational drugs, overeating, consumerism, and sex. If we are not eating ourselves to death, we forfeit our future by purchasing ourselves into such deep debt that our only relief comes through extraordinary measures like default or bankruptcy. What is worse, our favorite pastime comprises staring enthralled at Hollywood celebrities doubling as icons for our moral breakdown. Their addictions and bad behavior feed our insatiable appetite for scandal. When one starlet dies from a drug overdose, another emerges to take their place on the road to ruin. Celebrities, to employ Elton John's magnificent metaphor, burn out like candles in the wind.

What can satisfy the hunger of our souls? Popular religions spin cosmologies more outlandish and over the top than ever. Pseudo-spiritual movements hype their mystical solutions for these tempestuous times. The 2012 phenomenon, now behind us, generated scads of books and self-help DVDs during the first part of the twenty-first century. Study shows, however, the core issue for those captivated by 2012 was not the end of the world, but the crisis of personal and political choice. In many ways, this 'movement' amounted to nothing more than a relabeling of new age pseudo-religion which dominated spiritual discussions during the last third of the twentieth century. Those that *tuned into* this new spirituality *turned on* to drugs, yoga, meditation, and spiritual disciplines whose practice promised *psychic reality*—a titillating 'high' absent in religious experience of common folk. Even more telling, belief in the supernatural grows exponentially. Movies and television shows based on the paranormal are now legion. The History Channel, that bastion of well-documented truths, celebrates belief in extraterrestrials as nurturing parents to the human race. UFO documentaries are replete with undeniable encounters of the unknown. How the scene has changed from the secularism and skepticism of the 1960s and '70s! Once upon a time, we strained to believe anything out of the ordinary. Now we accept whatever seems weird, whacky, and 'out of this world'—all in due course.

FROM DEADLY DESPAIR TO THE DELUSION OF DIVINITY

Underlying these gimmicks to discover life's meaning lurks a 'creeping death'—a deep despair regarding Western civilization rooted in our dissatisfaction with the old ways of thinking.

Decades ago (a century in Europe), we advocated principles originating in the Bible. We accepted a transcendent basis for law that guaranteed absolute truth. Practicing ethics in business mattered to most because we did not separate spirituality from secular pursuits. Since we accepted the notion of an all-seeing, all-knowing God whose laws demanded justice and compassion, we expended considerable time and effort in charitable activities.

Not that long ago in America, accountability was not consciously evaded but implicitly embraced. Taking responsibility personally or corporately to 'make things right' or 'do the right thing' was standard operating procedure for all but the most brazen business interests. Today, however, we first calculate the downside: "Why worry about it? To whom do we answer? If we can cheat and get away with it, why wouldn't we?" Ethics surely comprises an outdated concept if not a lost art altogether.

Nowadays, we much prefer to think of God as a reality 'residing within.' Harkening to ages old metaphysics, plagiarized from eastern mysticism then mixed with modern physics, we have chopped God down to size. Our notion of God serves only as a subtle encouragement to be 'centered' and thoughtful—but primarily directed at the persons we care about most—*ourselves*. We have adopted a near-perfect pantheistic piety. Today, *it is all about us*. Consequently, when we choose to acknowledge the divine, we can now place His (his) name in lower case. What is more, since we perceive our deepest problems result from our failure to be *in touch with ourselves*, only *we* need take responsibility for our reclamation. By accepting our personal divinity, conventional wisdom now teaches we gain power to live, love, and be happy. Oprah makes us feel affirmed daily—everything is coming up roses!

However, there are some gurus and spiritual guides who advocate a much more radical departure from our Western religious past. They promise new answers to satisfy our personal needs and rectify our political problems once we cast away the archaic notions of the *old order*—guidelines that are inflexible, materialistic, and legalistic. In some cases (such as in the movement self-named "Awakening as One"), subtle threats laid buried within its hopeful but mystical message that challenged all inquirers to change to this new way of thinking or face the devastating consequences! Those who did not fall in line—who do *not* choose 'to sing out of the same hymnbook' with these pantheistic spiritualists—would not make the transition to the 'new age' (an epoch they incorrectly predicted to arrive on or soon after the end of 2012). The 'non-illuminated' were to be eliminated.

What were the means to exterminate the uncommitted? The answer remains unknown—the would-be 'next inquisition' toolkit was never disclosed. But since the philosophy behind this program was rooted in the same mysticism as Nazism (to be specific, esoteric *Theosophy*), a second holocaust might *not* have been out of the question for these activists.[2] It still lurks under other names. The messages broadcast from their website talked off an event reminiscent of a rapture in which those not inclined to advance into the new age will simply disappear from the earth. Poof! Universal forces magically eliminate the stick-in-muds refusing to transition.

SIZING UP THE REAL AMERICA

When we turn to social and political matters, do we find hope there? Are the old ways, those principles upon which America was founded, truly outdated? Is the dismissal of God from our government (virtually a *fait accompli* at this moment), likely to benefit our populace from whom the consent to be governed is derived? As a nation, do we still desire, "In God We Trust" to be printed on our currency?

Assume for a moment that Jesus Christ was invited to speak to a joint session of the United States Congress. Would He praise our

---

[2] I discuss this in depth in my book, *Decoding Doomsday*, in the chapter on "Esotericism, UFOs, and Nazism." This suspicion was also advanced by the authors of *The Stargate Conspiracy,* Lynn Picknett and Clive Prince.

government for the way it manages things? Or would Jesus challenge our nation's leaders to see the signs indicating America's future slumps toward demise? Would He praise us for our democratic ideals or rebuke us for our failure to live up to the principles our political philosophy advocates? Would He champion the American cause or criticize us for turning America's 'Exceptionalism' into a disingenuous ideal justifying whatever self-serving course of action we forcibly implement to further wrap the world around our little finger? Would He predict good times ahead or warn that the consequences of our chosen path portend calamity?

During 2013, Oliver Stone (a director not frightened by the prospects for confronting conventional wisdom), offered a ten program series entitled, "The Untold History of America." Presenting a multitude of matters glossed over by the standard history books, Stone argues conclusively that America feigns allegiance to democracy for the nations. Instead, it exploits opportunities predominantly to advance the aims of the 'military industrial' complex—corporations that make their living by producing munitions, often relying on the CIA to exacerbate if not commence conflicts in 'hot spots' all over the world which eventually lead us into war.

This author has presented a series of books documenting many of the same points along with numerous others Stone does not mention, which exceed the worst case scenarios of what one could imagine a runaway government could engineer—all accomplished on behalf of furthering the American empire. *Power Quest, Books One and Two*, as well as *The Final Babylon*, all testify to the real agenda of America which consists in dominating the world and maintaining markets for America goods and services. The almost unanimous acceptance of our hard-nosed declaration that America no longer operates from a Judeo-Christian intellectual (or moral) basis has truly surprised my co-authors and me. Evangelicals, typically very conservative politically as well as theologically, have slipped into a growing malaise of disbelief in the inherent goodness of America. Ten years ago this was not true. It is true today.

What type of issues testify to the failure of the United States to be true to its founding ideals? Take the mission statements of The World Bank and the International Monetary Fund (IMF) (sponsored predominantly by America's bankers). These visionary credos read as if they sincerely seek to help the Third World in the same guise as the Marshall Plan helped a devastated Europe after World War II. Nothing could be further from the truth. While doubtless the World Bank and the IMF have alleviated pain and suffering in some regards, they have placed all their customers in such a massive mountain of debt that these nations are forever 'beholdin' to the United States—more specifically to the bankers of the United States and England. Unending interest payments fuel the profits of the Anglo-Americans bankers whose headquarters reside on Wall Street or in 'The City' of London. Readers should be mindful that third-world countries that default on their debt (or second-world nations like Greece or Cyrus), hardly upset the equilibrium of international affairs or even harm their standing for continuing on the dole. Defaults are virtually meaningless as debt is simply refinanced and the interest payments commence once again.

Why do defaults matter so little? One must remember that 'the principal' for such debts was invented to begin with by leveraging the Fractional Banking System at the base of these machinations. The banks never lose real money. That is because the 'principal' is literally invented out of thin air. It is a greatest scam in the history of humankind. What is so pathetic is that most of humanity remains ignorant that they are being raped and pillaged by the rich.

DO MYTHS AND MORAL LAPSES CAUSE OUR PROBLEMS?

And yet, the citizenry as well as its leadership merit blame. The populace spends too much time caught up in 'life as usual'—soaking up entertainment rather than taking stock of what stands wrong with society and *how we can correct it*. Social responsibility stands in need of rejuvenation for our notion of freedom today infers the disregard of duty. Perhaps we consciously choose to ignore what is happening out of apathy; or worse, we do nothing because we have been brainwashed to accept 'it is what it is' with no recourse.

Another popular series of movies achieved some level of consciousness raising. The first film was entitled, *Zeitgeist: The Movie*.[3] The producer of the film, Peter Joseph endeavored to teach several fundamental truths.

First, religion is merely a means to gain social control. It instigates war and conflict. He argues we must realize that all religion is based upon sun worship and that each religion has the same identical 'solar savior' at its core whether its protagonist be Horus, Mithras, or Jesus Christ. However, Christians should not be fooled. The 'facts' presented are easily refuted by any credentialed religious historian, nevertheless, the film mounts a compelling (although incorrect) *apologia*.[4]

Joseph next contends that we must face the fact that social engineering drives our government. He presents another overwhelming barrage of 'facts' on the tragedy of 911, demonstrating to the horror of the viewer that the U.S. government played no small part in facilitating the destruction of the Twin Towers under the cover of a terrorist attack. The smoking gun, as many other researchers and investigators have proposed, is the collapse of World Trade Center, Tower 7. The tower crumbled at the end of that fateful day as if the subject of a controlled demolition. The reader may remember that WTC-7 was not hit by a jet. It received some damage on one side of the building with the fall of the two mega-towers, but it was *purportedly* destroyed by fire alone, an outcome which caused architects and engineers alike to cast grave suspicion toward the truth of what really caused the building to collapse upon itself at

---

[3] There were a total of three movies: *Zeitgeist, the M0vie* in 2008, *Zeitgeist, the Addendum,* in 2008, and *Zeiteist: Moving Forward* in 2011. See http://www.zeitgeist-movie.com/.

[4] A formal, well-structured argument.

near 'free-fall' speed—an impossibility without pre-set explosives facilitating a 'controlled' demolition.

Finally, Peter Joseph argued that the culprit we should rise up against is the *shadow government* facilitated by the Federal Reserve monetary system. The system thrives by creating scarcity, controlling the money supply, and—through intentional inflation managed by the central banking system—devaluing currency over time. The goal: make debtors and slaves of us all. Earning wages amounts to nothing more than a pittance to pacify us—a small payment in exchange for the slavery to which we have allowed ourselves to become obligated.

Society, Joseph argues, should not be based on money and debt, but on the abundance of resources. His is a picture of a utopian possibility built upon hidden confidence in the goodness of humankind. Freed from the tyranny of money and government controlled by corporate interests, human beings can create a society in which all prosper having the basic necessities of life available for free. This prescription for hope hardly constitutes a feasible remedy. However, because it builds upon a problematic humanism, the potential to make an impact upon our society comprises a 'million-to-1' shot.

IS THERE CHANGE WE CAN REALLY BELIEVE IN?

For those who might challenge whether our plight is as dismal of Joseph asserts, we must at least admit that as it now stands politically, we are a nation divided. We debate almost every substantive issue with the outcome predetermined based on 'party lines' (i.e., whoever holds the majority wins). This 'double-mindedness' in America stokes the fire of distrust and contempt, reinforcing political paralysis. The only fix for what remains wrong with our political and social structures rests in a 'vocal majority' to emerge demanding real transformation; for only broad agreement can foster dramatic movement in our values. But can harmony be found? Can we discover common ground upon which to reform our government?

Unless dramatic modification in the viewpoints of a super majority occurs within our nation, hopes for change will remain ephemeral. Any real transformation must address (1) the moral fabric comprising who we are individually, (2) what values we extol culturally, and (3) what ideals drive our goals politically. Without focusing on matters both personal and social, we will not garner sufficient leverage to change course for the better.

Again, this is certainly where Peter Joseph's proposal for a just society breaks down. Human beings act out of self-interest most of the time. *We are sinners.* Coveting what someone else has is as much a part of our nature as other carnal appetites that require frequent satiation. Even if everyone were to have the 'bare necessities' we would grow to demand a standard of living that satisfied all our cravings, much of which entails stealing what someone else has to make it our own. An old and paradoxically worded adage remains true: *Nothing is ever enough.*

Nevertheless, our national *raison d'être* seems set in concrete. International government continues toward full manifestation. America's persistent economic and military strength guarantee its eventual achievement despite the desire of the 'rank and file' that we retain national sovereignty, disavow the authority of the United Nations, put distance between our country and other 'noble pursuits' (i.e., global initiatives) of well financed NGOs[5] and

---

[5] NGO is a Non-Governmental Organization (NGO). Here is a definition from the NGO website: "Though it has no internationally recognized legal definition, an NGO generally refers to an organization that operates independently from any government – though it may receive funding from a government but operates without oversight or representation from that government. According to the University of London, the history of NGOs date back to 1839 and by 1914 there were already more than 1,000 NGOs with international scope. Today, there are more than 40,000 NGOs that operate internationally, while millions more are active at the national level. For instance, the Chicago Tribune reported in 2008 that Russia had 277,000 such groups, while India has 3.3 million. NGOs have grown at a phenomenal pace, especially in the last two decades, creating a need for millions of jobs – both paid and volunteer based. But the modern "non-governmental organization" as we know it

their expert social engineers. The elite drive toward one-world rule while the population waves the flag and chants "U.S.A." The two perspectives could not be more incongruent or misaligned.

However, we should not assume that the elite are solely motivated by greed and corruption. In their mind, the globalist agenda demands their commitment. They believe it holds the only means to world peace. Without a coordinated plan to bring the governments of the world together, war will rage and multitudes will starve. The master plan foisted by 'the Captains and the Kings'[6] seeks to make conditions better for everyone on the planet. At least that is what they tell us. But can an elite supposedly motivated by altruism and 'reason instead of religion' resolve our problems?[7]

Certainly, the sheep dare not speak against these unelected shepherds, lest we be accused of paranoia or intransigence. Furthermore, since most folk do not suspect the wealthy of such malfeasance, they remain mostly silent. So it should be no surprise that our government, supposedly of the people, by the people, and for the people, unwittingly and progressively relinquishes sovereignty to the elite few—believing that bankers, international corporations, NGOs, and media moguls will build a better world for us all.

An honest study of political science in the United States over the past 100 years shows that our Constitution, the high water mark of

---

today only came about with the establishment of the United Nations in 1945." See http://ngos.org/.

[6] A book by this title, authored by Taylor Caldwell, was made into mini-series in 1976. It was loosely based on the Kennedy's and presented a case that financiers are the real protagonists on the world stage. Democracy is illusory.

[7] This is the stated goal of Freemasonry, Rosicrucianism, and other secret societies seeking world domination, however righteous they purpose their influence to be. The writings of Albert Pike and Manly Hall, 33° Freemasons, and intellectual founders of the 'Craft' as Freemasonry refers to it, make this goal plain.

human government, no longer remains the bulwark against tyranny that our elementary schooling so naively promised it to be.[8] Unfortunately, politics and 'change we can believe in' will not likely lead to real change in our social order. While the poor and dispossessed will settle for any government that feeds and medicates them, most folk with just a modest education and modicum of social responsibility, do not expect government to change things. Past (poor) performance *does* predict future returns. A crisis of faith in our leaders and our system of government appears inevitable.

It is not that the Constitution of the United States does not deserve our oath of loyalty. It assuredly does and true patriots know this. However, many now realize that our leaders pay little attention to the founding documents of our nation anymore. They have become experts at circumventing the compact of the People.

- The current President issues Executive Orders working around the Congress—now over one thousand in number—exceeding all 43 other U.S. President's Executive Orders combined. On many matters, for all intents and purposes, he has become Caesar.

- Congress cannot agree on a budget to run the country. The legislative branch remains caught in a quagmire brought about by career politicians who get paid lots for accomplishing little.

- The CIA routinely breaks the law internationally, and likely conducts illegal domestic operations, while failing to obtain actionable intelligence on far too many matters. They are lucky that the nation has not performed a risk-reward analysis on their results.

- The NSA, always a questionable entity within our democratic society, leverages the Patriot Act making a mockery of the constitutional privacy rights of the citizens. With safe-keeping like this, who needs government-based security?

---

[8] Unfortunately, our elementary school teaching on American history and civics, presented in rose-colored hues, stands as an education most have never surpassed.

- Bolstered by their lobbyists, the military-industrial complex works overtime to ensure that our military fights endless wars. With over 1,000 bases located globally, we are the police of the world and the enforcers for the New World Order.

- The State Department allows its officers in the Foreign Service to become pawns in deadly international politics, intrigue, and secret strategies to overthrow other governments. The Benghazi scandal is the latest case in point.

- The Attorney General runs guns in plans of which, at best, he is ignorant. Then he ignores congressional requests for information, stonewalls investigations, and selectively enforces laws that suit his politics. This was the essence of 'Fast and Furious.'

- The Supreme Court, when it must stand up to the obvious tyranny of the Executive Branch, backs away from the conflict and punts, resting upon a makeshift rule not written in the constitution: *elections have consequences!* Methinks this was actually a rejoinder boasting Supreme Court Justices are not responsible to the electorate—they can do or not do as they pretty well please.

To expand further on this last point: even if there are reasons to doubt the legality of legislation on nationalizing healthcare as structured in ObamaCare (a 1,100 page law passed so the Speaker of the House could find the time to finally read it)—even if there are reasons to challenge the law since a virtual majority of the 50 States found the law impossible to implement—the last bastion of sanity, our Supreme Court, thanks to the failure of the recently appointed Chief Justice, refused to save us from a government run amuck. Millions of persons that were to become insured, weren't. And millions of others that had healthcare insurance, lost it and became the newly uninsured. Applaud the moral victory for the socialist planners serving at the pleasure of the President.[9]

---

[9] Allow me to provide my personal point of view. I happen to favor a national healthcare program. That is because I have no illusions about the philanthropic

Consequently, is there really any hope left that our government can correct its ineffectiveness and dishonesty, and get back to the business of acting on behalf of its patrons? As is often the case, real change happens when it constitutes the only choice available. Unfortunately, even if faced with the mandate for change, the rich and powerful will still come out on top. The best interests of the People are forever unlikely to be well-served.

THE ONLY HOPE—THE KINGDOM OF GOD MUST COME

The Kingdom of God stands as the only hope for our world. This does not mean that there is no hope for change until Christ returns. Substantial change can occur, but only with dramatic differences in what should rightly motivate most people, those in key positions that have the power to force real change in society. Believing in a purely humanist ideal—whether it be described as 'the audacity of hope,' 'hope we can believe in,' or realizing the 'divinity of human beings' (e.g., the new age gospel)—is destined to fail. Secular Humanism, based upon an unrealistic view of goodness in people, has never worked before and it never will.

The only manifesto that can achieve genuine change in society must be based upon the view derived from the principles of a Judeo-Christian cosmology. These principles must be internalized by those who acknowledge them and pledge to follow them with the ongoing help of the Spirit of God. That stands as the biblical prescription for authentic and lasting change in our world.

---

qualities of health insurance companies, the giant Pharmaceutical companies (so-called 'Big Pharma') and ambulance chasing attorneys. The existing system is corrupt, unnecessarily expensive, and unethically structured (with 'tiered levels of care'—he who can pay most gets the best care). The U.S. Healthcare system is NOT the best in the world despite having some of the world's greatest physicians and nurses. However, the attempt of the current administration to change the system has made it far worse. Little hope exists that the system will be changed in such a way to make it what it ought to be while protecting the fiscal interests of all involved.

Short of that, nothing will bring about meaningful change other than the apocalypse itself.

Christ calls His disciples, however, to model the Kingdom *today*, even though the ultimate fulfillment of that Kingdom will never be achieved until Christ dwells again on this earth. Only when His will is done on earth as it is in Heaven, can we expect a perfect (or even a substantially better) world. Only when those who choose to be His disciples truly become His disciples—by giving up their lives for the sake of others, by electing not to place their financial well-being ahead of everyone else's, by treating others as they would themselves want to be treated—can we achieve a world that we would truly want to live in. It would not be perfect. But as Christian intellectual Francis Schaeffer maintained, the world would experience substantial healing through the power of Jesus Christ. It would be measurable. It would be meaningful. And it would promise (through its portrayal) what the final state of the Kingdom of God would resemble. [10]

Christ taught that the Kingdom of God would turn the world upside down. Those that who were poor now would become rich. Those that are meek (and weak) will be powerful when the Kingdom of God comes. This will finally be realized in the Kingdom because those *that hunger and thirst for righteousness will be satisfied*. Only when the craving to live an exemplary life rises above other cravings in the lives of those in power, will social institutions change, and the downtrodden and dispossessed achieve an acceptable quality of life. The inner transformation must come first. Then outward transformation can take place.

---

[10] Of course, the reality of sickness and death would still be with us. The tragedies of natural disasters would still occur unpredictably, and harm would come to those who are its victims. But enormous improvements for the better could be accomplished this side of the coming of the Kingdom of God through transformed social institutions, sufficient charities to help those in need, and the means to pursue happiness as the 'God-given right' Jefferson extolled in the Declaration of Independence.

THE LESSON OF ZACCHAEUS

Allow me to share a story from the Gospel of Luke to better explain how Christ's disciples are to understand the meaning and implication of salvation in the fallen world in which we live. In this account in Luke, we have a short-story about a very short-man named Zacchaeus. He was a *publican* (not republican, although if he were alive today, he likely would be one!) We understand this position was a public official, most likely a tax-collector. He was hated and was considered in the conventional wisdom of his day 'a sinner.' But his story illustrates the hope that an authentic representation of the Gospel of Jesus Christ offers to any society.

The account occurs in Jericho, one of the oldest cities in the world, the city that Joshua and the armies of Israel marched around seven times, before 'the walls came tumbling down' at the sound of their trumpets. Perhaps this particular venue was not accidental to the meaning of the story. We have an older man, a sinner, hanging from a Sycamore tree (sometimes a symbol of Israel), in Israel's oldest city. Could it be the change that occurs in the heart of Zacchaeus suggests that no matter how 'set in his or her ways' a person is, that no matter how old the institution is, or corrupt the politics of a particular city or state, transformation can still be achieved when the people in charge change? This constitutes part of the meaning that should be derived from Luke's tale.

We read, from Luke, chapter 19:

[1] And Jesus entered and passed through Jericho.

[2] And, behold, there was a man named Zacchaeus, which was the chief among the publicans, and he was rich.

[3] And he sought to see Jesus who he was; and could not for the press, because he was little of stature.

[4] And he ran before, and climbed up into a sycomore tree to see him: for he was to pass that way.

> [5] And when Jesus came to the place, he looked up, and saw him, and said unto him, "Zacchaeus, make haste, and come down; for to-day I must abide at thy house."
>
> [6] And he made haste, and came down, and received him joyfully.
>
> [7] And when they saw it, they all murmured, saying, "That he was gone to be guest with a man that is a sinner."
>
> [8] And Zacchaeus stood, and said unto the Lord: "Behold, Lord, the half of my goods I give to the poor; and if I have taken anything from any man by false accusation, I restore him fourfold."
>
> [9] And Jesus said unto him, "This day is salvation come to this house, forsomuch as he also is a son of Abraham."
>
> [10] For the Son of man is come to seek and to save that which was lost.

Jesus indicates as a token which expresses that salvation has come to Zacchaeus, he now also is 'as a son of Abraham' (in good standing no less!) Of course, virtually every race living in Israel (not just the Hebrews who traced their lineage to Jacob) were racially children of Abraham (coming as they did from Ismael or from Isaac, then from Jacob or his brother Esau). The Jews considered themselves God's chosen because they were *children of Abraham* (Luke 3:8, John 8:39). Jesus celebrates Zacchaeus reclamation by reaffirming that he was 'included back in the fold' just like any other good child of Abraham. He proclaims that an inner change has truly occurred. Salvation has come to the place where Zacchaeus lives (not just a particular house mind you, but through his actions—how he *lives in his community* from now on). That is, repentance has led to a reform, because Zacchaeus will hereafter alter how he accomplishes his duties of political office.

OCCUPY UNTIL I COME

But the lesson is not yet complete. Jesus spins a parable on the spot to explain the timing of the Kingdom of God and the responsibility to accomplish the Kingdom's work even while the King remains far away in a distant country. It also involves public officials. The parable was no doubt actually told when Jesus was in Jericho, because contemporary issues there gave rise to the details of the parable.

The background of the story: Jericho was the hometown of Herod the Great and his son Archelaus. Jericho was where Archelaus had rebuilt his palace not long before Jesus sojourned to Jericho. However, Archelaus was not there when Jesus was teaching. He had left to go to Rome to receive his kingdom officially. And just as the nobleman in the parable meted out funds to each of his servants, Archelaus actually left money in trust with his servants to keep the business of the estate going. To 'occupy until I come' was likely a contemporary catchphrase conveying that the servants should busy themselves by completing tasks pertinent to the affairs of the estate. In Archelaus' case this may have included activities in the community no doubt partly related to the 'state,' i.e., its governance.

> *11 And as they heard these things, he added and spake a parable, because he was nigh to Jerusalem, and because they thought that the kingdom of God should immediately appear.*
>
> *12 He said therefore, "A certain nobleman went into a far country to receive for himself a kingdom, and to return.*
>
> *13 And he called his ten servants, and delivered them ten pounds, and said unto them, 'Occupy till I come.'*
>
> *14 But his citizens hated him, and sent a message after him, saying, 'We will not have this man to reign over us.'* [Which happened as the citizens of Jericho sent a message to Caesar complaining of the horrible actions of Archelaus and their plan to reject his rule.]
>
> *15 And it came to pass, that when he was returned, having received the kingdom, then he commanded these servants to be called unto him, to whom he had given the money, that he might know how much every man had gained by trading.*
>
> *16 Then came the first, saying, 'Lord, thy pound hath gained ten pounds'.*

17 And he said unto him, 'Well, thou good servant: because thou hast been faithful in a very little, have thou authority over ten cities.'

18 And the second came, saying, 'Lord, thy pound hath gained five pounds.'

19 And he said likewise to him, 'Be thou also over five cities.'

20 And another came, saying, 'Lord, behold, here is thy pound, which I have kept laid up in a napkin:

21 For I feared thee, because thou art an austere man: thou takest up that thou layedst not down, and reapest that thou didst not sow.'

22 And he saith unto him, 'Out of thine own mouth will I judge thee, thou wicked servant. Thou knewest that I was an austere man, taking up that I laid not down, and reaping that I did not sow:

23 Wherefore then gavest not thou my money into the bank, that at my coming I might have required mine own with usury?'

24 And he said unto them that stood by, 'Take from him the pound, and give it to him that hath ten pounds.'

26 For I say unto you, That unto every one which hath shall be given; and from him that hath not, even that he hath shall be taken away from him."

As in the story, like the nobleman, Archelaus was hated and resented. His only right to rule was due to his inheritance. And in the end, despite this, the servants realized that they must give account to what they had done for the good of 'the household.'

The connections between Jesus' parable and the matter of how His disciples are to conduct themselves 'in the meantime' stands as our de facto manifesto. We are to 'occupy until He comes.' We are to invest the gifts He has given us that there might be a measurable return on the investment, one that will allow us to receive praise from the King.

* * * * * * *

We began this book by talking about the paradoxes we are charged to accept as Christians. We must realize that only when the Kingdom comes will all the problems of our world be rectified. And yet, we are required to do what we can to make the world as it is (with all its problems), a model of the coming Kingdom. We are to live as if each day comprises our very last day on this earth. However, we are to consider the fact that the King remains away for an indefinite season and we are to be about His business, earnestly, while we wait for His return.

The signs of the apocalypse, therefore, are not meant to imply that we should stop running the race at full speed, as if our lead over our competition is now insurmountable. Instead, we are to keep running at an all-out gallop. For the signs of the Coming Kingdom are meant to be like the bell that rings when we are on our last lap letting us know that only one more time around the track remains. That is the nature of the Christian life. We are on the 'bell lap.' We may be gasping for breath, but the bell has rung. We are to intensify our efforts, give it all we got ('leave it all out on the field' as they say nowadays), because the victory tape stretches across the track in plain sight just ahead.

We can almost taste the victory—winning now stands within our grasp. We must keep running and not let up, for we can hear the pounding of steps behind us, clearly the rapid approach of our closest competitors. It is not time to quit—not yet. We must run and run hard, until... until...

APPENDIX ONE

In my Father's House are many mansions, I go to prepare a place for you. And if I go to prepare a place for you I will come again and receive you to myself, that where I am there ye may be also.
(John 4:2-3)

REASONS TO BELIEVE THE RAPTURE COMES SOMETIME BEFORE CHRIST'S RETURN AT ARMAGEDDON

IMPLIED IN THE 'COMING OF THE SAINTS' AS DESCRIBED BY JOEL, JUDE, ENOCH, AND PAUL IS THAT THE *SAINTS* (ALL WHO BELIEVE AND HAVE ACCEPTED JESUS CHRIST AS THEIR SAVIOR) COME FROM heaven, not immediately from the earth at the climatic time of Jesus' return to fight the Antichrist at Armageddon. Logically, if they come from heaven, the Saints first have to leave the earth behind. This implies a gap of some length between these events. But there are many other factors which also infer a necessary gap of time to fulfill Bible truths.

As a reminder, there are essentially three groups who believe in the rapture but differ as to when it occurs. Group one believes it happens before the final seven years, Daniel's 70th Week, aka the *Tribulation*, the *Time of Jacob's Trouble*, and sometimes *The Great Tribulation*. Group two believes it happens no earlier than half-way through this period of time and precisely before God unleashes His wrath upon the earth. The 'gap' between the rapture and the Second Coming may be a few months to a few years.[1] Group three believes that the rapture and the Second Coming happen at virtually the same moment. Jesus returns for His saints a 'split-second' before His Saints then return with Him to fight the Battle of Armageddon. This last battle occurs at the very end of the seven years. My argument here should find support from groups one and two, while being challenged by group three. The third group, those that believe the rapture happens immediately before Christ physically returns to judge the ungodly (the 'post-tribulation' view) must address some logical challenges as follows:

(1) Why do not the biblical accounts of the rapture include the detail of 'translation and judgment' happening simultaneously? This sequence seems rather significant. These actions are never spoken of by Jesus or Paul as concurrent events. If they actually transpire a split second apart, that is quite an oversight. Additionally, since there are so many references to this event, it is remarkable that never once do biblical statements tie these events together.

(2) If there are other events such as the 'judgment seat of Christ'[2] where each believer's 'works' are judged after they are resurrected (or raptured). Does the 'judgment seat of Christ' also happen in the same instance as the 'translation and the judgment of the unrighteous?' That would mean *all three events occur in the same moment.* Again, each action stands separate and the New Testament authors (and Jesus in His parables) speak of these

---

[1] There is also a view that suggests that Jesus first returns to Jerusalem and takes ten days to fight battles throughout the area surrounding Jerusalem before concluding these 10 days in the Valley of Megiddo—at the 'Mount of Megiddo,' aka Har-megiddon. These ten days may be the fulfillment of Jewish holiday period known as *The Ten Days of Awe* between Rosh Hashanah and Yom Kippur. If true, *Rosh Hashanah*, the Feast of Trumpets, would be when Jesus returns visibly to the entire world while the Battle of Armageddon transpires ten days later on Yom Kippur, known by Jews as the Day of Judgment. This is discussed in David Busch's book, *The Assyrian* (See *For Further Reading*).

[2] See Romans 14:10 and 2 Corinthians 5:10. Again, this is the *bēma* seat judgment.

events as distinct actions. There is no insinuation that they happen concurrently, in that very same moment we know as 'in the twinkling of an eye.' Indeed, Paul depicts the rapture occurring in a split second. Consequently, must all these other events happen consecutively in the very same instant?

(3) Perhaps the following objection should not be considered since I may be 'thinking from a human perspective.' I offer it nonetheless. The issue: when do the Saints get their 'marching orders?' If we have not first gone to be with Christ, would we not be a bit overwhelmed with the transformation to immortal beings in one second, being judged by Christ in the next moment, and then returning with Christ to judge the unrighteous one second later? To be 'Mighty Ones' we should be equipped with knowledge of our powers, duties, and 'the battle plan' well-rehearsed.

(4) If Christ has gone to prepare a place for us (remember that *mansion in the sky?*—See John 14: 2, 3); when do we get to check out the real estate? Is it only the 'dead in Christ' that died before the rapture who inherit a mansion? Are raptured believers left out? Do not the 'raptured' (aka, the 'quick') obtain a mansion too?

(5) With all these staggering events and wonderful experiences crowded together, there is no time for a celebration! There is no 'homecoming'—no party with that 'great cloud of witnesses' that has been cheering us on. (Hebrews 12:1) We have been waiting for this momentous day all our lives only to discover, no opportunity exists to appreciate what just happened? This would certainly be poor planning and frankly, not in character for our Father in heaven. I doubt the LORD overlooked a celebration for us. After all, He has always been enthusiastic about feasts. Just look at the Mosaic Law and all the Jewish 'holy convocations' (*holidays*—there are seven of them if you care to count). All are times of remembrance and rejoicing. Christ often compared His coming to a feast. Our God enjoys sharing wonderful occasions with His people.

(6) Next, we are promised *a time of rest*. We are to live worthy lives so we might enter into that time of rest. Paul says, *"Let us labour therefore to enter into that rest, lest any man fall after the same example of unbelief"* (Hebrews 4:11). But with all these events happening so quickly, 'one, two, three' it sounds like we must 'get to work' immediately. Is there 'no rest for the weary?'

(7) If the rapture occurs at the same instant that Christ returns *physically* to the earth, then no 'humans' exist to inherit the earth. All believers have just been raptured—and all unbelievers are eliminated. How do humans enter into the Millennial Kingdom when none are left on earth? The description of the Kingdom plainly indicates human beings dwell on earth and are ruled by Jesus from Jerusalem (See Ezekiel 40-47). Note: the same phenomenon would have happened if Noah and his family had been translated as Enoch was. Noah's offspring had to remain on earth to repopulate (replenish) the earth. Otherwise, the righteous would have been all been *snatched up* and all unbelievers would have been destroyed in the Flood. That is why believers converted during the period known as the Tribulation (equivalent to that class of humanity who refused to accept the Mark of the Beast), are analogous to Noah's family, and become the 'starting point' for repopulating the earth. These believers 'missed the rapture' and were *left behind*, so to speak, but became believers during the Tribulation and lived through it. Therefore, they inherit the Kingdom of Christ as mortals. Once more, mortals will be asked to 'replenish the earth.'

(8) Lastly, we have established the premise that God removes His righteous servants before unleashing judgment. This was discussed in several chapters in this book notably in the discussion of Lot and the example of Enoch. The example of Noah is disqualified for reason number seven above. If this principle is rejected, then those who believe otherwise must offer a rebuttal demonstrating why this principle is 'the exception and not the rule.'

APPENDIX TWO

*"Let no man deceive you by any means; for that day shall not come, except there come a **falling away** (apostasia) first, and that man of sin be revealed, the son of perdition (apoleia)"*
(2 Thessalonians 2:3)

THE GREEK WORD APOSTASIA AND ITS IMPLICATIONS FOR THE RAPTURE OF THE CHURCH

WHILE WE HAVE DISCUSSED A NUMBER OF ARGUMENTS FOR THE 'PRE-TRIBULATION RAPTURE'—THAT CHRIST RETURNS FOR HIS CHURCH SOMETIME BEFORE THE TRIBULATION period (or at least before God unleashes His wrath upon the world)—there is another argument to consider that hangs entirely upon the meaning of the Greek word *apostasia*, which is often translated, 'falling away' in the manner of an apostasy. Certainly, the Greek root for the word 'apostasy'—*apostasia*, appears rather obvious. In English, we define the word *apostasy* as "the renunciation of a religious or political belief or allegiance, typically in the sense of moving from an orthodox or traditional position to a heterodox or non-traditional view." But does a sound argument exist that the word *apostasia* can mean something other than 'a falling away' or 'apostasy?'

Because of the English definition, accompanied by a common interpretation and translation of the Greek word *apostasia* in most versions of the Bible, it would appear a stretch to consider any other alternative. In context, Paul's message has normally been understood as 'the Antichrist cannot appear, until an apostasy comes first.' Given this passage refers to the Antichrist as 'the MAN OF SIN' and 'SON OF PERDITION' (remembering the linkage discussed earlier between the word translated 'perdition' [*apoleia* in Greek], and the Greek / Roman god *Apollo*, the destroyer god), it seems logical to interpret *apostasia* in this way.

And yet, there are a number of evangelical scholars who argue forcefully that the better English word to express *apostasia* lies with the word *departure*. If this word constitutes the more accurate translation, it would strengthen the Pre-Tribulationist view. The passage would read, *"Let no man deceive you, for that day cannot come unless a departure comes first, in order that the son of perdition can be revealed."*

Terry James, editor of a fairly recent book on various prophetic topics, entitled, *The Departure*, cites Dr. Thomas Ice, a top scholar on biblical eschatology who "presents well-researched thought on the term 'departure'" as well as Gordon Lewis from his paper, *"Biblical Evidence for Pretribulationism."*[1] The article focuses on why this alternate (and perhaps proper) translation of 2 Thessalonians 2:3 would clarify the sequence of the rapture in regards to other crucial eschatological events.

Quoting Lewis:

> The verb [*apostasia*] may mean to remove spatially. There is little reason, then, to deny that the noun can mean such a spatial removal or departure... The verb is used fifteen times in the New Testament. Of these fifteen, only three have anything to do with a departure from the faith (Luke 8:13; I Timothy 4:1; Hebrews 3:12). [Otherwise] The word is used for departing from iniquity (II Timothy 2:19), from ungodly men (I Timothy 6:5), from the Temple (Luke 2:27), from the body (2

---

[1] See *Bibliotheca Sacra,* (vol. 125, no. 499; July 1968) pg. 218.

Corinthians 12:8), and from persons (Acts 12:10; Luke 4:13). (Emphasis added)[2]

Terry James identifies a series of other authorities and cites their research into the meaning of this term. One selection in particular quoted by James of a Dr. (Wayne) House seems especially helpful:

> Remember, the Thessalonians had been led astray by the false teaching (2:2-3) that the Day of the Lord had already come. This was confusing because Paul offered great hope, in the first letter, of a departure to be with Christ and a rescue from God's wrath. Now a letter purporting to be from Paul seems to say that they would first have to go through the Day of the Lord. Paul then clarified this prior teaching by emphasizing that they had no need to worry. They could again be comforted because the departure he had discussed in his first letter, and in his teaching while with them, was still the truth. The departure of Christians to be with Christ, and the subsequent revelation of the lawless one, Paul argues, is proof that the Day of the Lord had not begun as they had thought. This understanding of *apostasia* makes much more sense than the view that they are to be comforted (v. 2) because a defection from the faith must precede the Day of the Lord. The entire second chapter (as well as I Thess. 4:18; 5:11) serves to comfort (see v. 2, 3, 17) supplied by a reassurance of Christ's coming as taught in [Paul's] first letter.

Could this translation, therefore, comprise an accurate rendering of the word *apostasia*? Given the context it certainly seems to be a reasonable and acceptable rendering.

---

[2] Quoted from Terry James, editor: *The Departure*, Defender Books, Crane, MO. From the essay, "In the Twinkling," pg. 369. Originally published in *When the Trumpet Sounds: Today's Foremost Authorities Speak Out on End-Time Controversies* (Eugene, OR: Harvest House, 1995), p. 270. (Wayne) House, "Apostesia," p. 270.

As with any doctrine, however, we must be mindful that individual verses confirm a doctrine only when they collectively reinforce it. 'One verse does not a doctrine make' without support from several others and general biblical principles. By itself, this argument may not be totally compelling. Taken together, however, with all of the other biblical references cited in this book, it adds solid support to the pre-tribulation and pre-wrath rapture positions. This verse hardly stands alone as the many verses included in the chapter "Escaping the Wrath to Come" demonstrate.

If we agree that the Children of God do not experience God's wrath, then they must be 'removed' from the earth before the Great Tribulation (or prior to the time God's judgments commence.) Accordingly, the translation of *apostasia* as 'departure' is, in my opinion, a sound one. It connects to the context of Paul's rationale for writing to the Church at Thessalonica and to the many other passages which taken together uphold the same truth.

FOR FURTHER READING

Becker, Ernst, *The Denial of Death,* Free Press Paperbacks, New York, 1973, 314 pages.

Biltz, Mark, *Blood Moons: Decoding the Imminent Heavenly Signs*, Washington D.C., WND Books, 2014, 188 pages.

Bonhoeffer, Dietrich, *The Cost of Discipleship*, New York, NY. Simon & Schuster, Touchstone Edition, 1995. 304 pages.

Busch, David Winston, *The Assyrian: Satan, His Christ, and the Return of the Shadow of Degrees,* Xulon Press, United States, 2007, 339 pages.

Church, J.R., *Daniel Reveals the Blood Line of the Antichrist,* Prophecy Publications, Oklahoma City, OK. 2010, 330 pages.

Custance, Arthur C., *Without Form and Void: A Study of the Meaning of Genesis 1:2*, Classic Reprint Press, Windber, PA., 1970, 275 pages.

Dake, Finis, *Another Time, Another Place, Another Man*, Dake Publishing, 1997, Kindle Edition.

Ehrman, Bart D., *Jesus: Apocalyptic Prophet of the New Millennium*, Oxford University Press, 1999, 246 pages.

Flynn, David, *Temple at the Center of Time: Newton's Bible Codex Deciphered and the Year 2012,* Official Disclosure, A Division of Anomalous Publishing House, Crane, MO., 2008, 296 pages.

Hagee, John, *Four Blood Moons: Something is about to Change*, Brentwood, TN. Worthy Publishing, 2013, Kindle Edition.

Heron, Patrick, *The Nephilim and the Pyramid of the Apocalypse,* Citadel Press, Kensington Publishing Corp., New York, 2004, 241pages.

Hitchcock, Mark, *2012: The Bible and the End of the World,* Harvest House Publishers, Eugene, OR. 2009, 184 pages.

Hitchcock, Mark, *Blood Moon Rising, Bible Prophecy, Israel, and the Four Blood Moons*, Tyndale House, Carol Stream, IL., 2014, 196 pages.

Horn, Thomas R., *Apollyon Rising: 2012*, Anomalous Publishing, Crane, MO., 2009, 352 pages.

Horn, Tom and Nita, *Forbidden Gates*, Defender Publishing Group, Crane, MO., 2011, 350 pages.

James, Terry (Editor), *The Departure: God's Next Catastrophic Intervention into Earth's History,* Defender Publishing, Crane, MO., 2010, 411 pages.

Jeffrey, Grant R., *Countdown to the Apocalypse*, WaterBrook Press (Colorado Springs, Co.), 2008, 227 pages.

Jeffrey, Grant R., *The New Temple and the Second Coming*, WaterBrook Press, Colorado Springs, 2007, 204 pages.

Krieger, Douglas W., *Signs in the Heavens and on the Earth: Man's Days are Numbered*, Sacramento: TribNet Publications, 2014, 418 pages.

Lawrence, Joseph E., *Apocalypse 2012: An Investigation into Civilization's End*, Broadway Books (New York), 2007, 2008, 262 pages.

Lowe, David W., *Then His Voice Shook the Earth: Mount Sinai, the Trumpet of God, and the Resurrection of the Dead in Christ*, Seimos Publishing, 2006, 167 pages.

Lumpkin, Joseph B., *The Lost Book of Enoch, A Comprehensive Transliteration of the Forgotten Book of the Bible*, Fifth Estate Publishers, Blountsville, AL., 2004, 180 pages.

Marzulli, L.A., *Politics, Prophecy, and the Supernatural: The Coming Great Deception and the Luciferian Endgame*, Anomalous Publishing, Crane, MO., 2007, 248pages.

Rosenberg, Joel C., *Epicenter 2.0*, Tyndale House Publishers, Carol Stream, IL. 401 pages.

Ryrie, Charles C., *Dispensationalism, Revised and Expanded*, Moody Bible Institute, 2007, 265pages.

Pember, G.H., *Earth's Earliest Ages*, First published by Hodder and Stoughton, London, England, 1876, 380 pages.

Steyn, Mark, *After America: Get Ready for Armageddon*. Washington D.C.: Regnery Publishing, 2011.

Thomas, I.D.E., *The Omega Conspiracy: Satan's Last Assault on God's Kingdom*, Anomalous Publishing, Crane, MO., 2008, 195 pages.

Woodward, S. Douglas, *Are We Living in the Last Days? The Apocalypse Debate in the 21st Century*, Faith Happens, Woodinville, WA. 2009, 312 pages.

Woodward, S. Douglas, *Decoding Doomsday: The 2012 Prophecies, the Apocalypse, and the Perilous Days Ahead*, Woodinville, WA. Faith Happens, 380 pages.

Woodward, S. Douglas, *Lying Wonders of the Red Planet: Exposing the Lies of Ancient Aliens*, Oklahoma City, OK: Faith Happens, 2014, 336 pages.

Woodward, S. Douglas (with Douglas W. Krieger and Dene McGriff), *The Final Babylon: America and the Coming of Antichrist*, Oklahoma City, FaithHappens, 2013, 336 pages.

ABOUT THE AUTHOR

S. Douglas Woodward ("Doug") is an author and currently an independent consultant serving emerging companies. Over the past twelve years, Doug has served as CEO, COO, and CFO of numerous software and Internet companies. Prior to his tenure in entrepreneurial efforts, he worked as an executive for Honeywell, Oracle, Microsoft, and as a Partner at Ernst & Young LLP.

Doug grew up in Oklahoma City, going to high school and college nearby (Norman). At 15, Doug was struck with a serious form of adolescent cancer, *Rhabdomyosarcoma*, which forced him to lose his left leg as a means to treat the disease. At the time of his illness (1969), recovery was likely in less than 10% of the cases diagnosed. The experience had a dramatic impact upon Doug's spiritual life, linking him with dozens of family members, friends, ministers, nurses and doctors who showed great compassion and provided him with remarkable support.

Doug attended the University of Oklahoma where he received an Honors Degree in *Letters* (Bachelor of Arts), graduating Cum Laude. His studies focused principally on religious philosophy and theology as well as European history and Latin. Doug actively participated in *Young Life* and *Campus Crusade for Christ* throughout his college experience. Upon graduation, Doug served as a Youth Minister and Associate Pastor in the Methodist and Reformed Churches for three years before experimenting with the computer industry as another possible career choice. During his experience at Oracle and Microsoft, much of his efforts were devoted to education and introducing new approaches for better efficiency, making use of distanced learning technologies. Through the years, Doug has served in various capacities in Methodist, Presbyterian, and Reformed Churches. Most recently, Doug served as Elder in the Presbyterian Church.

Doug is married to Donna Wilson Woodward and together they are celebrating thirty-eight years of marriage. The Woodward's now live once more in Oklahoma after living six years in New England and twenty-one years in Woodinville, Washington, a suburb of Seattle. They have two children, Corinne, 35, and Nicholas, 30, and two dogs treated far too well.

POWER QUEST, BOOK ONE
Now in eBook Format. See Kindle, iBook, Lulu and Barnes and Noble.

POWER QUEST, BOOK TWO

Now in eBook Format. See Kindle, iBook, Lulu and Barnes and Noble.

LYING WONDERS OF THE RED PLANET
Now in eBook Format. See Kindle, iBook, Lulu and Barnes and Noble.